# 175 Best
# Air Fryer
## Recipes

# Camilla V. Saulsbury

Robert
**ROSE**

**For complete cataloguing information, see page 288.**

*Disclaimer*
The recipes in this book have been carefully tested by our kitchen and our tasters. To the best of
our knowledge, they are safe and nutritious for ordinary use and users. For those people with food
or other allergies, or who have special food requirements or health issues, please read the suggested
contents of each recipe carefully and determine whether or not they may create a problem for you.
All recipes are used at the risk of the consumer. Consumers should always consult their air fryer
manufacturer's manual for recommended procedures and cooking times.

We cannot be responsible for any hazards, loss or damage that may occur as a result of any
recipe use.

For those with special needs, allergies, requirements or health problems, in the event of
any doubt, please contact your medical adviser prior to the use of any recipe.

Design and production: Daniella Zanchetta/PageWave Graphics Inc.
Layout: Alicia McCarthy/PageWave Graphics Inc.
Editor: Sue Sumeraj
Recipe editor: Jennifer MacKenzie
Proofreader: Kelly Jones
Indexer: Gillian Watts
Photographer: Colin Erricson
Associate photographer: Matt Johannsson
Food stylist: Michael Elliott
Prop stylist: Charlene Erricson

Cover image: Buttermilk Fried Chicken (page 40) with Classic French Fries (page 22)

Published by Robert Rose Inc.
120 Eglinton Avenue East, Suite 800, Toronto, Ontario, Canada M4P 1E2
Tel: (416) 322-6552 Fax: (416) 322-6936
www.robertrose.ca

Printed and bound in Canada

10 MI 24 23 22 21 20 19 18

**To Nick**

# Contents

# Introduction

**Many of us** look forward to the occasional deep-fried indulgence. Crispy, crunchy and utterly craveable, fried foods — french fries, battered fried chicken, onion rings, hand pies and dozens of other delights — are comforting, tried and true, and oh-so-satisfying.

The reasons for limiting our fried food feasting to special occasions or every-once-in-a-while indulgences are all too obvious: high calories, high fat and high cholesterol. Further, despite the enticing taste, traditional fried foods can be heavy on both the palate and the stomach.

Now imagine a revolutionary cooking method, one that captures all of the wonderful characteristics of deep-frying — sizzling, crisp, delectable textures and golden-brown exteriors — to create meals and treats that are equally satisfying but also lighter and healthier, with significantly less fat and calories. It's quick and easy to use, too, without any of the fuss of traditional frying, including freedom from messy cleanup and no worries about the dangers of hot oil.

If it sounds too good to be true, think again. Thanks to modern ingenuity and engineering, the solution is here: air-frying.

# Air-Frying: Hot Air in Place of Hot Oil

## A Bit of Air Fryer History

Frying with air instead of oil? It sounds like a lot of hot air, and that is what air-frying is all about.

The first air fryer was the Quik n' Crispy Greaseless Fryer, a product designed and patented in 1990 by QNC, a Texas-based company. The box-like appliance was designed expressly for commercial settings as an alternative to traditional deep-frying. The machines are still in use today, mostly in fast-food and convenience-food kitchens, where they are used to air-fry fully cooked frozen foods, such as french fries and chicken strips, that closely resemble deep-fried foods in taste, texture and appearance.

It wasn't until 2006 that air fryers became available to home cooks in Europe and North America. The first home models were circular, with a turntable-style grate and a sweeping arm designed to keep foods, especially fries, in motion for even browning and cooking.

The latest air fryers more closely resemble compact deep fryers, complete with deep, removable baskets. Sleek and upright in design, they are approximately the size and shape of a football helmet and, because of their small footprint, they are ideal for keeping on the countertop.

## How Home Air Fryers Work

To best understand the unique abilities of an air fryer and how it works, it helps to know how it compares to oil frying.

Almost all cooking methods depend on two factors: heat transfer (from the heat source through the food) and removal of water from the food. Traditional oil-frying works so well because it performs both factors with aplomb. Oil holds heat well, plus it can be heated to a consistent temperature throughout, both of which characteristics facilitate even, efficient heating of food. Oil's consistent heat is also very effective at removing water from the surface of the food. Removing water is critical because it can slow heat transfer, which affects both the overall consistency of the cooked food (it might be too dry, too wet, undercooked, overcooked) and the browning and texture of the food's surface.

In contrast to frying in hot oil, air fryers use a combination of radiant and convection heat. Radiant heat in air fryers, like the heat in almost all standard ovens, refers to the infrared radiation emitted by both the heating element and the hot oven walls. When this radiation makes contact with the food in the oven, its energy agitates the food's molecules into a frenzy, which raises the temperature of the food.

But it is the convection aspect of air fryers that yields results akin to oil frying. Air fryers, like all convection ovens, have a fan that continuously circulates air through the oven. The moving air speeds up the rate of heat transference that naturally occurs when air of two different temperatures converges. Just as you feel colder when cold air blows against you on a blustery winter day, as opposed to a windless day of the same temperature, food gets hotter (and cooks more quickly) when hot air produced by the convection fan converges with the radiant heat of the oven. Air fryers have especially rapid fans (many of which use patented technology). Extra-fast fans plus a unique air fryer chamber design make the air fryer the equivalent of a convection oven on steroids.

This acceleration effect is one reason for the superior results you get from air-frying. The rush of heat speeds up the chemical reactions that occur as food cooks. In a conventional oven, the water in food is difficult to heat up, which slows heat transfer and reduces the ability of the surface to crisp. The turbo-speed air fryer fan moves water away from the food surface more quickly, thereby greatly increasing surface crisping and rendering finished effects close to those of oil-frying.

# Beyond Air-Frying

Air fryers can do so much more than re-create the flavor and texture of fried foods. The quick, even, dry heat is ideal for other everyday kitchen cooking tasks, too. For example, the rapidly circulating hot air in air fryers eliminates hot and cold spots in the cooking chamber. This promotes even, efficient cooking, which is perfect for roasting meats and vegetables, but also for creating a grilled-food flavor for everything from shrimp to hamburgers to fish fillets.

If you want to create professional-quality baked goods, the extra-rapid circulating hot air of the air fryer delivers. The butter or fat in puff pastry releases its steam quickly, creating flaky layers. The sugars in a mini batch of cookies or muffins begin caramelizing sooner, creating deep flavors and crisp edges. Moreover, baking in an air fryer is usually accomplished about 15% to 20% faster than in a conventional oven.

The air fryer is also an ideal tool for reheating leftovers. Simply preheat the air fryer to 300°F (150°C), place the food in the air fryer basket (without overcrowding it) and heat for 10 to 15 minutes or until heated to the desired temperature.

Finally, when summer temperatures soar, eschew firing up the oven (and subsequently heating the entire kitchen). Instead, rely on the efficiency of air-frying to save on both energy and time.

## A Safe, Practical Option

Air-frying has additional advantages beyond the considerable reduction of fat and calories. Topping the list is safety: frying in hot oil is intrinsically dangerous. Serious burns can result from splatters or spills, and the risk of fire is likewise a major concern. Air-frying "fries" with air instead of oil, eliminating the risk of oil spills, splatters and fires. Air-frying also eliminates the lingering smell associated with conventional hot-oil frying, as well as the messy cleanup of the fryer and surrounding surfaces.

# Getting Started

## Choosing an Air Fryer

All of the recipes in this collection were tested using an air fryer with an inner cooking chamber, removable cooking basket and adjustable thermostat. Air fryer options are broad, but almost all have the same essential design, with some variations in basket size, wattage and accessories.

### Wattage

Air fryers typically require between 800 and 1400 watts. Before buying an air fryer, it's a good idea to check if your kitchen outlet can support this kind of wattage.

### Size and Basket Capacity

Air fryers are relatively compact and easy to fit on a kitchen counter; simply choose what works for your space and your aesthetics.

Most air fryers have baskets with a capacity between $1\frac{1}{2}$ and $2\frac{1}{2}$ pounds (750 g and 1.25 kg). The recipes in this collection were all tested in air fryers that fell within this range. Larger air fryers are available, which is convenient for making larger batches of food. Cooking times are not affected by basket capacity, so choose the size that best suits your needs.

### A Removable Basket

When selecting an air fryer, check to make sure the basket is easily removable, since it will be inserted and removed many times. Removing the basket should be as simple as pressing the release button and lifting or sliding it out of the cooking chamber.

### Settings

Air fryers typically have a temperature range in the neighborhood of 150°F (75°C) to 200°F (100°C) for the lowest setting to a maximum setting of 390°F (200°C). Temperature controls are more variable. For example, some models have analog dials with preset temperature intervals, while some of the newest models have digital programmable settings.

Additional settings may include timers as well as preset options for different frozen or fresh foods (such as fries, bacon, fish and breaded chicken strips). Choose which bells and whistles best suit your needs and preferences.

### Other Features to Consider

- **Safety features:** Some air fryer models include additional safety features, such as a removable pan with a cool-touch handle, nonslip feet, overheat protection, temperature light, ready signal and automatic switch-off.

- **Dishwasher safety:** Dishwasher-safe baskets make cleanup simple and convenient. Dishwasher-safe parts are fast becoming the standard in home air fryers, but with more and more models on the market, it is worth double-checking.

- **Nonstick surfaces:** Nonstick surfaces are particularly beneficial when it comes to cleaning air fryer parts, even though only a small amount of oil is used. Like dishwasher safety, nonstick basket surfaces are the norm in many air fryer models, but you may still want to check before purchase.

- **Additional accessories:** Some air fryers come with optional removable accessories, such as a removable rack that sits inside the basket and can be used to lift meats, fish and other foods off the bottom of the basket.

### Preheating

It takes only 3 to 5 minutes to preheat most air fryers. Check your air fryer's manual to determine the preheating time for your particular model.

# Air Fryer Cooking Tips

Successful cooking is easy with an air fryer. The following troubleshooting tips will guarantee it.

- **Avoid overcrowding.** Overcrowding foods in the basket prevents them from cooking and browning evenly, and will result in less crispy foods.

- **Shake the basket.** Occasional shaking of the basket can facilitate evenly browned, crispy food — but only do so when the recipe directs you to. To shake the ingredients, pull the pan out of the appliance by the handle and shake it (be sure to wear oven mitts when you do this). Do not press the basket release button during shaking.

- **Spray with nonstick cooking spray.** Spraying foods with a light coating of nonstick cooking spray helps them achieve a light, crispy, crunchy texture. Do not skip it if the recipe calls for it! (But likewise, do not spray unless the recipe tells you to.)

- **Check early.** Check the food for doneness at the earliest cooking time given in the recipe.

- **Use the correct bakeware.** As mentioned earlier, the air fryer can be used for baking and roasting in addition to air-frying. Glass, metal, ceramic and silicone bakeware can all be used in the air fryer, so long as it is the correct size. Round or square bakeware should be no larger than 6 inches (15 cm) in diameter to allow some space on either side of the pan. It should also be no higher than 2.95 inches (7.5 cm) high. Doubled foil or paper cupcake liners, or single silicone muffin liners, can be used to bake muffins and breads.

- **Use foil correctly.** Foil is perfectly safe to use in the air fryer, and several recipes in this collection call for its use in lining the air fryer basket. Be sure to leave at least $\frac{1}{2}$ inch (1 cm) between the foil and the inside edge of the basket. This will ensure that there is enough space to allow the circulating hot air to pass through. Never cover the bottom of the basket completely with foil or any other material; this reduces the airflow in the basket, which diminishes the cooking performance of the air fryer. Further, do not put the foil in the basket while the air fryer preheats. The foil can be sucked into the heater and could start to burn.

# Air Fryer Safety Tips

Air fryers are far safer than frying with hot oil, but they should still be used with care and caution. What follows are general tips for using your air fryer safely.

- **Mind the heat.** Air fryers become very hot, especially when heated to maximum temperature. Use oven pads or mitts when touching the appliance and when opening and closing the basket.
- **Mind the steam.** Hot air and steam will release from the air fryer throughout the cooking cycle. If your face is in close proximity to the appliance during the cooking cycle or when you are opening the basket, you risk being scalded by the release of accumulated steam.
- **Heed the hot basket.** The basket will be especially hot once the cooking cycle is complete. Avoid placing it on countertops or dishcloths, as it may cause damage.
- **Avoid overflow.** It is important to avoid any contact between food and the heating element. Before closing the basket to cook food, double-check that no ingredients have spilled out of the basket into the air fryer chamber.
- **Keep it clear.** Do not place anything on top of the air fryer or over the air inlets during the cooking cycle. Also, move the air fryer at least 6 inches (15 cm) from the wall before use.
- **Stick around.** Do not leave the air fryer unattended when it is in use. Unplug the air fryer when cooking is complete.

- **Do not use if damaged.** It may sound obvious, but never use the air fryer if there is any noticeable damage to the cord, plug, basket or any other parts.
- **Dry your hands.** Make sure your hands are not wet when using the air fryer.

# Cleaning Your Air Fryer

Air fryer cleanup is a breeze, especially when compared to the greasy mess of conventional hot-oil fryers. Nevertheless, it is important to clean the air fryer after each use to prevent buildup of grease or stuck-on food particles.

## Cleaning the Basket

1. Let the air fryer cool to room temperature.
2. If the air fryer basket is dishwasher-safe, wash it in a normal dishwashing cycle. Otherwise, remove the air fryer basket, place it in a plugged sink or a large bowl and fill with hot water and a drop or two of liquid dishwashing soap. Let soak for 10 to 15 minutes. Use a nonabrasive sponge or dishwashing cloth to gently clean the walls and bottom of the basket. Invert the basket and gently clean the bottom.

## Cleaning the Inside and Outside of the Appliance

1. Let the air fryer cool to room temperature.

2. Use a nonabrasive sponge or dishwashing cloth and hot water to clean the outside and the inner chamber of the air fryer.

## Cleaning the Heating Element

1. Let the air fryer cool to room temperature.

2. Gently clean off any grease or food residue with a soft to medium bristle brush and hot water. It is important not to use a hard or steel bristle brush, as it can damage the coating on the heating element.

3. Dry the heating element with paper towels.

### Suggested Tools and Equipment

Air-frying requires very little equipment to achieve success. The following items will ensure that you can make every recipe in this collection.

- 6-inch (15 cm) round metal cake pan
- ¾-cup (175 mL) ramekins
- Foil or paper muffin/cupcake liners
- Foil
- Tongs (preferably silicone-tipped, to prevent scratching if the basket has a nonstick coating)
- Pancake turner/spatula
- Slotted spoon
- Wire cooling rack

# The Air Fryer Pantry

**The recipes in this collection** largely rely on fresh vegetables, fruits, lean meats, poultry, eggs and seafood, plus a short list of ingredients you likely already have in your pantry. Here are some of the most commonly used pantry ingredients to keep at the ready for a variety of air-frying recipes.

## Eggs, Dairy and Nondairy Milks

### Eggs

All of the recipes in this book were tested with large eggs. Select clean, fresh eggs that have been handled properly and refrigerated. Do not use dirty, cracked or leaking eggs, or eggs that have a bad odor or unnatural color when cracked open; they may have become contaminated with harmful bacteria, such as salmonella.

### Dairy Milk

All of the recipes in this collection calling for milk were tested with lower-fat (2%) milk. However, milk of any fat level can be used in its place, as can any of the nondairy milk options listed below.

### Nondairy Milks

Nondairy milks are essential for vegans, as well as those who are lactose intolerant or are allergic to dairy. The variety and availability of nondairy milks is vast; soy milk, rice milk, hemp milk and almond milk are readily available options in most well-stocked grocery stores. Opt for plain nondairy milk when substituting for milk in any of the recipes in this collection.

### Buttermilk

Tangy buttermilk is a traditional ingredient in a wide range of fried foods, and it works wonders with air-fried foods, too. Commercially prepared varieties are made by culturing 1% milk with bacteria. When added to batters and baked goods, it yields a tender result and a slightly buttery flavor.

> **Buttermilk Substitute**
>
> If you do not have buttermilk, it's easy to make a substitute. Mix 1 tbsp (15 mL) lemon juice or white vinegar into 1 cup (250 mL) milk. Let stand for at least 15 minutes before using, to allow the milk to curdle. Any extra can be stored in the refrigerator for the same amount of time as the milk from which it was made.

### Yogurt

All of the recipes in this collection call for either plain yogurt or plain Greek yogurt. Greek yogurt is a thick, creamy yogurt similar in texture to sour cream.

# Flours and Grains
## All-Purpose Flour

Made from a blend of high-gluten hard wheat and low-gluten soft wheat, all-purpose flour is fine-textured flour milled from the inner part of the wheat kernel and contains neither the germ nor the bran. All-purpose flour comes either bleached or unbleached; they can be used interchangeably.

## Gluten-Free All-Purpose Flour

Gluten-free all-purpose flour is readily available in most supermarkets, either in the health foods section or in the baking aisle. No single gluten-free flour performs exactly like wheat flour, so gluten-free all-purpose flours are a blend, most often of rice flours, other flours (such as millet or chickpea flour) and some form of starch, such as tapioca or potato starch. Gluten-free all-purpose flour works well as a substitute for all-purpose wheat flour for dredging before air-frying.

## Cornmeal

Cornmeal is simply ground dried corn kernels. There are two methods of grinding. The first is the modern method, in which milling is done by huge steel rollers, which remove the husk and germ almost entirely; this creates the most common variety of cornmeal found in supermarkets. The second is the stone-ground method, in which some of the hull and germ of the corn is retained; this type of cornmeal is available at health food stores and in the health food sections of most supermarkets. The two varieties can be used interchangeably, but I recommend using the stone-ground variety, as it has a much deeper corn flavor and is also more nutritious.

## Rolled Oats

Two types of rolled oats are called for in these recipes. Large-flake (old-fashioned) rolled oats are oat groats (hulled and cleaned whole oats) that have been steamed and flattened with huge rollers. Quick-cooking rolled oats are groats that have been cut into several pieces before being steamed and rolled into thinner flakes. For the best results, it is important to use the type of rolled oats specified in the recipe.

# Breading
## Panko (Japanese Bread Crumbs)

Panko bread crumbs are made from loaves of white bread that have had the crusts removed. The crumbs are larger in size than regular bread crumbs and have a light texture that becomes especially crunchy with air-frying. Look for panko in the Asian or international foods section of well-stocked supermarkets.

## Dry Bread Crumbs

Dry bread crumbs are available in the baking section of the supermarket. They have a fine texture (finer than panko) that is ideal for coating a wide range of foods. Both plain bread crumbs and bread crumbs with Italian seasoning are used in this collection.

## Corn Flakes Cereal

Crumbled corn flakes cereal — crispy toasted flakes of corn — can be used as a substitute for panko or dry bread crumbs in any of the recipes in this collection. It will take 3 cups (750 mL) whole corn flakes cereal to yield 1 cup (250 mL) corn flake crumbs.

### Gluten-Free Corn Flakes

If using corn flakes cereal specifically as a gluten-free alternative to bread crumbs, be sure to choose a brand that is specifically labeled "gluten-free." Although corn is naturally gluten-free, many brands of corn flakes cereal include glutinous ingredients, such as malt syrup (which is made from barley and contains gluten).

# Sweeteners

## Granulated Sugar

Granulated sugar (also called white sugar) is refined cane or beet sugar and is the most common sweetener used in this book. Once opened, store granulated sugar in an airtight container in a cool, dry place.

## Brown Sugar

Brown sugar is granulated sugar with some molasses added to it. The molasses gives the sugar a soft texture. Light brown sugar (also known as golden yellow sugar) has less molasses and a more delicate flavor than dark brown sugar. Once opened, store brown sugar in an airtight container or a resealable plastic food bag, to prevent clumping.

## Confectioners' (Icing) Sugar

Confectioners' (icing) sugar (also called powdered sugar) is granulated sugar that has been ground to a fine powder. Cornstarch is added to prevent the sugar from clumping together. It is used in recipes where regular sugar would be too grainy.

## Honey

Honey is plant nectar that has been gathered and concentrated by honeybees. Any variety of honey may be used in the recipes in this collection.

## Maple Syrup

Maple syrup is a thick liquid sweetener made by boiling the sap from maple trees. It has a strong, pure maple flavor. Maple-flavored pancake syrup is just corn syrup with coloring and artificial maple flavoring added, and it is not recommended as a substitute for pure maple syrup.

### Storing Honey and Maple Syrup

Unopened containers of honey and maple syrup may be stored at room temperature. After opening, store honey and maple syrup in the refrigerator to protect against mold. Honey and maple syrup will both keep indefinitely when stored properly.

# Fats and Oils

Fats and oils are used sparingly in air-frying, largely because they simply aren't needed. Where they are used, make sure to choose good-quality fats to ensure optimum flavor.

## Butter

Butter is used most in the desserts chapter of this book; it is used sparingly throughout the remainder of the collection.

Butter quickly picks up off-flavors during storage and when exposed to oxygen, so once the carton or wrap is opened, place it in a sealable plastic food bag or other airtight container. Store it away from foods with strong odors, such as onions or garlic.

### Freezing Butter

If you only use butter occasionally, I recommend storing it in the freezer. Wrap entire sticks, or use a method I developed in my student days: cut the butter into 1-tbsp (15 mL) pats and place them on a baking sheet lined with plastic wrap. Place in the freezer for 30 to 60 minutes, until frozen, then transfer the frozen pats to an airtight container. Butter can be frozen for up to 6 months. Remove pats of butter as needed and thaw in the refrigerator or at room temperature.

## Margarine

Margarine is not recommended as a replacement for butter because it is lacking in flavor, but it can stand in for butter as a dairy-free option. If margarine is used as a replacement in any of the baking recipes, it is important to use 100% vegetable oil varieties in stick form. Margarine spreads — in tub or stick form — contain a significant amount of water, which will alter the results of the recipe.

## Vegetable Oil

Vegetable oil is a generic term used to describe any neutral plant-based oil that is liquid at room temperature. You can use a vegetable oil blend, canola oil, light olive oil, grapeseed oil, safflower oil, sunflower oil, peanut oil or corn oil.

## Olive Oil

Olive oil is a monounsaturated oil that is prized for a wide range of cooking preparations. I recommend using plain olive oil (simply labeled "olive oil"), which contains a combination of refined olive oil and virgin or extra virgin oil. The subtle nuances of extra virgin olive oil are not very noticeable after cooking in the air fryer.

## Toasted (Dark) Sesame Oil

Toasted sesame oil, also known as dark sesame oil, has a dark brown color and a rich, nutty flavor. It is used sparingly, mostly in Asian recipes, to add a tremendous amount of flavor.

## Nonstick Cooking Spray

Nonstick cooking spray is used extensively in this collection to coat foods in an even yet minimal layer of fat to promote a golden-brown, crispy exterior. While any type of cooking spray may be used, I recommend using an organic spray for two reasons: first, these sprays are typically made with higher-quality oils (in many cases expeller-pressed or cold-pressed oils) than most commercial brands; second, they are more likely to use compressed gas to expel the propellant, so no hydrocarbons are released into the environment. Read the label and choose wisely.

# Leavening Agents
## Baking Powder

Baking powder is a chemical leavening agent made from a blend of alkali (sodium bicarbonate, known commonly as baking soda) and acid (most commonly calcium acid phosphate, sodium aluminum sulfate or cream of tartar), plus some form of starch to absorb any moisture so a reaction does not take place until a liquid is added.

## Baking Soda

Baking soda is a chemical leavener consisting of bicarbonate of soda. It is alkaline in nature and, when combined with an acidic ingredient, such as buttermilk, yogurt, citrus juice or honey, it creates carbon dioxide bubbles, giving baked goods a dramatic rise.

# Flavorings

When fat is kept to a minimum in sweet and savory recipes such as these, it is especially important to amplify other flavors. Here are my top recommendations for ingredients that will accentuate a range of air-frying recipes.

## Salt

Unless otherwise specified, the recipes in this collection were tested using common table salt. An equal amount of fine sea salt can be used in its place.

## Black Pepper

Black pepper is made by grinding black peppercorns, which have been picked when the berry is not quite ripe and then dried until it shrivels and the skin turns dark brown to black. Black pepper has a strong, slightly hot flavor, with a hint of sweetness. Both freshly cracked and freshly ground black pepper are used in this collection.

## Spices and Dried Herbs

Spices and dried herbs can elevate healthy air-fried foods to delectable heights with minimal effort. They should be stored in light- and air-proof containers, away from direct sunlight and heat, to preserve their flavors.

Co-ops, health food stores and mail order sources that sell herbs and spices in bulk are all excellent options for purchasing very fresh organic spices and dried herbs, often at a low cost.

With ground spices and dried herbs, freshness is everything. To determine whether a ground spice or dried herb is fresh, open the container and sniff. A strong fragrance means it is still acceptable for use.

Note that ground spices, not whole, are used throughout this collection. On page 18 you'll find a list of my favorite ground spices and dried herbs.

## Ground Spices

- Cardamom
- Cayenne pepper
  (also labeled "ground red pepper")
- Chili powder
- Chinese five-spice powder
- Chipotle chile powder
- Cinnamon
- Coriander
- Cumin
- Garam masala
- Ginger
- Hot pepper flakes
- Mild curry powder
- Nutmeg
- Paprika
- Smoked paprika (both hot and sweet)
- Turmeric

## Dried Herbs

- Bay leaves
- Oregano
- Rosemary
- Rubbed sage
- Thyme

## Citrus Zest

"Zest" is the name for the colored outer layer of citrus peel. The oils in zest are intense in flavor. Use a zester, a Microplane-style grater or the small holes of a box grater to grate zest. Avoid grating the white layer (pith) just below the zest; it is very bitter.

## Hot Pepper Sauce

Hot pepper sauce is a spicy condiment made from chile peppers and other common ingredients, such as vinegar and spices. It is available in countless heat levels and flavors, so pick the multipurpose sauce that best suits your taste.

### An Instant Dipping Sauce

Marinara sauce — a highly seasoned Italian tomato sauce made with onions, garlic, basil and oregano — makes a great instant dipping sauce for many air-fried appetizers and snacks. You'll find a quick and easy recipe for marinara sauce on page 255. If using jarred marinara sauce, choose a variety with minimal ingredients that is low in sodium and free of sweeteners and preservatives for the best tomato flavor and the most versatility.

## Sriracha

Sriracha is a multipurpose hot sauce made from red chile peppers, garlic, vinegar, salt and sugar. It is hot and tangy, with a slight sweetness that distinguishes it from other hot sauces. Sriracha is often served as a condiment in Thai, Vietnamese and Chinese restaurants, but it can be used in a wide range of cuisines and preparations.

## Thai Curry Paste

Available in small jars, Thai curry paste is a blend of Thai chiles, garlic, lemongrass, galangal, ginger and wild lime leaves. It is a fast and delicious way to add Southeast Asian flavor to a broad spectrum of recipes in a single step. Panang and yellow curry pastes tend to be the mildest. Red curry paste is medium hot, and green curry paste is typically the hottest.

## Soy Sauce and Tamari

Soy sauce is a dark, salty sauce made from fermented soybeans, water, salt and sometimes added wheat or barley. If you're avoiding gluten, look for soy sauce specifically labeled as gluten-free.

Tamari is a natural, aged soy sauce with a more intense flavor than regular soy sauce. It can be used in place of regular soy sauce and vice versa.

## Vanilla Extract

Vanilla extract adds a sweet, fragrant flavor to dishes, especially baked goods. It is produced by combining an extraction from dried vanilla beans with an alcohol-and-water mixture. It is then aged for several months.

## Mayonnaise

Mayonnaise is a thick and creamy dressing or sauce made from emulsified oil, eggs, seasonings and lemon juice or vinegar. Either regular or reduced-fat mayonnaise (ranging from 25% to 50% less fat than regular) can be used in the recipes in this collection.

## Mustard

Mustard is most commonly used in this collection for dips to add instant depth of flavor. I recommend either Dijon mustard or brown mustard for their versatility.

## Vinegars

Vinegars are multipurpose flavor powerhouses used to intensify sauces and dips and to brighten the flavor of a variety of air-fried dishes. Store vinegars in a dark place, away from heat and light.

Inexpensive and versatile, apple cider vinegar is an excellent multipurpose choice. It is made from the juice of crushed apples. After the juice is collected, it is allowed to age in wooden barrels. Red or white wine vinegars — produced by fermenting wine in wooden barrels — are also good multitasking options.

## Ready-to-Use Broths

Ready-made chicken and vegetable broths are handy for adding flavor to dishes without making stock from scratch. Opt for broths that are all-natural, reduced-sodium (you can always add more salt) and MSG-free. For chicken broth, look for brands that are made from chicken raised without hormones and antibiotics.

For convenience, look for broths in Tetra Paks, which typically come in 32-oz (1 L), 48-oz (1.5 L) and occasionally 16-oz (500 mL) sizes. Once opened, these can be stored in the refrigerator for up to 1 week. You can also freeze small amounts (2 tbsp/30 mL up to $\frac{1}{4}$ cup/60 mL) in ice-cube trays. Once frozen, simply pop out the cubes and store in an airtight bag for up to 6 months (thaw in the microwave or the refrigerator).

## Measuring Ingredients

Accurate measurements are important for air fryer recipes, to achieve the right balance of flavors. So take both time and care as you measure.

### Dry Ingredients

When measuring a dry ingredient, such as flour, cocoa powder, sugar, spices or salt, spoon it into the appropriate-size dry measuring cup or measuring spoon, heaping it up over the top. Slide a straight-edged utensil, such as a knife, across the top to level off the extra. Be careful not to shake or tap the cup or spoon to settle the ingredient, or you will have more than you need.

### Moist Ingredients

Moist ingredients, such as brown sugar, coconut and dried fruit, must be firmly packed in a measuring cup or spoon to be measured accurately. Use a dry measuring cup for these ingredients. Fill the measuring cup to slightly overflowing, then pack down the ingredient firmly with the back of a spoon. Add more of the ingredient and pack down again until the cup is full and even with the top of the measure.

### Liquid Ingredients

Use a clear plastic or glass measuring cup or container with lines up the sides to measure liquid ingredients. Set the container on the counter and pour the liquid to the appropriate mark. Lower your head to read the measurement at eye level.

# Top 20 Fried Favorites

# Classic French Fries

Is there a person anywhere who doesn't love french fries? Now you can make them with ease and enjoy them without guilt, too!

## Makes 2 servings

### Tips

A single large russet potato may weigh 1 lb (500 g).

Soaking the potatoes in hot water before roasting removes some of their starch, ensuring extra-crisp fries without deep-frying.

Use oven mitts when opening and closing the basket.

### Variations

*Garlic Parmesan Fries:* Add 2 tsp (10 mL) minced garlic when tossing the potatoes in step 3. Toss the finished fries with 1 tbsp (15 mL) freshly grated Parmesan cheese and 1 tbsp (15 mL) minced fresh parsley (optional) before serving.

*Cajun Fries:* Replace the salt with 1 tsp (5 mL) Cajun seasoning. Sprinkle with 1 tbsp (15 mL) minced fresh parsley before serving.

*Rosemary Fries:* Add 1 tsp (5 mL) minced fresh rosemary when tossing the potatoes in step 3.

| 1 lb | russet potatoes | 500 g |
|------|-----------------|-------|
| | Hot (not boiling) water | |
| 1 tbsp | vegetable or olive oil | 15 mL |
| 1/2 tsp | salt | 2 mL |

1. Peel potatoes and cut lengthwise into 1/4-inch (0.5 cm) thick sticks. Place in a large bowl and add enough hot water to cover. Let stand for 10 minutes. Drain, pat dry and return to dry bowl. Add oil and salt, tossing to coat.

2. Preheat air fryer to 360°F (180°C).

3. Place half the potatoes in a single layer in air fryer basket. Air-fry for 5 minutes. Open basket and, using tongs, gently toss the potatoes. Increase temperature to 390°F (200°C) and air-fry for 12 to 16 minutes, opening basket twice more to toss, until golden brown. Serve immediately. Repeat with the remaining potatoes.

# Onion Rings

Air-frying onion rings allows their sweet onion flavor to shine through. They are wonderful as a side dish but equally great as a stand-alone snack. Less is more when you're dipping the rings in the flour mixture and panko; a thin coating of each is all you need. Serve with Creole Mayonnaise (page 278).

## Makes 4 servings

### Variation

*Gluten-Free Onion Rings:* Replace the all-purpose flour with an all-purpose gluten-free flour blend, and replace the panko with crushed gluten-free corn flakes cereal.

• Preheat air fryer to 390°F (200°C)

| 1 | large Vidalia onion | 1 |
|---|---|---|
| 1 cup | all-purpose flour | 250 mL |
| 1 tsp | baking powder | 5 mL |
| 1 tsp | salt | 5 mL |
| 1 cup | panko (Japanese bread crumbs) | 250 mL |
| 2 | large eggs | 2 |
| | Nonstick cooking spray | |

1. Cut onion into ¼-inch (0.5 cm) slices and separate into rings.

2. Place flour, baking powder and salt in a large sealable plastic bag. Seal bag and shake to combine. Add onion rings, seal and toss until coated.

3. Spread panko in a shallow dish.

4. In another shallow dish, whisk eggs.

5. Working with 1 onion ring at a time, remove from flour, shaking off excess. Dip in egg, shaking off excess, then dredge in panko, pressing gently to adhere. As they are dredged, place 4 to 7 onion rings (depending on size) in air fryer basket, leaving space in between. Spray with cooking spray.

6. Air-fry for 5 to 7 minutes or until golden brown. Serve immediately.

7. Repeat steps 5 and 6 with the remaining onion rings, egg and panko. Discard any excess flour mixture, egg and panko.

# Tempura-Style Vegetables

Vegetable tempura is irresistible — you simply can't eat just one — and thanks to the air fryer, you no longer have to limit it to rare occasions. Serve with Citrus Soy Dipping Sauce (page 265), if desired.

## Makes 4 servings

### Variation

*Gluten-Free Tempura Vegetables:* Replace the all-purpose flour with an all-purpose gluten-free flour blend, and replace the panko with crushed gluten-free corn flakes cereal.

| | | |
|---|---|---|
| ⅔ cup | cornstarch | 150 mL |
| ⅓ cup | all-purpose flour | 75 mL |
| ¼ tsp | salt | 1 mL |
| 1 | large egg, lightly beaten | 1 |
| ¾ cup | club soda, chilled | 175 mL |
| 1½ cups | panko (Japanese bread crumbs) | 375 mL |
| 1 cup | broccoli florets | 250 mL |
| 1 | red bell pepper, cut into ¼-inch (0.5 cm) thick strips | 1 |
| 1 | small sweet potato, peeled and cut into ¼-inch (0.5 cm) thick slices | 1 |
| 1 | small zucchini, cut into ¼-inch (0.5 cm) thick slices | 1 |
| 12 | green beans, trimmed | 12 |
| | Nonstick cooking spray | |

1. In a medium bowl, whisk together cornstarch, flour and salt. Whisk in egg and club soda until blended and smooth. Cover loosely with plastic wrap and refrigerate for 30 minutes to thicken.

2. Preheat air fryer to 390°F (200°C).

3. Spread panko in a shallow dish.

4. Working with 1 vegetable piece at a time, dip in batter, shaking off excess, then dredge in panko, pressing gently to adhere. As they are dredged, place 5 to 6 vegetables in air fryer basket, leaving space in between. Spray with cooking spray.

5. Air-fry for 5 to 8 minutes or until golden brown. Serve immediately.

6. Repeat steps 4 and 5 with the remaining vegetables, batter and panko. Discard any excess batter and panko.

# Jalapeño Poppers

The pleasantly spicy bite of fresh jalapeños finds perfect complement with a creamy, double-cheese stuffing — a game-day party is incomplete without them. This version makes the preparation a snap.

**Makes 20 appetizers**

## Tip

For spicier poppers, leave some of the ribs inside the peppers.

## Variations

*Gluten-Free Jalapeño Poppers:* Replace the panko with crushed gluten-free corn flakes cereal.

*Bacon Jalapeño Poppers:* Add 3 slices cooked bacon, chopped, to the cheese mixture.

*Sweet Pepper Poppers:* Replace the jalapeños with miniature bell peppers (typically sold in bags in supermarket produce departments).

• *Preheat air fryer to 360°F (180°C)*

| | | |
|---|---|---|
| 10 | medium jalapeño peppers | 10 |
| 8 oz | brick-style reduced-fat cream cheese, softened | 250 g |
| 1 cup | shredded sharp (old) Cheddar cheese | 250 mL |
| 1 tsp | chipotle chile powder | 5 mL |
| 1/2 cup | panko (Japanese bread crumbs) | 125 mL |
| | Nonstick cooking spray | |

1. Cut each jalapeño in half lengthwise. Use a spoon to scoop out any seeds and ribs. (If the peppers have stems, leave them intact.)

2. In a medium bowl, combine cream cheese, Cheddar cheese and chipotle powder. Spoon cheese mixture into jalapeños, dividing evenly.

3. Place panko in a shallow dish. Press cheese side of each filled jalapeño into panko.

4. Place 5 to 8 jalapeños (depending on size), filling side up, in air fryer basket, leaving space in between. Spray with cooking spray. Air-fry for 10 to 12 minutes or until cheese is melted and bread crumbs are golden. Serve immediately. Repeat with the remaining jalapeños. Discard any excess panko.

# Crispy-Gooey Mozzarella Sticks

This dish combines gooey mozzarella and Parmesan cheese with the crunch and flavor of herb-seasoned bread crumbs. Be sure to invite a crowd when you make them; it's hard to stop at just a few! Serve with Easy Marinara Sauce (page 255), if desired.

**Makes 6 to 8 servings**

## Tips

The eggs can be replaced by 4 large egg whites. In step 5, whisk the egg whites until slightly frothy.

Air fryers become very hot, especially when heated to maximum temperature. Use oven pads or mitts when touching the appliance and when opening and closing the basket.

• *Small rimmed baking sheet*

| | | |
|---|---|---|
| 1 | package (12 oz/375 g) mozzarella string cheese (about 12 sticks) | 1 |
| 2/3 cup | all-purpose flour | 150 mL |
| 2 cups | dry bread crumbs with Italian seasoning | 500 mL |
| 1/2 cup | freshly grated Parmesan cheese | 125 mL |
| 2 | large eggs | 2 |
| | Nonstick cooking spray | |

1. Remove string cheese from its packaging and cut each cheese stick in half crosswise. Place cheese sticks on baking sheet. Cover with plastic wrap and place in the freezer for 30 to 45 minutes or until very cold (do not freeze solid).

2. Preheat air fryer to 390°F (200°C).

3. Place flour in a large sealable plastic bag.

4. In a shallow dish, combine bread crumbs and Parmesan.

5. In another shallow dish, whisk eggs until blended.

6. Add 6 cheese sticks to bag of flour, seal and toss until coated. (Keep the remaining cheese sticks in the freezer until ready to coat and air-fry.)

## Variations

*Gluten-Free Mozzarella Sticks:* Replace the bread crumbs with crushed gluten-free corn flakes cereal, and replace the all-purpose flour with an all-purpose gluten-free flour blend.

*Cheddar Cheese Sticks:* Replace the mozzarella cheese sticks with Cheddar cheese sticks.

*Pesto Cheese Sticks:* Replace one of the eggs with 3 tbsp (45 mL) basil pesto.

7. Working with 1 stick at a time, dip in egg, shaking off excess, then roll in bread crumb mixture, pressing gently to adhere. As they are coated, place cheese sticks in air fryer basket, leaving space in between. Spray with cooking spray.

8. Air-fry for 3 minutes. Open basket and, using tongs or a spatula, carefully turn cheese sticks over. Air-fry for 3 to 5 minutes or until golden brown. Serve immediately.

9. Repeat steps 6, 7 and 8 with the remaining cheese sticks, flour, egg and bread crumb mixture. Discard any excess flour, egg and bread crumb mixture.

# Triple-Cheese Rice Balls

Triple-cheese rice balls are an appetizer akin to Italian arancini, but simplified with the use of frozen fully-cooked rice in place of leftover risotto. Enriched with ricotta and Parmesan, then stuffed with cubes of provolone, they are hearty yet refined bites of decadence. Serve with Easy Marinara Sauce (page 255), if desired.

**Makes 4 servings**

## Tips

If packaged frozen rice is not available, substitute 2 cups (500 mL) cooled cooked white rice.

Whole-milk, reduced-fat or nonfat ricotta may be used with equally good results.

| | | |
|---|---|---|
| 1 | clove garlic, minced | 1 |
| 2/3 cup | ricotta cheese | 150 mL |
| 1/2 cup | freshly grated Parmesan cheese | 125 mL |
| 1 | package (12 oz/375 g) frozen white rice, thawed | 1 |
| | Salt and freshly cracked black pepper | |
| 20 | 1/2-inch (1 cm) cubes provolone or mozzarella cheese | 20 |
| 2 | large eggs | 2 |
| 1 1/2 cups | panko (Japanese bread crumbs) | 375 mL |
| | Nonstick cooking spray | |

1. In a medium bowl, stir together garlic, ricotta and Parmesan until blended. Stir in rice until combined. Season to taste with salt and pepper.

2. Scoop about 2 tbsp (30 mL) rice mixture into your palm and place 1 cheese cube on top. Form rice mixture into a ball around cheese. Place on a plate. Repeat with the remaining rice mixture and cheese. Cover loosely with plastic wrap and place in the freezer for 20 to 30 minutes or until firm.

3. Preheat air fryer to 390°F (200°C).

4. In a shallow dish, whisk eggs until blended. Spread panko in another shallow dish.

## Variation

*Gluten-Free Rice Balls:* Replace the panko with crushed gluten-free corn flakes cereal.

5. Remove 5 rice balls from the freezer. (Keep the remaining rice balls in the freezer until ready to coat and air-fry.) Working with 1 ball at a time, dip in egg, shaking off excess, then roll in panko, pressing gently to adhere. As they are coated, place rice balls in air fryer basket, leaving space in between. Spray with cooking spray.

6. Air-fry for 7 to 11 minutes or until golden brown. Serve immediately.

7. Repeat steps 5 and 6 with the remaining rice balls, egg and panko. Discard any excess egg and panko.

# Egg Rolls

This master egg roll recipe has a lot of flexibility; feel free to use up leftover meat or chicken in place of the shrimp and vary the vegetables according to what you have in the crisper. One fundamental tip: Don't overstuff! Egg roll wrappers are pliable, but they will tear if you stretch them too much.

## Makes 10 egg rolls

### Tips

The egg rolls can be assembled up to 1 day in advance. Refrigerate in an airtight container until ready to use. Increase the cooking time by 1 to 2 minutes for chilled egg rolls.

While assembling the egg rolls, keep the stack of wrappers moist by covering them with a damp towel.

| | | |
|---|---|---|
| 1 tbsp | cornstarch | 15 mL |
| 1 tsp | granulated sugar | 5 mL |
| 1/2 tsp | ground ginger | 2 mL |
| 2 1/2 tbsp | soy sauce | 37 mL |
| 1 tsp | white or cider vinegar | 5 mL |
| 2 tsp | vegetable oil | 10 mL |
| 3 cups | coleslaw mix | 750 mL |
| 1/3 cup | drained canned water chestnuts, chopped | 75 mL |
| 1/3 cup | chopped green onions | 75 mL |
| 1 cup | chopped cooked shrimp | 250 mL |
| 10 | refrigerated or thawed frozen 6 1/2-inch (16 cm) square egg roll wrappers | 10 |
| | Nonstick cooking spray | |

1. In a small cup, whisk together cornstarch, sugar, ginger, soy sauce and vinegar.

2. In a large skillet, heat oil over medium heat. Add coleslaw mix, water chestnuts and green onions. Cook, stirring, until cabbage is wilted, about 3 minutes. Stir in shrimp and cornstarch mixture. Cook, stirring, for 1 to 2 minutes or until thickened. Remove from heat and let cool for 10 minutes.

3. Preheat air fryer to 390°F (200°C).

## Variations

*Mushroom Egg Rolls:*
Omit the shrimp and add
8 oz (250 g) mushrooms,
chopped, with the green
onions in step 2. Cook,
stirring, for 6 to 7 minutes
or until most of the liquid
from the mushrooms has
evaporated.

Replace the shrimp with an
equal amount of chopped
cooked chicken, cooked
ground pork or drained
extra-firm tofu.

4. Place 1 wrapper on work surface, with an edge facing you. Spoon $\frac{1}{4}$ cup (60 mL) cabbage mixture onto bottom third. Fold the sides in toward the center and roll tightly away from you, enclosing filling. Repeat with the remaining wrappers and filling.

5. Place 3 to 4 egg rolls, seam side down, in air fryer basket. Spray generously with cooking spray. Air-fry for 5 to 7 minutes or until golden brown. Serve immediately. Repeat with the remaining egg rolls.

# Tex-Mex Egg Rolls

These deeply flavorful egg rolls are an iconic menu item in restaurants well beyond my state of Texas. One bite and you'll understand their popularity. Serve with Cilantro Lime Dipping Sauce (page 264), if desired.

**Makes
14 egg rolls**

## Tips

For the beans, purchase a 14- to 19-oz (398 to 540 mL) can, drain and rinse the beans, then measure out 1⅓ cups (325 mL).

An equal amount of pinto beans can be used in place of the black beans.

| | | |
|---|---|---|
| 8 oz | turkey or pork sausage (bulk or casings removed) | 250 g |
| ½ cup | packed fresh cilantro leaves, chopped | 125 mL |
| 1 tsp | ground cumin | 5 mL |
| 1⅓ cups | rinsed drained canned black beans | 325 mL |
| 1 cup | shredded Monterey Jack cheese | 250 mL |
| ¾ cup | thick and chunky salsa | 175 mL |
| 14 | refrigerated or thawed frozen 6½-inch (16 cm) square egg roll wrappers | 14 |
| 1 | large egg, lightly beaten | 1 |
| | Nonstick cooking spray | |

1. In a large skillet, cook sausage over medium-high heat, breaking it up with the back of a spoon, until no longer pink. Drain off any excess fat.

2. Transfer sausage to a large bowl and stir in cilantro, cumin, beans, cheese and salsa. Let cool for 10 minutes.

3. Preheat air fryer to 390°F (200°C).

4. Place 1 wrapper on work surface, with an edge facing you. Spoon ¼ cup (60 mL) filling onto bottom third. Fold the sides in toward the center and roll tightly away from you, enclosing filling. Repeat with the remaining wrappers and filling.

5. Place 3 to 4 egg rolls, seam side down, in air fryer basket. Spray generously with cooking spray. Air-fry for 5 to 7 minutes or until golden brown. Serve immediately. Repeat with the remaining egg rolls.

# Beer-Battered Fried Fish

Air-frying beer-battered fish is not only easier and less messy than frying, but it also has the distinct advantages of a splatter-free stovetop and no fried fish smell when the cooking and eating is complete. The key to getting the crunchiest coating is to coat the fish with batter as thinly as possible, shaking off any excess.

**Makes 4 servings**

### Variation

*Gluten-Free Fried Fish:* Replace the all-purpose flour with an all-purpose gluten-free flour blend and replace the panko with an equal amount of crushed gluten-free corn flakes cereal.

| | | |
|---|---|---|
| 1/4 cup | cornstarch | 60 mL |
| 1/4 cup | all-purpose flour | 60 mL |
| 1/4 tsp | salt | 1 mL |
| 1 | large egg white, lightly beaten | 1 |
| 1/2 cup | beer (not dark), chilled | 125 mL |
| 1 cup | panko (Japanese bread crumbs) | 250 mL |
| 4 | skinless pollock or other firm white fish fillets (each 8 oz/250 g), patted dry | 4 |
| | Nonstick cooking spray | |
| | Malt vinegar (optional) | |

1. In a medium bowl, whisk together cornstarch, flour and salt. Whisk in egg and beer until blended and smooth. Cover loosely with plastic wrap and refrigerate for 30 minutes to thicken.

2. Preheat air fryer to 390°F (200°C).

3. Spread panko in a shallow dish.

4. Working with 1 fish fillet at a time, dip in batter, shaking off excess, then dredge in panko, pressing gently to adhere. As they are dredged, place 2 fillets in air fryer basket, leaving space in between. Spray with cooking spray.

5. Air-fry for 10 to 12 minutes or until coating is golden brown and fish flakes easily when tested with a fork. Serve immediately with malt vinegar, if desired.

6. Repeat steps 4 and 5 with the remaining fish, batter and panko. Discard any excess batter and panko.

# Light and Crispy Fried Catfish

Panko — light and crisp bread crumbs — is one of the secrets to creating perfectly crispy catfish in the air fryer. Add your favorite herbs or spices in place of the seafood seasoning to vary this essential dish in countless ways.

## Makes 2 servings

### Tips

Tilapia fillets may be used in place of the catfish.

The fish can be prepared through step 3 and frozen (this will work only with fresh fish, not fish that has been previously frozen and thawed). Wrap the fish pieces in plastic wrap, then foil, completely enclosing them, and freeze for up to 3 months. When ready to cook, unwrap the frozen fish (do not thaw), place in air fryer basket and air-fry at 390°F (200°C) for 12 to 16 minutes or until coating is golden brown and fish flakes easily when tested with a fork.

### Variation

*Gluten-Free Fried Catfish:* Replace the panko with crushed gluten-free crackers or crushed gluten-free crisp rice cereal.

• *Preheat air fryer to 390°F (200°C)*

| | | |
|---|---|---|
| 1 cup | panko (Japanese bread crumbs) | 250 mL |
| 1 tsp | Old Bay or other seafood seasoning | 5 mL |
| 1 | large egg | 1 |
| 1/4 tsp | salt | 1 mL |
| 1/8 tsp | freshly cracked black pepper | 0.5 mL |
| 2 | skinless catfish fillets (each 6 oz/175 g), patted dry | 2 |

1. In a shallow dish, combine panko and Old Bay seasoning.

2. In another shallow dish, whisk together egg, salt and pepper.

3. Working with 1 fish fillet at a time, dip in egg, shaking off excess, then dredge in panko mixture, pressing gently to adhere. As they are dredged, place fillets in a single layer in air fryer basket. Discard any excess panko mixture and egg.

4. Air-fry for 10 to 14 minutes or until coating is golden brown and fish flakes easily when tested with a fork. Serve immediately.

# Fried Calamari with Sriracha Mayonnaise

Delicately crisp, tender as can be and fueled by a piquant mayonnaise alongside, these calamari are perfection with a tall glass of iced tea or lemonade on a sultry day.

## Makes 4 servings

### Tips

Regular tortilla chips can be used in place of the baked tortilla chips.

You can substitute 1¼ cups (300 mL) panko (Japanese bread crumbs) for the crushed tortilla chips.

Air fryers become very hot, especially when heated to maximum temperature. Use oven pads or mitts when touching the appliance and when opening and closing the basket.

- *Preheat air fryer to 390°F (200°C)*
- *Food processor*

| | | |
|---|---|---|
| 1½ lbs | cleaned squid | 750 g |
| 5 cups | baked tortilla chips | 1.25 L |
| | Nonstick cooking spray | |
| | Sriracha Mayonnaise (page 278) | |
| | Lemon wedges (optional) | |

1. Separate the squids' tentacles from their bodies (if it has not already been done). Slice the bodies into ½-inch (1 cm) rings and cut the tentacles in half if they are large. Rinse squid in a colander and drain. Pat dry with paper towels.

2. In food processor, process tortilla chips until finely ground. Spread crumbs in a shallow dish.

3. Working with 1 piece at a time, lightly spray squid with cooking spray, then dredge in crumbs, pressing gently to adhere. As they are dredged, place 6 to 8 pieces in air fryer basket, leaving space in between. Spray with cooking spray.

4. Air-fry for 3 minutes. Open basket and, using tongs or a spatula, carefully turn pieces over. Air-fry for 3 to 5 minutes or until golden brown. Serve immediately with Sriracha Mayonnaise and, if desired, lemon wedges.

5. Repeat steps 3 and 4 with the remaining squid and crumbs. Discard any excess crumbs.

# Crab Rangoon

This favorite Asian restaurant appetizer is simple as can be when made in an air fryer. Turn it into a light meal by pairing it with a fresh fruit salad or Asian slaw.

## Makes 20 pieces

### Tips

Either regular or reduced-fat cream cheese can be used in this recipe.

While assembling the crab Rangoon, keep the stack of wrappers moist by covering them with a damp towel.

The crab Rangoon can be assembled up to 1 day in advance. Refrigerate in an airtight container until ready to use. Increase the cooking time by 1 to 2 minutes for chilled crab Rangoon.

• *Preheat air fryer to 390°F (200°C)*

### Crab

| | | |
|---|---|---|
| 4 oz | cream cheese, softened | 125 g |
| 1 tbsp | minced gingerroot | 15 mL |
| 1 tbsp | Sriracha | 15 mL |
| 8 oz | fully cooked backfin (lump) crabmeat, picked over | 250 g |
| 1/4 cup | finely chopped green onions | 60 mL |
| | Salt and freshly ground black pepper | |
| 20 | 3 1/2-inch (9 cm) square wonton wrappers | 20 |
| 1 | large egg, beaten | 1 |
| | Nonstick cooking spray | |

### Dipping Sauce (Optional)

| | | |
|---|---|---|
| 3 tbsp | soy sauce | 45 mL |
| 1 tbsp | liquid honey | 15 mL |
| 1 tbsp | Sriracha | 15 mL |
| 1 tsp | rice vinegar or cider vinegar | 5 mL |
| 1/4 tsp | toasted (dark) sesame oil | 1 mL |

1. *Crab:* In a medium bowl, stir together cream cheese, ginger and Sriracha until blended and smooth. Gently stir in crab and green onions until combined. Season to taste with salt and pepper.

## Variation

Replace the crabmeat with an equal amount of finely chopped cooked shrimp or chicken.

2. Place 7 wrappers on work surface. Spoon 2 tsp (10 mL) crab mixture into the center of each wrapper. Using a brush or fingertip, brush the edges of each wrapper with egg. Fold up opposite corners of wrappers, pinching centers, to create an X shape. Press edges together to seal.

3. Place wontons in a single layer in air fryer basket, leaving about 1 inch (2.5 cm) space in between. Spray with cooking spray. Air-fry for 8 to 12 minutes or until golden brown.

4. Repeat steps 2 and 3 with the remaining wonton wrappers and crab mixture.

5. *Dipping Sauce:* If desired, in a small bowl, combine soy sauce, honey, Sriracha, vinegar and sesame oil. Serve immediately with wontons.

# Southern Fried Shrimp with Creole Mayonnaise

This peppery, cornmeal-crusted approach is a common method of frying shrimp throughout the American South, and it is every bit as delicious when air-fried. It is perfect for snacking, as an appetizer or as a meal with some fresh vegetables or a salad alongside.

**Makes 4 servings**

### Variation

*Gluten-Free Fried Shrimp:* Replace the all-purpose flour with an all-purpose gluten-free flour blend and be sure to use certified gluten-free cornmeal.

- Preheat air fryer to 390°F (200°C)

| | | |
|---|---|---|
| ⅔ cup | all-purpose flour | 150 mL |
| 1 cup | cornmeal | 250 mL |
| 2 | large eggs, lightly beaten | 2 |
| ¾ tsp | salt | 3 mL |
| ¼ tsp | freshly cracked black pepper | 1 mL |
| 1 lb | large shrimp, peeled and deveined | 500 g |
| | Nonstick cooking spray | |
| | Creole Mayonnaise (page 278) | |

1. Place flour in a large sealable plastic bag.

2. Spread cornmeal in a shallow dish.

3. In another shallow bowl, whisk together eggs, salt and pepper.

4. Add 8 shrimp to flour, seal and toss until coated. Working with 1 shrimp at a time, remove from flour, shaking off excess. Dip in egg, shaking off excess, then dredge in cornmeal, pressing gently to adhere. As they are dredged, place shrimp in air fryer basket, leaving space in between. Spray with cooking spray.

5. Air-fry for 4 to 7 minutes or until golden brown. Serve immediately with Creole Mayonnaise.

6. Repeat steps 4 and 5 with the remaining shrimp, flour, egg and cornmeal. Discard any excess flour, egg and cornmeal.

# Air-Fried Coconut Shrimp

The marriage of shrimp and coconut is a blissful one, made even better with a hint of fresh lime zest. It's a quick, satisfying dinner that requires little accompaniment beyond a fresh green or fruit salad alongside.

## Makes 4 servings

### Tip

Large shrimp typically have a count of 35 to 45 per pound (500 g).

### Variation

*Gluten-Free Coconut Shrimp:* Replace the panko with crushed gluten-free corn flakes cereal.

• Preheat air fryer to 390°F (200°C)

| | | |
|---|---|---|
| 1/3 cup | cornstarch | 75 mL |
| 1/2 tsp | salt | 2 mL |
| 1/8 tsp | cayenne pepper | 0.5 mL |
| 3/4 cup | sweetened flaked coconut | 175 mL |
| 3/4 cup | panko (Japanese bread crumbs) | 175 mL |
| 2 tsp | finely grated lime zest | 10 mL |
| 2 | large egg whites | 2 |
| 1 lb | large shrimp, peeled and deveined, tails on | 500 g |
| | Nonstick cooking spray | |

1. In a shallow dish, combine cornstarch, salt and cayenne.

2. In another shallow dish, combine coconut, panko and lime zest.

3. In a small bowl, whisk egg whites until foamy.

4. Working with 1 shrimp at a time, dredge in cornstarch mixture, dip in egg whites, shaking off excess, then dredge in coconut mixture, pressing gently to adhere. As they are dredged, place 7 shrimp in air fryer basket, leaving space in between. Spray generously with cooking spray.

5. Air-fry for 5 to 8 minutes or until golden brown. Serve immediately.

6. Repeat steps 4 and 5 with the remaining shrimp, cornstarch mixture, egg whites and coconut mixture. Discard any excess cornstarch mixture, egg whites and coconut mixture.

# Buttermilk Fried Chicken

In this lighter, simpler version of fried chicken, chicken drumsticks and thighs are marinated in spicy seasoned buttermilk before being tossed in a flavorful coating. A spritz of cooking spray is all it takes to deliver a crispy, crunchy "fried" texture.

**Makes 2 servings**

## Tips

If you prefer, you can use 2 bone-in chicken breasts (totaling no more than 1 lb/500 g) in place of the thighs and drumsticks.

You can use all drumsticks or all thighs in place of a combination.

Air fryers become very hot. Use oven pads or mitts when touching the appliance and when opening and closing the basket.

| | | |
|---|---|---|
| 2 | chicken drumsticks (about 8 oz/ 250 g total), patted dry | 2 |
| 2 | small chicken thighs (about 8 oz/ 250 g total), patted dry | 2 |
| $2/3$ cup | buttermilk | 150 mL |
| | Salt and freshly ground black pepper | |
| $1/8$ tsp | cayenne pepper | 0.5 mL |
| $2/3$ cup | all-purpose flour | 150 mL |
| 1 tsp | garlic powder | 5 mL |
| 1 tsp | paprika | 5 mL |
| 1 tsp | baking powder | 5 mL |
| | Nonstick cooking spray | |

1. In a large sealable plastic bag, combine drumsticks, thighs, buttermilk, $1/4$ tsp (1 mL) salt, $1/8$ tsp (0.5 mL) black pepper and cayenne. Press out most of the air, seal and gently squeeze bag to combine. Refrigerate for at least 20 minutes or for up to 12 hours.

2. Preheat air fryer to 380°F (200°C).

3. In another large sealable plastic bag, combine flour, garlic powder, paprika, baking powder, $3/4$ tsp (3 mL) salt and $3/4$ tsp (3 mL) black pepper.

## Variation

*Gluten-Free Fried Chicken:* Replace the all-purpose flour with an all-purpose gluten-free flour blend.

4. Remove 2 chicken pieces from buttermilk, shaking off excess, and place in bag with flour mixture. Seal and shake well, coating completely. Place in air fryer basket. Repeat with the remaining chicken and flour mixture, spacing chicken pieces evenly in a single layer in basket. Discard buttermilk marinade and any excess flour mixture. Spray chicken with cooking spray.

5. Air-fry for 20 minutes. Open basket and, using tongs or a spatula, carefully turn chicken over. Spray with cooking spray. Air-fry for 8 to 12 minutes or until coating is golden brown and an instant-read thermometer inserted in the thickest part of a drumstick registers 165°F (74°C). Serve immediately.

# Air-Fried Chicken Strips

These chicken strips require so little time but taste so good that it raises the bar for all other chicken strips, breasts and nuggets. Buttermilk adds a pleasant tang to each tender bite, and panko adds crispness without heaviness.

## Makes 4 servings

### Tips

In place of the chicken tenders, you can use 1 lb (500 g) boneless skinless chicken breasts, trimmed and cut into thick fingers.

Air fryers become very hot, especially when heated to maximum temperature. Use oven pads or mitts when touching the appliance and when opening and closing the basket.

### Variation

*Gluten-Free Chicken Strips:* Replace the all-purpose flour with an all-purpose gluten-free flour blend, and replace the panko with crushed gluten-free corn flakes cereal.

*• Preheat air fryer to 390°F (200°C)*

| | | |
|---|---|---|
| ½ cup | all-purpose flour | 125 mL |
| ½ tsp | salt | 2 mL |
| ¼ tsp | freshly ground black pepper | 1 mL |
| 1 lb | chicken tenders, trimmed and patted dry | 500 g |
| 1½ cups | panko (Japanese bread crumbs) | 375 mL |
| 1 | large egg | 1 |
| ½ cup | buttermilk | 125 mL |
| | Nonstick cooking spray | |

1. Place flour, salt and pepper in a large sealable plastic bag. Seal bag and shake to combine. Add chicken, seal and toss until coated.

2. Spread panko in a shallow dish.

3. In a medium bowl, whisk together egg and buttermilk until blended.

4. Working with 1 chicken tender at a time, remove from flour, shaking off excess. Dip in egg mixture, shaking off excess, then dredge in panko, pressing gently to adhere. As they are dredged, place 3 to 4 tenders (depending on size) in air fryer basket, leaving space in between. Spray with cooking spray.

5. Air-fry for 5 minutes. Open basket and, using tongs or a spatula, carefully turn tenders over. Air-fry for 3 to 7 minutes or until golden brown. Serve immediately.

6. Repeat steps 4 and 5 with the remaining tenders, egg mixture and panko. Discard any excess egg mixture and panko.

# Buffalo Chicken Wings

According to most accounts, no actual buffaloes were involved in the creation of Buffalo chicken wings; rather, they were "invented" at the Anchor Bar in Buffalo, New York. They are the official food of countless sporting events, but with this streamlined version, you can savor them any time the craving strikes. Serve with Blue Cheese Dressing (page 274) and celery sticks, if desired.

## Makes 2 servings

### Variations

For a milder sauce, replace 1½ tbsp (22 mL) of the hot pepper sauce with ketchup or canned tomato sauce.

For a sweet and spicy sauce, replace 1 tbsp (15 mL) of the hot pepper sauce with liquid honey.

• Preheat air fryer to 360°F (180°C)

| 6 | chicken wings, tips removed and wings cut into drumettes and flats | 6 |
| --- | --- | --- |
| ¼ cup | unsalted butter, cut into small pieces | 60 mL |
| 2 tbsp | hot pepper sauce | 30 mL |
| ¾ tsp | Worcestershire sauce | 3 mL |
| ¾ tsp | cider vinegar | 3 mL |

1. Place chicken wings in a single layer (with some overlap) in air fryer basket. Air-fry for 24 to 28 minutes, shaking basket twice, until skin is browned and crisp and juices run clear when chicken is pierced.

2. Meanwhile, in a small saucepan set over medium heat, combine butter, hot pepper sauce, Worcestershire sauce and vinegar. Cook, stirring, until butter is melted and mixture comes to a low boil. Remove from heat.

3. Transfer wings to a bowl. Add sauce and toss to coat. Serve immediately.

# Asian Pot Stickers

Some versions of pot stickers are oily and overly rich, but this air-fried variation is light, fresh and well-balanced. Serve with Asian Dipping Sauce (page 268), if desired.

## Makes 48 pot stickers

### Tips

You can use an equal amount of ground turkey or chicken in place of the pork.

Air fryers become very hot, especially when heated to maximum temperature. Use oven pads or mitts when touching the appliance and when opening and closing the basket.

| | | |
|---|---|---|
| 2 tbsp | cornstarch | 30 mL |
| 1 tsp | granulated sugar | 5 mL |
| 1½ tbsp | soy sauce | 22 mL |
| 1 tbsp | water | 15 mL |
| 8 oz | lean ground pork | 250 g |
| 8 oz | mushrooms, chopped | 250 g |
| 2½ cups | chopped cabbage | 625 mL |
| ½ cup | finely chopped green onions | 125 mL |
| 2 tsp | minced gingerroot | 10 mL |
| 1 tbsp | toasted (dark) sesame oil | 15 mL |
| 48 | 3½-inch (9 cm) square wonton wrappers | 48 |
| | Nonstick cooking spray | |

1. In a small cup, combine cornstarch, sugar, soy sauce and water until blended.

2. In a large skillet, cook pork over medium-high heat, breaking it up with the back of a spoon, until no longer pink. Add mushrooms, cabbage, green onions, ginger and sesame oil; cook, stirring, for 4 to 5 minutes or until mushrooms are soft and cabbage is wilted. Add cornstarch mixture and cook, stirring, for 1 to 2 minutes or until thickened. Remove from heat and let cool in skillet, then transfer to a bowl, cover and refrigerate until cold.

3. Preheat air fryer to 390°F (200°C).

4. Working with 1 wonton wrapper at a time (see tip, at left), spoon 2 tsp (10 mL) pork mixture into the center of the wrapper. Moisten the edges of the wrapper with water. Fold in half into a triangle, pinching edges together to seal. Loosely cover filled dumplings with plastic wrap or a kitchen towel to prevent drying. Repeat with 7 more wrappers and filling.

5. Place potstickers in air fryer basket, leaving space in between. Spray generously with cooking spray. Air-fry for 5 minutes. Open basket and, using tongs or a spatula, carefully turn potstickers over. Air-fry for 4 to 6 minutes or until golden brown. Serve immediately.

6. Repeat steps 4 and 5 with the remaining wonton wrappers and pork mixture.

# Mini Latkes with Multiple Toppings

These are everything a good latke should be: crisp-edged with a creamy interior, plus a fresh potato and onion flavor that usually gets lost when latkes are fried in a copious amount of oil. For the best results, make the batter for these just before frying and serve immediately.

**Makes 4 servings**

**Tip**

For best results and especially crispy latkes, stick with russet potatoes; waxy potatoes will yield creamy but less crispy results.

• *Preheat air fryer to 390°F (200°C)*

| 2 | large russet potatoes, peeled (about 1½ lbs/375 g) | 2 |
|---|---|---|
| 1 | small onion | 1 |
| 3 tbsp | all-purpose flour | 45 mL |
| 1 tsp | baking powder | 5 mL |
| ¾ tsp | salt | 3 mL |
| ¼ tsp | freshly ground black pepper | 1 mL |
| 1 | large egg | 1 |
| | Nonstick cooking spray | |

### Suggested Toppings

Sour cream + applesauce

Thinly sliced pastrami + thinly sliced dill pickles

Plain Greek yogurt + pomegranate seeds

Smoked salmon + chopped fresh parsley or chives

1. Place potatoes in a medium saucepan and add enough water to cover. Bring to a boil over high heat. Boil for 9 to 11 minutes or until potatoes are still firm but tender enough to easily pierce with a fork. Drain and let cool until cool enough to handle.

## Variation

You can replace half the amount of potatoes with an equal amount of parsnips, celery root or butternut squash.

2. Using a box grater, coarsely grate potatoes and onion. Place grated potatoes and onion in the center of a clean dish towel. Working over the sink, gather the ends of the towel together and twist the towel tightly around the potatoes and onion. Squeeze out as much liquid as possible.

3. Transfer potatoes and onion to a medium bowl. Add flour, baking powder, salt, pepper and egg, stirring to combine. Form $1/4$-cup (60 mL) measures of potato mixture into $1/2$-inch (1 cm) thick patties.

4. Place 2 to 3 patties in air fryer basket, leaving space in between. Spray with cooking spray. Air-fry for 13 to 17 minutes or until deep golden brown. Repeat with the remaining patties. Serve warm with any of the suggested toppings, as desired.

# Old-Fashioned Cake Donuts

Homemade donuts can be a bit of a project, but not so when you air-fry. The results are great: hot, crisp donuts with less fat and calories than deep-fried donuts. Moreover, the cleanup is a breeze! Once you've made this basic recipe once or twice, you can do pretty much anything you like in terms of glazes and toppings.

**Makes 6 to 8 donuts**

## Tips

A 2½-inch (6 cm) round biscuit or cookie cutter can be used in place of the donut cutter. Use a 1-inch (2.5 cm) cutter to cut out "holes."

Air fryers become very hot, especially when heated to maximum temperature. Use oven pads or mitts when touching the appliance and when opening and closing the basket.

- 2½-inch (6 cm) donut cutter

| | | |
|---|---|---|
| 1⅔ cups | all-purpose flour | 400 mL |
| 1½ tsp | baking powder | 7 mL |
| ½ tsp | salt | 2 mL |
| ⅛ tsp | ground nutmeg (optional) | 0.5 mL |
| ⅔ cup | granulated sugar | 150 mL |
| 2 | large eggs, at room temperature | 2 |
| 2½ tbsp | milk, at room temperature | 37 mL |
| 2 tbsp | unsalted butter, melted and cooled slightly | 30 mL |
| 1 tsp | vanilla extract | 5 mL |
| | Nonstick cooking spray | |
| | Confectioners' (icing) sugar | |

1. In a medium bowl, whisk together flour, baking powder, salt and nutmeg (if using).

2. In another medium bowl, using an electric mixer on medium-high speed, beat granulated sugar and eggs for 3 to 5 minutes or until thick and pale yellow. With mixer on low speed, beat in milk, butter and vanilla. Gently stir in flour mixture until just blended. Cover bowl with plastic wrap and refrigerate for 30 minutes or until dough is firm enough to roll.

3. Preheat air fryer to 390°F (200°C).

## Variation

*Cinnamon Sugar Donuts:* Replace the nutmeg with ¼ tsp (1 mL) ground cinnamon. Replace the confectioners' (icing) sugar with 3 tbsp (45 mL) granulated sugar combined with 1½ tsp (7 mL) ground cinnamon.

4. On a floured surface, roll or press out dough to a thickness of about ¼ inch (0.5 cm). Using the donut cutter, cut out circles (dough will be very soft). Place donuts and holes on a piece of parchment paper, keeping them separate. Gather up the scraps, roll and cut out more donuts and holes.

5. Place 2 to 3 donuts in air fryer basket, leaving 1 inch (2.5 cm) in between. Air-fry for 3 minutes. Open basket and, using tongs or a spatula, carefully turn donuts over. Air-fry for 2 to 5 minutes or until golden brown and a tester inserted in the thickest part of a donut comes out clean. Repeat with the remaining donuts. Let cool on a wire rack for at least 5 minutes.

6. Place 8 donut holes in air fryer basket, leaving space in between. Air-fry for 3 to 6 minutes or until golden brown and a tester inserted in the thickest part of a donut hole comes out clean. Let cool on a wire rack for at least 5 minutes.

7. Sift confectioners' sugar over donuts and donut holes. Serve warm or at room temperature.

# Breakfast and Brunch

# Golden Raisin and Coconut Muesli

This muesli is just one of many good reasons to stock both golden raisins and coconut in your pantry. My favorite spice to use is ground ginger, but an equal amount of ground cardamom, allspice or cinnamon is welcome, too.

**Makes about three ¹/₂-cup (125 mL) servings**

## Tips

An equal amount of vegetable oil, olive oil or unsalted butter, melted, can be used in place of the coconut oil.

Dark raisins or any chopped dried fruit can be used in place of the golden raisins.

## Storage Tip

Store the cooled muesli in an airtight container at room temperature for up to 3 weeks or in the freezer for up to 3 months.

• *Preheat air fryer to 300°F (160°C)*

| | | |
|---|---|---|
| 1 tbsp | liquid honey | 15 mL |
| 1 tbsp | virgin coconut oil, melted | 15 mL |
| ¹/₂ tsp | ground ginger | 2 mL |
| ¹/₈ tsp | salt | 0.5 mL |
| 1 cup | large-flake (old-fashioned) rolled oats | 250 mL |
| ¹/₄ cup | unsweetened flaked coconut | 60 mL |
| ¹/₄ cup | golden raisins | 60 mL |

1. In a medium bowl, whisk together honey, coconut oil, ginger and salt until well blended. Stir in oats and coconut until well coated.

2. Spread mixture in a single layer in air fryer basket. Air-fry for 15 to 20 minutes, stirring twice, until oats are golden brown.

3. Transfer muesli to a medium bowl and let cool completely. Stir in raisins.

# Cranberry Pecan Granola

The cereal bowl is just one destination for this delectable granola. Grab or pack a handful for a snack, stir it into Greek-style yogurt or sprinkle it on vanilla ice cream.

**Makes about four ¹/₂-cup (125 mL) servings**

## Tips

An equal amount of virgin coconut oil, melted, vegetable oil or olive oil can be used in place of the butter.

An equal amount of pure maple syrup can be used in place of the honey.

Any other dried fruit (such as raisins, cherries, chopped apricots or chopped figs) can be used in place of the cranberries.

Any variety of chopped nuts (such as hazelnuts, walnuts, almonds or cashews) or seeds (such as sunflower, green pumpkin or hemp) can be used in place of the pecans.

## Storage Tip

Store the cooled granola in an airtight container at room temperature for up to 3 weeks or in the freezer for up to 3 months.

• *Preheat air fryer to 300°F (160°C)*

| | | |
|---|---|---|
| 1 cup | large-flake (old-fashioned) rolled oats | 250 mL |
| ¹/₂ cup | chopped pecans | 125 mL |
| ¹/₄ tsp | ground cinnamon | 1 mL |
| ¹/₈ tsp | salt | 0.5 mL |
| 3 tbsp | liquid honey | 45 mL |
| 2 tbsp | unsalted butter, melted | 30 mL |
| 1 tsp | vanilla extract | 5 mL |
| ¹/₃ cup | dried cranberries | 75 mL |

1. In a large bowl, stir together oats, pecans, cinnamon and salt.

2. In a medium bowl, whisk together honey, butter and vanilla until well blended.

3. Add the honey mixture to the oats mixture, stirring until well coated.

4. Spread mixture in a single layer in air fryer basket. Air-fry for 13 to 18 minutes, stirring twice, until oats are golden brown.

5. Transfer granola to a medium bowl and let cool completely. Stir in cranberries.

# Air-Baked Oatmeal to Go

One of my favorite ways to enjoy oatmeal is these individual baked oatmeal cups. They are completely customizable, based on what you do or do not stir into them, so you can add in seasonal fruits, spices, nuts or whatever else suits your fancy.

## Makes 4 servings

**Tip**

For the dried fruit, try raisins, cranberries or chopped apricots, or a combination.

**Storage Tip**

Store the cooled oatmeal in an airtight container in the refrigerator for up to 1 week. Enjoy cold or at room temperature, or warm in the microwave on Medium-High (70%) for 60 to 75 seconds.

- *Preheat air fryer to 330°F (160°C)*
- *8 standard-size foil or paper muffin cup liners*

| | | |
|---|---|---|
| 1¼ cups | large-flake (old-fashioned) rolled oats | 300 mL |
| 1 tsp | baking powder | 5 mL |
| ½ tsp | ground cinnamon | 2 mL |
| ¼ tsp | salt | 1 mL |
| 1 | large egg | 1 |
| 1 tbsp | packed light brown sugar | 15 mL |
| 2 tsp | unsalted butter, melted | 10 mL |
| 1 tsp | vanilla extract | 5 mL |
| 1¼ cups | milk (dairy or plain nondairy) | 300 mL |

### Suggested Stir-Ins (Choose One)

| | | |
|---|---|---|
| ½ cup | fresh or thawed frozen blueberries or raspberries | 125 mL |
| 3 tbsp | miniature semisweet chocolate chips | 45 mL |
| 3 tbsp | dried fruit (see tip, at left) | 45 mL |
| 3 tbsp | chocolate or vanilla protein powder | 45 mL |
| 1 tbsp | ground flax seeds (flaxseed meal) | 15 mL |

1. Place one muffin cup liner inside another. Repeat to create 4 doubled liners.

2. In a medium bowl, stir together oats, baking powder, cinnamon and salt.

3. In a large bowl, whisk egg. Whisk in brown sugar, butter and vanilla until blended. Whisk in milk.

## Variations

*Banana Baked Oatmeal:* Replace ½ cup (125 mL) of the milk with mashed very ripe banana.

*Pumpkin Spice Baked Oatmeal:* Replace ½ cup (125 mL) of the milk with pumpkin purée (not pie filling). Add ¼ cup (60 mL) dried cranberries in step 4, skipping any additional stir-ins.

4. Add the oats mixture to the egg mixture, stirring until combined. Add any of the suggested stir-ins, as desired.

5. Divide batter equally among the doubled liners.

6. Place filled liners in air fryer basket, spacing them evenly. Air-fry for 20 to 25 minutes or until golden brown at the edges and just set at the center. Serve warm or let cool completely and serve cold or at room temperature.

# Crunchy Granola Cups with Yogurt and Fruit

Because these crunchy granola cups are so portable, you can fill them and carry them with you out the door and eat as you head to work or the gym, or to walk the dog. They're great for summer picnics as well: simply pack the cups in an airtight container and the yogurt and fruit in the cooler. Once you've reached your destination, fill and enjoy!

## Makes 4 servings

### Tips
The ground flax seeds can be replaced by 1½ tbsp (22 mL) chia seeds.

An equal amount of unsalted butter, melted, can be used in place of the coconut oil.

### Storage Tip
The granola cups can be stored in an airtight container at room temperature for up to 3 days or frozen for up to 3 months.

### Variation
For an easy dessert, replace the yogurt with softly whipped cream, frozen yogurt or ice cream.

• *Preheat air fryer to 320°F (160°C)*
• *8 standard-size foil or paper muffin cup liners*

| | | |
|---|---|---|
| 3 tbsp | liquid honey or brown rice syrup | 45 mL |
| 1½ tbsp | virgin coconut oil, melted | 22 mL |
| 1 tsp | vanilla extract | 5 mL |
| ⅛ tsp | salt | 0.5 mL |
| 1 cup | large-flake (old-fashioned) or quick-cooking rolled oats | 250 mL |
| 2 tbsp | ground flax seeds (flaxseed meal) | 30 mL |
| **Filling** | | |
| ¾ cup | vanilla yogurt | 175 mL |
| ½ cup | berries (such as blueberries or raspberries) or diced fruit | 125 mL |

1. Place one muffin cup liner inside another. Repeat to create 4 doubled liners.

2. In a medium bowl, whisk together honey, coconut oil, vanilla and salt until blended. Stir in oats and flax seeds, stirring until completely coated.

3. Divide mixture evenly among the doubled liners, gently pressing down in the center of each to compact and make a cup shape.

4. Place filled liners in air fryer basket. Air-fry for 14 to 18 minutes or until golden brown. Carefully transfer to a wire rack and let cool completely.

5. When ready to eat, fill each granola cup with yogurt and fruit. Serve immediately.

# Spicy-Sweet Bacon

Do you need a reason to love this recipe? Absolutely not! And because it is so quick and easy to make in the air fryer, you do not need a special occasion, either — any weekday will do!

## Makes 2 servings

### Tip
If you do not want the spice, simply omit the cayenne pepper.

### Variation
*Air-Fried Bacon:* Prepare as directed, but omit the brown sugar mixture.

• Preheat air fryer to 360°F (180°C)

| | | |
|---|---|---|
| 4 oz | thick-cut bacon slices | 125 g |
| 1½ tbsp | packed light brown sugar | 22 mL |
| ¼ tsp | cayenne pepper | 1 mL |

1. Cut strips of bacon crosswise into thirds (to more easily fit into air fryer).

2. In a small cup, stir together brown sugar and cayenne pepper.

3. Arrange half the bacon slices in a single layer in air fryer basket. They should be close together, but not overlapping. Sprinkle evenly with half the brown sugar mixture. Air-fry for 5 to 8 minutes or until bacon is crisp and glazed. Transfer to a plate or wire rack and let cool for 5 minutes before serving. Repeat with the remaining bacon and brown sugar mixture.

# Air-Fried Sausages

**Frying up sausages for everyone in the family this morning? It's no longer a chore. Lightly browned, with crispy skins, these air-fried sausages are great for breakfast in a hurry or a leisurely weekend brunch.**

**Makes 4 servings**

### Variation

*Maple Sausages:* Lightly brush sausages with 1½ tbsp (22 mL) pure maple syrup during the final 2 minutes of air-frying.

- Preheat air fryer to 390°F (200°C)

| 8 | small breakfast sausage links | 8 |
|---|---|---|

1. Place sausages in a single layer in air fryer basket, spacing evenly. Air-fry for 5 to 8 minutes or until sausages are cooked through.

# Parmesan Air-Baked Eggs

**Forget fried: you'll love these air-baked eggs best of all. A bit of cream and Parmesan yields ethereal eggs that are great eaten with a spoon or scooped up with fingers of crisp toast.**

**Makes 2 servings**

## Tips

If you have fresh herbs on hand, use them! Use 1 tbsp (15 mL) minced fresh chives, parsley or basil in place of the dried Italian seasoning.

An equal amount of grated Romano, manchego, Asiago or sharp (old) Cheddar cheese can be used in place of the Parmesan.

- Preheat air fryer to 360°F (180°C)
- Two ⅔-cup (150 mL) ramekins, sprayed with nonstick cooking spray

| | | |
|---|---|---|
| ¼ cup | light (5%) cream | 60 mL |
| ½ tsp | dried Italian seasoning | 2 mL |
| 4 | large eggs | 4 |
| 2 tbsp | freshly grated Parmesan cheese | 30 mL |
| | Salt and freshly cracked black pepper | |

1. Divide cream and Italian seasoning evenly between prepared ramekins. Carefully crack 2 eggs into each ramekin, without breaking the yolks. Sprinkle each with half the cheese.

2. Place ramekins in air fryer basket. Air-fry for 6 to 9 minutes or until egg whites are set and yolks are just beginning to set. Remove ramekins from basket and let stand for 5 minutes before serving.

# Portobello and Prosciutto Air-Fried Eggs

Portobello mushrooms are perfect vessels for eggs. When they are filled with prosciutto and Parmesan cheese, this quick and easy breakfast tastes restaurant-worthy.

**Makes 2 servings**

### Tips

If you can only find large or extra-large portobello mushrooms, simply air-fry one mushroom at a time.

If desired, leave out the prosciutto to make this a vegetarian dish.

• *Preheat air fryer to 390°F (200°C)*

| | | |
|---|---|---|
| 2 | medium portobello mushrooms, stems removed and dark gills scraped out | 2 |
| 2 tsp | olive oil | 10 mL |
| | Salt and freshly ground black pepper | |
| 2 | large eggs | 2 |
| ¼ cup | chopped prosciutto or deli ham | 60 mL |
| 2 tbsp | freshly grated Parmesan cheese | 30 mL |
| | Chopped fresh basil or parsley (optional) | |

1. Brush mushrooms with oil and season with salt and pepper. Place, cut side up and close together (but not touching), in air fryer basket. Crack 1 egg into each mushroom. Season with salt and pepper. Sprinkle evenly with prosciutto and cheese.

2. Air-fry for 10 to 14 minutes or until mushrooms are tender and egg whites and yolks are firm, not runny. Sprinkle with basil, if desired.

# Air-Fried Eggs and Hash

A shower of green onions on a fast air-frying of potatoes makes a traditional hash with unexpected ease, as well as fresh, bright flavor. Perfectly cooked eggs on top? It's all ready in no time.

**Makes 2 servings**

## Tips

The hash can be made without the eggs. Skip adding the eggs in step 3 and air-fry as directed in step 4.

Do not put the foil in the basket while the air fryer preheats. The foil can be sucked into the heater and could start to burn.

Air fryers become very hot. Use oven pads or mitts when touching the appliance and when opening and closing the basket.

• *Preheat air fryer to 360°F (180°C)*

| | | |
|---|---|---|
| | Nonstick cooking spray | |
| 3 | red-skinned potatoes, scrubbed and cut into $\frac{1}{4}$-inch (0.5 cm) dice | 3 |
| 1 tbsp | olive oil | 15 mL |
| | Salt and freshly cracked black pepper | |
| 2 | small green onions, chopped, white and green parts divided | 2 |
| 2 | large eggs | 2 |

1. Place a piece of foil in bottom of air fryer basket, leaving $\frac{1}{2}$ inch (1 cm) between the foil and the inside edge of the basket. Spray foil with nonstick cooking spray.

2. On prepared foil, toss potatoes with oil, $\frac{1}{4}$ tsp (1 mL) salt and $\frac{1}{8}$ tsp (0.5 mL) pepper. Spread in a single layer. Air-fry for 10 to 12 minutes or until potatoes are fork-tender.

3. Open basket and stir potatoes. Stir in white parts of green onions. Make 2 evenly spaced wells in the hash. Crack eggs into the wells and sprinkle with salt and pepper.

4. Air-fry for 4 to 6 minutes or until egg whites are opaque. Sprinkle with green parts of onions.

# Bacon and Swiss Hash Brown Casserole

This is indulgent brunch fare, transformed into svelte weekday morning eating. It's still great on a lazy Saturday; simply add a side of fresh fruit, endless cups of coffee and the magic of weekend relaxation.

**Makes 2 servings**

**Tip**
An equal amount of sour cream can be used in place of the yogurt.

- *Preheat air fryer to 390°F (200°C)*
- *6-inch (15 cm) round metal cake pan, sprayed with nonstick cooking spray*

| | | |
|---|---|---|
| 1¼ cups | frozen diced hash brown potatoes with peppers and onions, thawed | 300 mL |
| 2 | large eggs | 2 |
| ¼ tsp | salt | 1 mL |
| ⅛ tsp | freshly cracked black pepper | 0.5 mL |
| 3 tbsp | plain Greek yogurt | 45 mL |
| 2 | slices bacon, cooked and crumbled | 2 |
| ¼ cup | shredded Swiss cheese | 60 mL |

1. Spread hash browns in a single layer in prepared cake pan. Place pan in air fryer basket. Air-fry for 10 to 12 minutes until golden brown.

2. Meanwhile, in a small bowl, whisk eggs until blended. Whisk in salt, pepper and yogurt until blended. Stir in bacon.

3. Remove pan from air fryer and pour egg mixture evenly over hash browns. Sprinkle with cheese.

4. Return pan to air fryer and air-fry for 12 to 17 minutes or until eggs are just set (they will continue to cook from the heat of the pan). Let cool on a wire rack for at least 10 minutes before cutting in half and serving. Serve hot or warm.

# Cheesy Breakfast Strata

This master recipe for breakfast strata is both extremely flexible and extremely rewarding. It tastes rich but not heavy, is packed with bakery bread but not dense, and is reasonably low in fat and calories. The Gruyère and thyme are interchangeable with the cheese and herbs of your choice.

## Makes 2 servings

### Variations

*Ham and Cheese Strata:*
Add ½ cup (125 mL) chopped cooked ham with the bread in step 1.

*Italian Breakfast Strata:*
Add ½ cup (125 mL) drained cooked crumbled Italian sausage (pork or turkey) with the bread in step 1. Replace the Gruyère with shredded fontina or Italian cheese blend. Add ¼ tsp (1 mL) dried Italian seasoning with the salt in step 2.

- 6-inch (15 cm) round metal cake pan, sprayed with nonstick cooking spray

| | | |
|---|---|---|
| 2 | thick slices soft French- or Italian-style bakery bread, torn into small pieces (about 1½ cups/375 mL) | 2 |
| ½ cup | shredded Gruyère or Swiss cheese, divided | 125 mL |
| 1 | large egg | 1 |
| ½ cup | milk | 125 mL |
| ¼ tsp | dried thyme | 1 mL |
| ⅛ tsp | salt | 0.5 mL |
| ⅛ tsp | freshly cracked black pepper | 0.5 mL |

1. Place bread in prepared pan. Sprinkle with half the cheese.

2. In a small bowl, whisk egg until blended. Whisk in milk, thyme, salt and pepper until blended. Pour evenly over bread in pan. Sprinkle with the remaining cheese. Place a piece of parchment or waxed paper over pan and press down to help bread absorb liquid. Let stand for 15 minutes.

3. Meanwhile, preheat air fryer to 330°F (160°C).

4. Remove the parchment and place pan in air fryer basket. Air-fry for 13 to 16 minutes or until bubbling and golden brown. Transfer pan to a wire rack and let cool for 10 minutes before serving.

# Cherry Tomato and Parmesan Omelet

Here's a quick and easy, but so satisfying, breakfast, especially when summer tomatoes are in season. The method is equally friendly to other vegetables, such as chopped plum (Roma) tomatoes, finely chopped bell pepper or chopped mushrooms.

**Makes 2 servings**

### Variations

*Bacon, Cheddar and Chives Omelet:* Omit the cherry tomatoes and step 1. Replace the parsley with 1 tbsp (15 mL) chopped fresh chives and stir 2 tbsp (30 mL) crumbled cooked bacon into the egg mixture. Use 3 tbsp (45 mL) shredded sharp (old) Cheddar cheese in place of the Parmesan, adding all of it to the egg mixture in step 2.

*Green Chile and Pepper Jack Omelet:* Omit the cherry tomatoes and step 1. Add 1/2 tsp (2 mL) ground cumin with the salt and stir 3 tbsp (45 mL) drained canned green chiles into the egg mixture. Use 3 tbsp (45 mL) shredded pepper Jack or Monterey Jack cheese in place of the Parmesan, adding all of it to the egg mixture in step 2.

- Preheat air fryer to 390°F (200°C)
- 6-inch (15 cm) round metal cake pan, sprayed with nonstick cooking spray

| | | |
|---|---|---|
| 4 | cherry tomatoes, quartered | 4 |
| 2 tsp | olive oil | 10 mL |
| 3 | large eggs | 3 |
| 1/8 tsp | salt | 0.5 mL |
| Pinch | freshly ground black pepper | Pinch |
| 2 tbsp | chopped fresh flat-leaf (Italian) parsley | 30 mL |
| 2 tbsp | freshly grated Parmesan cheese, divided | 30 mL |

1. Place tomatoes in prepared pan and drizzle with oil. Place pan in air fryer basket. Air-fry for 2 minutes.

2. Meanwhile, in a medium bowl, whisk eggs, salt and pepper until blended. Stir in parsley and 1 tbsp (15 mL) cheese.

3. Open basket and pour egg mixture over tomatoes. Air-fry for 3 to 5 minutes or until eggs are just set. Using a spatula, transfer omelet to a plate. Sprinkle with the remaining cheese.

# So-Easy Spanish Frittata

You may doubt the use of kettle-cooked potato chips here, but this frittata is based on tortilla Española, which typically includes crispy fried potatoes. The chips make an ideal quick substitution, softening into tender bites of potato as the frittata cooks.

## Makes 2 servings

### Tips

Use either hot or sweet smoked paprika.

An equal amount of ground cumin can be used in place of the smoked paprika.

- *Preheat air fryer to 390°F (200°C)*
- *6-inch (15 cm) round metal cake pan, sprayed with nonstick cooking spray*

| | | |
|---|---|---|
| 2 | large eggs | 2 |
| ¼ tsp | smoked paprika (optional) | 1 mL |
| ⅔ cup | coarsely crushed kettle-cooked potato chips | 150 mL |
| ¼ cup | chopped drained roasted red bell peppers | 60 mL |
| 2 tbsp | grated manchego, Romano or Parmesan cheese | 30 mL |

1. In a medium bowl, whisk eggs and paprika (if using) until blended. Stir in potato chips and let stand for 10 minutes. Stir in roasted peppers and cheese. Pour into prepared pan.

2. Place pan in air fryer basket. Air-fry for 4 to 6 minutes or until eggs are just set (they will continue to cook from the heat of the pan). Transfer to a wire rack and let cool for 5 minutes. Serve warm or let cool completely.

# Migas

Who knew that corn tortilla chips and eggs could work in such perfect harmony? Add an artful mix of hot, creamy, crunchy and crisp elements on top for an extra-special south-of-the-border breakfast.

## Makes 2 servings

## Tips

Either regular or reduced-fat tortilla chips can be used. Alternatively, use 2 small corn tortillas, torn into small pieces.

An equal amount of finely chopped onions or shallots can be used in place of the green onions.

- Preheat air fryer to 390°F (200°C)
- 6-inch (15 cm) round metal cake pan, sprayed with nonstick cooking spray

| 2 | large eggs | 2 |
|---|---|---|
| ¼ tsp | ground cumin | 1 mL |
| ⅔ cup | coarsely crushed tortilla chips | 150 mL |
| 2 tbsp | chopped green onions | 30 mL |
| 2 tbsp | shredded Monterey Jack or pepper Jack cheese | 30 mL |

### Suggested Accompaniments

Salsa or hot sauce

Diced Hass avocado

Minced fresh cilantro

Thinly sliced green onions

1. In a medium bowl, whisk eggs and cumin until blended. Stir in tortilla chips and let stand for 10 minutes. Stir in green onions and cheese. Pour into prepared pan.

2. Place pan in air fryer basket. Air-fry for 4 to 6 minutes or until eggs are just set (they will continue to cook from the heat of the pan). Transfer to a wire rack and let cool for 5 minutes. Serve warm, with any of the suggested accompaniments, as desired.

# Huevos Rancheros

Having grown up in California, and now living in Texas, I am unabashedly fussy about Tex-Mex food. That's why I prefer to make it myself. The simplest dishes are typically my favorite, like this air-fried rendition of huevos rancheros. It's equally terrific for lunch or dinner as it is for breakfast.

## Makes 1 serving

### Tips

You can use ²⁄₃ cup (150 mL) rinsed drained canned black beans or pinto beans, mashed with a fork, in place of the refried beans.

A flour tortilla of the same size can be used in place of the corn tortilla.

• *Preheat air fryer to 390°F (200°C)*

| | | |
|---|---|---|
| ¹⁄₂ cup | canned fat-free refried beans | 125 mL |
| 3 tbsp | thick and chunky salsa, divided | 45 mL |
| 1 | 6-inch (15 cm) soft corn tortilla | 1 |
| | Nonstick cooking spray | |
| 1 | large egg | 1 |
| 1 tbsp | minced fresh cilantro | 15 mL |
| 1 tbsp | crumbled queso fresco or mild feta cheese | 15 mL |

### Suggested Accompaniments

| | | |
|---|---|---|
| ¹⁄₂ | lime (for squeezing) | ¹⁄₂ |
| | Diced Hass avocado | |
| | Thinly sliced green onions | |
| | Thinly sliced jalapeño peppers | |

1. In a small bowl, combine refried beans and 2 tbsp (30 mL) salsa until blended.

2. Lightly spray both sides of tortilla with cooking spray. Spread bean mixture to within ¹⁄₂ inch (1 cm) of the edge. Use the back of the spoon to create a slight well in the center.

3. Place tortilla in air fryer basket. Carefully break egg into well. Air-fry for 4 to 6 minutes or until egg whites and yolks are firm, not runny. Serve topped with cilantro, queso fresco, the remaining salsa and any of the suggested accompaniments, as desired.

# Air-Fried Egg Bullseyes

One of my favorite breakfasts from childhood just became easier and lighter thanks to air-frying. I'm always happy to eat an egg bullseye unadorned, but it's delicious fun to add a variety of colorful toppings, too.

## Makes 2 servings

**Tips**

If adding a sprinkle of cheese as a topping, add it during the last minute of cooking time.

When lining the basket with foil in step 1, be sure to leave at least 1/2 inch (1 cm) between the foil and the inside edge of the basket. This will ensure that there is enough space to allow the circulating hot air to pass through.

Do not put the foil in the basket while the air fryer preheats. The foil can be sucked into the heater and could start to burn.

Air fryers become very hot. Use oven pads or mitts when touching the appliance and when opening and closing the basket.

- Preheat air fryer to 360°F (180°C)
- 2- to 2½-inch (5 to 6 cm) cookie cutter or glass

| | Nonstick cooking spray | |
|---|---|---|
| 4 tsp | unsalted butter, softened | 20 mL |
| 2 | large slices multigrain or white sandwich bread | 2 |
| 2 | large eggs | 2 |
| | Salt and freshly cracked black pepper | |

**Suggested Toppings**

Shredded, grated or crumbled cheese (such as Cheddar, Parmesan or goat cheese)

Chopped fresh herbs

Diced or sliced Hass avocado

Chopped tomato

Salsa

1. Place a piece of foil in bottom of air fryer basket (see tips, at left). Spray foil with cooking spray.

2. Spread half the butter over both sides of 1 bread slice and place on foil. Using the cookie cutter, cut a round from the center of the bread slice. Place cut-out piece alongside bread slice. Air-fry for 4 minutes.

3. Open basket and flip bread and cut-out. Carefully crack 1 egg into the center of the bread slice. Sprinkle with salt and pepper. Air-fry for 4 to 6 minutes or until egg whites are set but yolks are still runny, or to desired doneness. Using a large pancake turner, transfer bread and egg to a plate.

4. Repeat steps 2 and 3 with the remaining bread, butter and egg. Serve with any of the suggested toppings, as desired.

# Air-Fried Egg Sandwich

Although egg sandwiches started out as healthy, homemade, portable breakfasts, many of the modern fast-food versions are not something you would want to eat to stay fit. But this version, packed with protein, will keep you satisfied and ready to conquer a mountain of tasks before lunchtime.

## Makes 1 serving

### Tip
Feel free to use other varieties of sliced deli meat and cheese in place of the ham and Cheddar.

### Variation
Omit the ham to make the sandwich vegetarian.

- Preheat air fryer to 390°F (200°C)
- ½- or ⅔-cup (125 or 150 mL) ramekin or custard cup, sprayed with nonstick cooking spray

| | | |
|---|---|---|
| 1 | English muffin, split | 1 |
| | Nonstick cooking spray | |
| 1 | large egg | 1 |
| | Salt and freshly ground black pepper | |
| 1 | thick slice deli ham (about the diameter of muffin) | 1 |
| 1 | thin deli slice Cheddar cheese | 1 |

1. Stack split halves of muffin together so that the cut sides are facing out. Lightly spray cut halves with cooking spray and place in air fryer basket.

2. Crack egg into prepared ramekin. Season with salt and pepper. Place ramekin and ham in basket beside muffin.

3. Air-fry for 3 minutes. Open basket and, using a spatula or tongs, turn muffin and ham over. Air-fry for 2 to 4 minutes or until egg white and yolk are firm, not runny.

4. Slide egg out of ramekin onto cut side of one muffin half. Top with cheese, ham and second muffin half. Serve immediately.

# Ham, Cheese and Egg Bread Boats

Deli ham, Cheddar cheese and eggs, all held in a perfectly portioned bread "boat," yield one of the easiest and most satisfying breakfasts imaginable. These are perfect for a fast dinner or lunch, too, with a green salad or a cup of soup on the side.

## Makes 2 servings

### Tips

You need to use lunch-size bread rolls for this; small dinner rolls are too small.

Other varieties of thinly sliced deli meat, such as roast beef, roast turkey or salami, can be used in place of the ham. Do not skip the meat liner or the egg will soak into the bread.

Refrigerate or freeze the leftover bread for making fresh bread crumbs or croutons.

• Preheat air fryer to 360°F (180°C)

| | | |
|---|---|---|
| 2 | soft or crusty lunch-size bread rolls (about 3 inches/7.5 cm in diameter) | 2 |
| 2 | small thin slices deli ham | 2 |
| 2 | large eggs | 2 |
| ¼ cup | shredded Cheddar, Swiss or mozzarella cheese | 60 mL |
| 2 tsp | minced fresh chives or parsley (optional) | 10 mL |

1. Using a serrated knife, cut ½ inch (1 cm) off the tops of the rolls; set aside. Scoop out centers, keeping sides about ½ inch (1 cm) thick, reserving the scooped-out bread for another use. Press 1 slice of ham into each roll. Crack an egg into each roll and sprinkle each with half the cheese.

2. Carefully place filled rolls in air fryer basket and replace tops of rolls. Air-fry for 7 to 13 minutes (7 to 9 minutes for runny yolks; 10 to 12 minutes for firm, just-set yolks; 13 to 15 minutes for firm yolks). If desired, remove the roll tops, sprinkle the filling with chives and replace the tops. Serve immediately.

# French Toast Sticks

With plenty of crispy corners, these custardy sticks of French toast are guaranteed to start your day with a smile. Start them soaking before you get ready for the day, then pop them in the air fryer for quick and delicious decadence in minutes.

**Makes 2 servings**

### Variation
An equal amount of ground ginger or cinnamon can be used in place of the cardamom.

| | | |
|---|---|---:|
| 1 | large egg | 1 |
| 3 tbsp | confectioners' (icing) sugar, divided | 45 mL |
| ¼ tsp | ground cardamom | 1 mL |
| ¼ tsp | salt | 1 mL |
| ½ tsp | vanilla extract | 2 mL |
| ⅔ cup | milk | 150 mL |
| 2 | slices (1 inch/2.5 cm thick) challah, brioche or other sturdy white bread | 2 |
| | Nonstick cooking spray | |
| | Pure maple syrup, warmed (optional) | |

1. In a shallow dish, whisk together egg, 1 tbsp (15 mL) confectioners' sugar, cardamom, salt and vanilla until blended. Whisk in milk until blended.

2. Cut each slice of bread crosswise into 1-inch (2.5 cm) wide "sticks." Arrange bread sticks in a single layer in egg mixture, gently pressing down on bread to help it absorb liquid. Turn bread slices over and gently press down again. Let stand for 15 minutes.

3. Meanwhile, preheat air fryer to 360°F (180°C).

4. Remove bread from egg mixture, discarding any excess egg mixture, and place in a single layer in air fryer basket, spacing evenly. Spray with cooking spray. Air-fry for 6 to 9 minutes or until golden brown. Sprinkle with the remaining confectioners' sugar. Serve with maple syrup, if desired.

# Dutch Baby for Two

This crackly-edged, fluffy-centered, puffy pancake is a winner for breakfast, brunch, lunch, dinner or dessert. And it takes no more than a few minutes to blend the batter. In sum, you will be making this recipe many times over!

**Makes 2 servings**

## Tips

An equal amount of neutral vegetable oil, ghee, olive oil or virgin coconut oil can be used in place of the butter. In step 2, add the oil or ghee to the pan as directed, so that it heats up before you add the batter.

If using nondairy milk, try hemp, almond, soy or rice milk.

## Variations

*Lemon Raspberry Dutch Baby:* Add 1 tsp (5 mL) finely grated lemon zest to the batter in step 1. Add 1/2 cup (125 mL) fresh raspberries after pouring the batter into the pan in step 3. Serve with additional confectioners' (icing) sugar and freshly squeezed lemon juice.

*Spiced Apple Dutch Baby:* Add 1/4 tsp (1 mL) pumpkin pie spice to the batter in step 1. Peel and thinly slice 1/2 of a small tart-sweet apple. Arrange in a single layer on top of melted butter in step 3, pour batter over top and proceed as directed.

- Preheat air fryer to 390°F (200°C)
- 6-inch (15 cm) round metal cake pan

| | | |
|---|---|---|
| 2 | large eggs | 2 |
| 1/2 cup | all-purpose flour | 125 mL |
| 2 tbsp | confectioners' (icing) sugar, divided | 30 mL |
| 1/8 tsp | salt | 0.5 mL |
| 1/2 cup | milk (dairy or plain nondairy), at room temperature | 125 mL |
| 1 tbsp | unsalted butter, cut into pieces | 15 mL |

### Suggested Accompaniments

Berries or diced fruit

Pure maple syrup, liquid honey or agave nectar

Jam, preserves or marmalade

1. In a medium bowl, whisk eggs until blended. Add flour, 1 tbsp (15 mL) confectioners' sugar, salt and milk; whisk vigorously until smooth. (The batter will be thin.)

2. Place butter in pan. Place pan in air fryer basket. Air-fry for 45 to 90 seconds or until butter is melted.

3. Remove pan from air fryer. Tilt pan to swirl butter and coat bottom. Pour batter into pan and immediately return pan to air fryer basket. Air-fry for 9 to 13 minutes or until Dutch baby is puffed and golden brown.

4. Cut Dutch baby in half and serve immediately, sprinkled with the remaining sugar and with any of the suggested accompaniments, as desired.

# Mini Biscuit Beignets

A blast of heat in the air fryer and a basting of golden butter does wonders for refrigerated buttermilk biscuits. A generous dusting of confectioners' sugar makes these mini beignets thoroughly New Orleans–worthy.

## Makes 8 servings

### Tip

An equal amount of ghee or virgin coconut oil, melted, can be used in place of the butter.

### Variation

*Sugar and Spice Beignets:* Omit the confectioners' sugar. In a small cup or bowl, combine ¼ cup (60 mL) granulated sugar and 1½ tsp (7 mL) pumpkin pie spice or ground cinnamon. Sprinkle 1 tbsp (15 mL) sugar mixture over biscuits after brushing with butter in step 2. Sprinkle with another 1 tbsp (15 mL) sugar mixture after transferring to a plate or wire rack in step 3. Repeat with the remaining biscuits, butter and sugar mixture.

*• Preheat air fryer to 390°F (200°C)*

| | | |
|---|---|---|
| 1 | can (12 oz/375 g) large refrigerated buttermilk biscuits | 1 |
| ¼ cup | unsalted butter, melted and cooled slightly | 60 mL |
| ½ cup | confectioners' (icing) sugar | 125 mL |

1. Open can and separate biscuits.

2. Brush tops of 2 of the biscuits with butter. Cut brushed biscuits into quarters.

3. Place biscuit quarters in air fryer basket, spacing them at least 1 inch (2.5 cm) apart. Air-fry for 3 to 6 minutes or until puffed and golden brown. Transfer to a plate or wire rack and sift confectioners' sugar over top. Serve immediately.

4. Repeat steps 2 and 3 with the remaining biscuits, butter and sugar.

# Buttery Biscuits

The cooking time for these biscuits is short, but still long enough for you to get dressed and ready for the day as they air-fry. When you return, you'll have a perfect breakfast of tender biscuits with toothsome crusts and fluffy interiors. Don't forget to anoint them with one or more of the suggested accompaniments.

**Makes 2 servings**

## Tips

You can replace $\frac{1}{3}$ cup (75 mL) of the all-purpose flour with whole wheat pastry flour.

Air fryers become very hot, especially when heated to maximum temperature. Use oven pads or mitts when touching the appliance and when opening and closing the basket.

* Preheat air fryer to 390°F (200°C)

|  |  |  |
|---|---|---|
|  | Nonstick cooking spray |  |
| $\frac{2}{3}$ cup | all-purpose flour | 150 mL |
| 1 tsp | baking powder | 5 mL |
| $\frac{1}{4}$ tsp | salt | 1 mL |
| 3 tbsp | cold unsalted butter, cut into small pieces | 45 mL |
| $\frac{1}{3}$ cup | milk or light (5%) cream | 75 mL |

### Suggested Accompaniments

Softened butter

Fruit jam, preserves, jelly, lemon curd or marmalade

Chocolate hazelnut spread

Liquid honey or light (fancy) molasses

1. Tear a piece of foil large enough to cover the bottom of the air fryer basket with $\frac{1}{2}$ inch (1 cm) between the foil and the inside edge of the basket. Spray foil with nonstick cooking spray.

2. In a medium bowl, whisk together flour, baking powder and salt. Using a pastry blender or your fingertips, cut in butter until mixture resembles fresh bread crumbs. Add milk and gently stir with a fork until dough is just moistened.

3. Drop dough into 2 mounds (each about $\frac{1}{2}$ cup/ 125 mL) on prepared foil, spacing them about 2 inches (5 cm) apart.

## Storage Tip

Store the cooled biscuits in an airtight container at room temperature for up to 2 days or in the freezer for up to 3 months. Let thaw at room temperature for 1 to 2 hours before serving.

4. Place foil with biscuits in air fryer basket. Air-fry for 7 to 11 minutes or until tops are golden brown and a tester inserted in the center of a biscuit comes out clean. Transfer to a wire rack and let cool for 5 minutes. Serve warm or let cool completely.

## Variations

*Cheddar Parmesan Biscuits:* Add 1/2 cup (125 mL) shredded sharp (old) Cheddar cheese and 1 1/2 tbsp (22 mL) freshly grated Parmesan cheese to the dough in step 2, after adding the milk.

*Buttermilk Biscuits:* Reduce the baking powder to 3/4 tsp (3 mL) and add 1/4 tsp (1 mL) baking soda. Replace the milk with an equal amount of buttermilk.

*Herbed Butter Biscuits:* Add 3 tbsp (45 mL) minced fresh chives or chopped fresh parsley, dill, cilantro or basil, or a combination, to the dough along with the milk.

# Lemon Drop Scones

The trick to great scones isn't in the ingredients, but in the bowl. Achieving a golden, tender crust outside and light, fluffy interiors takes a light hand: if the dough is mixed vigorously, the results will be leaden instead of ethereal. These lemony scones bypass the rolling and cutting steps, making them extra-simple to prepare.

## Makes 4 scones

### Tips

You can replace 1/3 cup (75 mL) of the all-purpose flour with whole wheat pastry flour.

The granulated sugar can be replaced with an equal amount of packed light brown sugar.

### Storage Tip

Store the cooled scones in an airtight container at room temperature for up to 2 days or in the freezer for up to 3 months. Let thaw at room temperature for 1 to 2 hours before serving.

### Variation

*Fruit Drop Scones:* Gently stir in 1/2 cup (125 mL) raspberries, blueberries, blackberries, diced peaches or diced strawberries at the end of step 3.

- *Preheat air fryer to 390°F (200°C)*

| | Nonstick cooking spray | |
|---|---|---|
| 1 cup | all-purpose flour | 250 mL |
| 1/2 tsp | baking soda | 2 mL |
| 1/4 tsp | salt | 1 mL |
| 1/4 cup | granulated sugar | 60 mL |
| 1/4 cup | unsalted butter, softened | 60 mL |
| 1 tsp | finely grated lemon zest | 5 mL |
| 1/3 cup | buttermilk | 75 mL |

1. Tear a piece of foil large enough to cover the bottom of the air fryer basket with 1/2 inch (1 cm) between the foil and the inside edge of the basket. Spray foil with nonstick cooking spray.

2. In a small bowl, whisk together flour, baking soda and salt.

3. In a medium bowl, cream sugar, butter and lemon zest until blended. Add the flour mixture alternately with the buttermilk, stirring gently with a fork until just blended.

4. Drop dough into 4 mounds (each about 1/3 cup/75 mL and about 2 inches/5 cm in diameter) on prepared foil, spacing them about 1 inch (2.5 cm) apart.

5. Place foil with scones inside air fryer basket. Air-fry for 6 to 10 minutes or until tops are golden brown and a tester inserted in the center of a scone comes out clean. Transfer to a wire rack and let cool for 5 minutes. Serve warm or let cool completely.

# Cherry Ricotta Danishes

These Danishes are a handmade homage to the kinds of fresh pastries that were once available at neighborhood bakeries. Prepared puff pastry makes them extra-simple to prepare, while the creamy cheese and cherry topping renders them irresistible.

## Makes 4 Danishes

### Tips

Any other flavor of jam, preserves or lemon curd can be used in place of the cherry jam.

The Danishes can be assembled ahead of time through step 5. Cover loosely with plastic wrap and refrigerate for up to 12 hours before air-frying.

For optimal crispness, serve the Danishes soon after they are cooled.

• *Preheat air fryer to 360°F (180°C)*

| | | |
|---|---|---|
| ¾ cup | ricotta cheese | 175 mL |
| 1½ tbsp | granulated sugar | 22 mL |
| ¼ tsp | almond extract | 1 mL |
| 1 | large egg | 1 |
| 2 tsp | water | 10 mL |
| | All-purpose flour | |
| 1 | sheet frozen puff pastry (half a 17.3-oz/490 g package), thawed | 1 |
| 4 tbsp | cherry jam or preserves | 60 mL |

1. In a small bowl, stir together ricotta, sugar and almond extract until blended and smooth.

2. In another small bowl or cup, whisk together egg and water until blended.

3. On a lightly floured surface, roll out puff pastry into a 12-inch (30 cm) square. Cut into four 6-inch (15 cm) squares.

4. Gently spread about 3 tbsp (45 mL) ricotta mixture in a 5-inch (12.5 cm) diagonal strip across each square. Spread 1 tbsp (15 mL) jam over cheese.

5. For each Danish, fold the corners over the filling toward the center (about 1 inch/2.5 cm from center). Brush top of dough with egg wash.

6. Place 2 Danishes in air fryer basket (refrigerate the others until ready to air-fry). Air-fry for 11 to 15 minutes or until pastry is puffed and golden brown and appears crisp. Transfer to a wire rack and let cool completely. Repeat with the remaining Danishes.

# Chocolate Croissant Donuts

It's hard to believe these donuts take mere minutes to prepare. Their combined texture and taste is remarkable, with light and crisp layers of pastry and a very chocolatey topping. Go ahead and have seconds!

## Makes 9 donuts

### Tips

A 3-inch (7.5 cm) round biscuit or cookie cutter can be used in place of the donut cutter. Use a 1-inch (2.5 cm) cutter to cut out "holes."

Commercial puff pastry loses it crispness quickly, so it is best to eat the donuts shortly after they are cooled and iced.

- Preheat air fryer to 360°F (180°C)
- 3-inch (7.5 cm) round donut cutter (see tip, at left)

**Donuts**

|   | All-purpose flour |   |
|---|---|---|
| 1 | sheet frozen puff pastry (half a 17.3-oz/490 g package), thawed | 1 |

**Chocolate Icing**

| 3 tbsp | unsweetened cocoa powder | 45 mL |
|---|---|---|
| 2 tbsp | boiling water | 30 mL |
| 1 tbsp | unsalted butter, cut into small pieces | 15 mL |
| 1 cup | confectioners' (icing) sugar | 250 mL |
| ½ tsp | vanilla extract | 2 mL |

1. *Donuts:* On a lightly floured surface, unfold pastry sheet. Using the donut cutter, cut out 9 donuts and donut holes. (Discard pastry scraps.)

2. Place 2 to 3 donuts in air fryer basket, leaving 1 inch (2.5 cm) in between (refrigerate remaining donuts and donut holes until ready to air-fry). Air-fry for 10 to 15 minutes or until donuts are puffed and golden brown. Let cool on a wire rack set over waxed paper for 15 minutes. Repeat with the remaining donuts.

3. Place donut holes in air fryer basket, leaving space in between. Air-fry for 7 to 10 minutes or until donuts are puffed and golden brown. Let cool on wire rack for 15 minutes.

4. *Icing:* In a small bowl, whisk together cocoa powder, boiling water and butter until butter is melted and mixture is smooth. Stir in confectioners' sugar and vanilla until blended and smooth. Drizzle over cooled donuts and donut holes.

# Honey Bran Muffins

These moist, hearty muffins have a satisfying, tender texture. They're subtly sweet from the honey and the bran. Although they are wonderful on the day you air-fry them, I think they taste even better the next day.

## Makes 4 muffins

### Tips

If using nondairy milk, try hemp, almond, soy or rice milk.

An equal amount of pure maple syrup or packed brown sugar can be used in place of the honey.

Melted unsalted butter, melted ghee, olive oil or melted virgin coconut oil can be used in place of the vegetable oil.

### Variation

Add ⅓ cup (75 mL) dried fruit (such as raisins, cherries, chopped apricots or cranberries) to the batter at the end of step 5.

• *8 standard-size foil or paper muffin cup liners*

| | | |
|---|---|---|
| ¾ cup | 100% bran pellet-style cereal | 175 mL |
| ½ cup | milk (dairy or plain nondairy) | 125 mL |
| ⅓ cup | all-purpose flour | 75 mL |
| 1 tsp | baking powder | 5 mL |
| ½ tsp | ground cinnamon | 2 mL |
| ⅛ tsp | salt | 0.5 mL |
| 1 | large egg white | 1 |
| 1½ tbsp | liquid honey | 22 mL |
| 1 tbsp | vegetable oil | 15 mL |

1. Place one muffin cup liner inside another. Repeat to create 4 doubled liners.

2. In a medium bowl, stir together cereal and milk. Let stand for 5 minutes or until cereal softens.

3. Meanwhile, preheat air fryer to 390°F (200°C).

4. In a small bowl, whisk together flour, baking powder, cinnamon and salt.

5. Stir egg white, honey and oil into the cereal mixture until very well blended. Add flour mixture, stirring until just combined.

6. Divide batter equally among the doubled liners.

7. Place filled liners in air fryer basket, spacing them evenly. Air-fry for 14 to 18 minutes or until a tester inserted in the center of a muffin comes out clean. Transfer to a wire rack and let cool completely.

# Blueberry Muffins

Homemade blueberry muffins are almost as fast and taste immeasurably better than even the best bakery versions. This vanilla-scented version, bursting with bright berry flavor, is delectable proof.

## Makes 4 muffins

### Tip

An equal amount of vegetable oil, melted ghee, olive oil or melted virgin coconut oil can be used in place of the butter.

### Variations

*Cranberry Orange Muffins:* Replace the vanilla with 1/2 tsp (2 mL) finely grated orange zest. Replace the blueberries with 1/3 cup (75 mL) dried cranberries.

*Chocolate Chip Muffins:* Replace the blueberries with 1/3 cup (75 mL) miniature semisweet chocolate chips.

*Lemon Poppy Seed Muffins:* Replace the vanilla with 1 1/2 tsp (7 mL) finely grated lemon zest. Replace the blueberries with 1 tbsp (15 mL) poppy seeds.

- *Preheat air fryer to 390°F (200°C)*
- *8 standard-size foil or paper muffin cup liners*

| | | |
|---|---|---|
| 1 cup | all-purpose flour | 250 mL |
| 1 1/2 tsp | baking powder | 7 mL |
| 1/4 tsp | baking soda | 1 mL |
| 1/4 tsp | salt | 1 mL |
| 1 | large egg | 1 |
| 1/4 cup | granulated sugar | 60 mL |
| 3 tbsp | unsalted butter, melted | 45 mL |
| 1/2 tsp | vanilla extract | 2 mL |
| 3/4 cup | buttermilk | 175 mL |
| 1/2 cup | blueberries | 125 mL |

1. Place one muffin cup liner inside another. Repeat to create 4 doubled liners.

2. In a medium bowl, whisk together flour, baking powder, baking soda and salt.

3. In a small bowl, whisk egg. Whisk in sugar, butter and vanilla until blended. Whisk in buttermilk.

4. Add the egg mixture to the flour mixture and stir until just blended. Gently stir in blueberries.

5. Divide batter equally among the doubled liners.

6. Place filled liners in air fryer basket, spacing them evenly. Air-fry for 14 to 18 minutes or until tops are golden and a tester inserted in the center of a muffin comes out clean. Transfer to a wire rack and let cool completely.

# Chai-Spice Banana Muffins

Here is a simple solution to use up the spotted bananas on the countertop, or those brown ones at the back of the freezer. For the best results, be sure not to overmix the ingredients, and use bananas that are very ripe.

## Makes 4 muffins

## Tips

For the best flavor and sweetness, opt for a banana that is very soft and squishy to the touch, with many brown spots on the peel. You'll need about 1 large banana to yield ¾ cup (175 mL) mashed.

Neutral vegetable oil, melted ghee, olive oil or melted unsalted butter can be used in place of the coconut oil.

An equal amount of pure maple syrup or granulated sugar can be used in place of the honey.

## Variations

*Peanut Butter–Filled Banana Muffins:* Omit all of the spices. Drop 2 tsp (10 mL) peanut butter on top of the batter after filling the doubled liners (it will sink as the muffins air-fry). Air-fry as directed.

*Chocolate Chip Banana Muffins:* Omit all of the spices except the cinnamon. Gently stir in ⅓ cup (75 mL) miniature semisweet chocolate chips at the end of step 4.

- *Preheat air fryer to 390°F (200°C)*
- *8 standard-size foil or paper muffin cup liners*

| | | |
|---|---|---|
| 1 cup | all-purpose flour | 250 mL |
| 1½ tsp | baking powder | 7 mL |
| ½ tsp | ground cinnamon | 2 mL |
| ¼ tsp | ground cardamom | 1 mL |
| ¼ tsp | ground ginger | 1 mL |
| ⅛ tsp | ground cloves | 0.5 mL |
| ¼ tsp | baking soda | 1 mL |
| ¼ tsp | salt | 1 mL |
| 1 | large egg | 1 |
| ¾ cup | mashed very ripe banana | 175 mL |
| 3 tbsp | virgin coconut oil, melted | 45 mL |
| 2 tbsp | liquid honey | 30 mL |
| ½ tsp | vanilla extract | 1 mL |

1. Place one muffin cup liner inside another. Repeat to create 4 doubled liners.

2. In a medium bowl, whisk together flour, baking powder, cinnamon, cardamom, ginger, cloves, baking soda and salt.

3. In a small bowl, whisk egg. Whisk in banana, coconut oil, honey and vanilla until blended.

4. Add the egg mixture to the flour mixture and stir until just blended.

5. Divide batter equally among the doubled liners.

6. Place filled liners in air fryer basket, spacing them evenly. Air-fry for 14 to 18 minutes or until tops are golden and a tester inserted in the center of a muffin comes out clean. Transfer to a wire rack and let cool completely.

# Maple-Glazed Pumpkin Muffins

These hearty pumpkin muffins are a sophisticated twist on traditional versions with the addition of maple syrup in both the batter and the glaze.

**Makes 4 muffins**

**Tip**

An equal amount of melted unsalted butter, melted ghee, olive oil or melted virgin coconut oil can be used in place of the vegetable oil in the muffins.

- *Preheat air fryer to 390°F (200°C)*
- *8 standard-size foil or paper muffin cup liners*

**Muffins**

| | | |
|---|---|---|
| ⅔ cup | whole wheat flour | 150 mL |
| ⅓ cup | all-purpose flour | 75 mL |
| 1 tsp | pumpkin pie spice | 5 mL |
| ¾ tsp | baking powder | 3 mL |
| ½ tsp | baking soda | 2 mL |
| ¼ tsp | salt | 1 mL |
| 1 | large egg | 1 |
| 3 tbsp | packed light brown sugar | 45 mL |
| ⅔ cup | pumpkin purée (not pie filling) | 150 mL |
| 2½ tbsp | vegetable oil | 37 mL |
| 2 tbsp | pure maple syrup | 30 mL |
| 1 tbsp | milk (dairy or plain nondairy) | 15 mL |

**Glaze**

| | | |
|---|---|---|
| ½ cup | confectioners' (icing) sugar, sifted | 125 mL |
| 1 tbsp | pure maple syrup | 15 mL |
| 2 tsp | unsalted butter, melted | 10 mL |
| 1 tsp | water | 5 mL |

1. Place one muffin cup liner inside another. Repeat to create 4 doubled liners.

2. *Muffins:* In a medium bowl, whisk together whole wheat flour, all-purpose flour, pumpkin pie spice, baking powder, baking soda and salt.

## Tip

If using nondairy milk, try hemp, almond, soy or rice milk.

3. In a small bowl, whisk egg. Whisk in brown sugar, pumpkin, oil, maple syrup and milk until blended.

4. Add the egg mixture to the flour mixture and stir until just blended.

5. Divide batter equally among the doubled liners.

6. Place filled liners in air fryer basket, spacing them evenly. Air-fry for 14 to 18 minutes or until a tester inserted in the center of a muffin comes out clean. Transfer to a wire rack set over waxed paper and let cool completely.

7. *Glaze:* In a small bowl, whisk together confectioners' sugar, maple syrup, butter and water until blended and smooth. Spoon or drizzle over tops of cooled muffins. Let stand for at least 5 minutes before serving.

# Cinnamon Crumb Coffee Cakes

Here is a streamlined take on a classic breakfast pastry, with a tender buttermilk cake and a crunchy cinnamon and butter topping. It comes together — from start to finish — in about 30 minutes; it typically disappears in under 5.

**Makes 4 cakes**

### Storage Tip

Store the cooled cakes, loosely wrapped in foil or waxed paper, at room temperature for up to 3 days. Alternatively, wrap them in plastic wrap, then foil, completely enclosing them, and freeze for up to 6 months. Let thaw at room temperature for 4 to 6 hours before serving.

- *Preheat oven to 360°F (180°C)*
- *8 standard-size foil or paper muffin cup liners*

### Cakes

| | | |
|---|---|---|
| 1 cup | all-purpose flour | 250 mL |
| 1¼ tsp | baking powder | 6 mL |
| ¼ tsp | salt | 1 mL |
| ½ cup | granulated sugar | 125 mL |
| 1 | large egg, at room temperature | 1 |
| ½ cup | buttermilk | 125 mL |
| 2½ tbsp | unsalted butter, melted and cooled slightly | 37 mL |
| 1 tsp | vanilla extract | 5 mL |

### Topping

| | | |
|---|---|---|
| ⅔ cup | all-purpose flour | 150 mL |
| ⅓ cup | packed light or dark brown sugar | 75 mL |
| 1 tsp | ground cinnamon | 5 mL |
| ⅛ tsp | salt | 0.5 mL |
| ¼ cup | unsalted butter, melted and cooled slightly | 60 mL |

1. Place one muffin cup liner inside another. Repeat to create 4 doubled liners.

2. *Cakes:* In a medium bowl, whisk together flour, baking powder and salt.

3. In another medium bowl, whisk together sugar, egg, buttermilk, butter and vanilla until well blended.

## Variation

*Blueberry Crumb Coffee Cakes:* Stir 1/2 cup (125 mL) fresh or frozen (not thawed) blueberries into the batter at the end of step 4.

4. Add the egg mixture to the flour mixture, stirring until just blended (do not overmix).

5. Divide batter equally among the doubled liners.

6. *Topping:* In the same bowl used to mix the batter (no need to clean it), combine flour, brown sugar, cinnamon and salt. Using a wooden spoon, stir in butter until coarse crumbs form. Sprinkle topping evenly over batter.

7. Place filled liners in air fryer basket, spacing them evenly. Air-fry for 16 to 20 minutes or until tops are golden and a tester inserted in the center of a cake comes out clean. Transfer to a wire rack and let cool completely.

# Appetizers and Snacks

# Bacon-Wrapped, Almond-Stuffed Dates

Plain dates have their place, but when stuffed with almonds, wrapped in bacon and air-fried to crispy succulence, they are irresistible.

**Makes 12 pieces**

## Tips

Almond butter can be used in place of the almonds. Use 1 tsp (5 mL) almond butter in place of each almond.

If Medjool dates are not available, other varieties of dates may be used. If the dates are not very soft, soak them in warm (not hot) water for 15 minutes, drain, then pat dry with paper towels.

## Variation

*Cheese-Stuffed Dates:* Use 1 tsp (5 mL) soft goat cheese or blue cheese in place of each almond.

• *Preheat air fryer to 390°F (200°C)*

| 12 | salted roasted almonds | 12 |
| 12 | pitted Medjool dates (about 8 oz/250 g) | 12 |
| 6 | slices bacon (not thick-cut), halved crosswise | 6 |

1. Stuff 1 almond into each date. Wrap 1 piece of bacon around each date, overlapping ends.

2. Arrange dates, seam side down, in air fryer basket, leaving space in between. Air-fry for 12 to 17 minutes or until bacon is cooked crisp. Serve immediately.

# Air-Fried Dill Pickles

Fried dill pickles are a time-honored treat in the American South, and now at many state and country fairs across North America. Here, they become an anytime treat, made even more enticing when served with Buttermilk Ranch Dressing (page 275).

## Makes 8 servings

### Variation

*Gluten-Free Air-Fried Dill Pickles:* Replace the all-purpose flour with an all-purpose gluten-free flour blend, and replace the panko with an equal amount of crushed gluten-free corn flakes cereal.

* Preheat air fryer to 390°F (200°C)

| | | |
|---|---|---|
| ²/₃ cup | all-purpose flour | 150 mL |
| 1 tsp | garlic powder | 5 mL |
| ⅛ tsp | freshly ground black pepper | 0.5 mL |
| 1 cup | panko (Japanese bread crumbs) | 250 mL |
| ½ cup | freshly grated Parmesan cheese | 125 mL |
| 2 | large eggs | 2 |
| 1 | jar (16 oz/500 mL) dill pickle slices | 1 |
| | Nonstick cooking spray | |

1. Place flour, garlic powder and pepper in a large sealable plastic bag. Seal bag and shake to combine.

2. In a shallow dish, stir together panko and Parmesan.

3. In another shallow dish, whisk eggs until blended.

4. Add 8 pickle slices to flour mixture, seal bag and toss until coated. Working with 1 pickle slice at a time, remove from flour, shaking off excess. Dip in egg, shaking off excess, then dredge in panko mixture, pressing gently to adhere. As they are dredged, place pickle slices in air fryer basket, leaving space in between. Spray with cooking spray.

5. Air-fry for 4 to 7 minutes or until golden brown. Serve immediately.

6. Repeat steps 4 and 5 with the remaining pickle slices, egg and panko mixture. Discard any excess flour mixture, egg and panko mixture.

# Blooming Onion with Creamy Chipotle Dip

Deep-frying aficionados will be amazed at the gorgeous results of this crispy-crunchy blooming onion. The accompanying chipotle dip has a smoky earthiness that perfectly complements the vegetal sweetness of the onion.

## Makes 4 servings

### Tips

The eggs can be replaced by 4 large egg whites. In step 4, whisk the egg whites until slightly frothy.

For a milder blooming onion, omit the Cajun seasoning or replace it with the seasoning blend of your choice.

| | | |
|---|---|---|
| 1 | large Vidalia or other sweet onion | 1 |
| | Ice water | |
| 2 | large eggs | 2 |
| ⅔ cup | panko (Japanese bread crumbs) | 150 mL |
| 2 tsp | Cajun seasoning | 10 mL |
| ¼ tsp | salt | 1 mL |
| | Nonstick cooking spray | |
| | Creamy Chipotle Dip (page 272) | |

1. Cut off top ¼ inch (0.5 cm) of the onion to reveal a few of the inside layers. Peel and remove outermost papery layers down to the root (leave root intact).

2. Place onion, flat side down, on a cutting board. Beginning ⅛ inch (3 mm) from the root end and keeping the root end intact, slice onion vertically into 16 sections. Place onion in a bowl of ice water and refrigerate for at least 4 hours or overnight (this allows the onion sections to "bloom").

3. Remove onion from water and thoroughly pat dry with paper towels. Preheat air fryer to 390°F (200°C).

4. In a small bowl, whisk eggs until blended.

5. In another small bowl, stir together panko, Cajun seasoning and salt.

## Variation

*Gluten-Free Blooming Onion:* Replace the panko with an equal amount of crushed gluten-free corn flakes cereal.

6. Brush egg evenly over all of the onion "petals." Immediately sprinkle with panko mixture. Generously spray onion with cooking spray and resprinkle with any panko mixture that may have fallen off. Discard any excess egg.

7. Place onion in air fryer basket, with "petals" up, and cover with foil shaped like a tent. Air-fry for 7 minutes. Carefully remove foil and air-fry for 9 to 14 minutes or until onion is soft and tips of "petals" appear crisp and golden brown.

8. Transfer onion to a serving plate and serve with Creamy Chipotle Dip.

# Air-Fried Pimento Cheese

Distinctively tangy pimento cheese is an iconic appetizer and sandwich filling in the American South. Here, it finds new life as golden, crisp-edged air-fried rounds.

**Makes about 30 rounds**

### Variation

*Gluten-Free Air-Fried Pimento Cheese:* Replace the all-purpose flour with an all-purpose gluten-free flour blend.

- Preheat air fryer to 350°F (180°C)
- 1½-inch (4 cm) round biscuit cutter

| | | |
|---|---|---|
| ¾ cup | all-purpose flour | 175 mL |
| ½ tsp | salt | 2 mL |
| ¼ tsp | cayenne pepper | 1 mL |
| 1¼ cups | shredded sharp (old) Cheddar cheese | 300 mL |
| ¼ cup | unsalted butter, softened | 60 mL |
| 2 tsp | Dijon mustard | 10 mL |
| 1 | jar (4 oz/114 mL) diced pimentos, drained, patted dry and finely chopped | 1 |
| | Nonstick cooking spray | |

1. In a medium bowl, whisk together flour, salt and cayenne. Gradually add pimentos, tossing to coat.

2. In another medium bowl, using an electric mixer on medium speed, beat cheese, butter and mustard until blended. Beat in pimentos. Gradually add pimento mixture, beating just until combined.

3. On a lightly floured surface, press or roll out dough to ¼-inch (0.5 cm) thickness. Use biscuit cutter to cut out rounds. Reroll or press dough scraps and cut out more rounds. Spray rounds with cooking spray.

4. Place 6 to 8 rounds in air fryer basket, spacing them 1 inch (2.5 cm) apart (loosely cover the remaining rounds and refrigerate until ready to air-fry). Air-fry for 6 to 9 minutes or until golden brown. Transfer rounds to a wire rack to cool. Repeat with the remaining rounds.

# Blue Cheese Olive Poppers

Olives are great solo, but when their flavor and texture are built up with a piquant blue cheese and chipotle–spiked coating, they become extraordinary.

**Makes 24 pieces**

## Variation

*Gluten-Free Blue Cheese Olive Poppers:* Replace the all-purpose flour with an all-purpose gluten-free flour blend.

- *Preheat air fryer to 390°F (200°C)*
- *Food processor*
- *Plate or baking pan lined with parchment paper*

| | | |
|---|---|---|
| ¾ cup | all-purpose flour | 175 mL |
| ½ tsp | chipotle chile powder | 2 mL |
| 4 oz | blue cheese, crumbled | 125 g |
| ¼ cup | butter, cut into pieces | 60 mL |
| 1 tbsp | milk | 15 mL |
| 24 | small green pimento-stuffed olives | 24 |
| | Nonstick cooking spray | |

1. In food processor, pulse together flour, chile powder, blue cheese and butter until mixture forms coarse crumbs. Add milk, pulsing until mixture just comes together into a dough.

2. Shape 1 heaping teaspoon (5 mL) dough around each olive, forming the dough into a ball. Place on prepared plate or baking pan and spray with cooking spray.

3. Place half the poppers in air fryer basket, leaving space in between (refrigerate the remaining poppers until ready to air-fry). Air-fry for 5 to 9 minutes or until golden brown. Transfer poppers to a serving plate and serve immediately. Repeat with the remaining poppers.

# Peppered Goat Cheese Poppers with Honey

Air-fry the tastiest goat cheese you can find, then turn your guests loose to help drizzle on the honey, sprinkle with chives and get fabulously messy. They'll have a wonderful time.

**Makes 24 pieces**

### Variation

*Gluten-Free Goat Cheese Poppers:* Replace the all-purpose flour with an all-purpose gluten-free flour blend, and replace the panko with an equal amount of crushed gluten-free corn flakes cereal.

• Baking sheet, lined with parchment paper

| | | |
|---|---|---:|
| 11 oz | soft goat cheese, softened | 312 g |
| 2/3 cup | all-purpose flour | 150 mL |
| 2/3 cup | panko (Japanese bread crumbs) | 150 mL |
| 1/4 tsp | freshly cracked black pepper | 1 mL |
| 1 | large egg | 1 |
| 1 tbsp | water | 15 mL |
| | Nonstick cooking spray | |
| 1 tbsp | liquid honey | 15 mL |
| 1 tbsp | minced fresh chives | 15 mL |

1. Roll goat cheese into 24 balls (each about 1 tbsp/ 15 mL). Place cheese balls on prepared baking sheet and place in the freezer for 15 minutes (no longer).

2. Preheat air fryer to 390°F (200°C).

3. Place flour in a large sealable plastic bag.

4. In a shallow dish, combine panko and pepper.

5. In another shallow dish, whisk egg and water until blended.

*Jalapeño Cream Cheese Poppers with Honey:* Replace the goat cheese with 12 oz (375 g) cream cheese, softened. Replace the cracked black pepper with 1½ tbsp (22 mL) finely chopped jalapeño peppers.

6. Add half the cheese balls to the flour, seal bag and toss until coated. (Keep the remaining cheese balls in the refrigerator until ready to coat and air-fry.) Working with 1 cheese ball at a time, remove from flour, shaking off excess. Dip in egg mixture, shaking off excess, then dredge in panko mixture, pressing gently to adhere. As they are dredged, place cheese balls in air fryer basket, leaving space in between. Spray with cooking spray.

7. Air-fry for 4 to 7 minutes or until golden brown. Transfer cheese balls to a serving plate, drizzle with half the honey and sprinkle with half the chives. Serve immediately.

8. Repeat steps 6 and 7 with the remaining cheese balls, flour, egg mixture, panko mixture, honey and chives. Discard any excess flour, egg mixture and panko mixture.

# Greek Feta Triangles

No premade appetizer can equal a simple homemade one, especially when the robust flavor of feta cheese and delicate layers of phyllo are added to the mix.

## Makes 15 triangles

**Tip**

An equal amount of soft goat cheese can be used in place of the feta.

**Variation**

*Blue Cheese and Fig Triangles:* Replace the green onions with an equal amount of finely chopped dried figs. Omit the dillweed and replace the feta with creamy blue cheese.

*• Preheat air fryer to 390°F (200°C)*

| | | |
|---|---|---|
| 1 | large egg yolk | 1 |
| ¼ cup | finely chopped green onions | 60 mL |
| ½ tsp | dried dillweed or oregano | 2 mL |
| ⅛ tsp | freshly cracked black pepper | 0.5 mL |
| 4 oz | feta cheese, crumbled | 125 g |
| 5 | sheets thawed frozen phyllo pastry | 5 |
| | Nonstick cooking spray | |

1. In a medium bowl, whisk egg yolk. Add green onions, dill, pepper and feta, mashing with a fork until blended.

2. Place 1 sheet of phyllo on work surface. Lightly spray with cooking spray and cut lengthwise into three equal strips. Place 1 tsp (5 mL) filling at the bottom of one strip. Fold pastry over filling to form a triangle, then continue folding the strip in a zigzag manner until the filling is wrapped in a triangle. Repeat with the remaining phyllo and filling. Lightly spray finished triangles with cooking spray.

3. Place 5 triangles in air fryer basket, leaving space in between. Air-fry for 3 to 5 minutes or until golden brown. Transfer triangles to a wire rack and let cool for 3 to 5 minutes before serving. Repeat with the remaining triangles.

Tempura-Style Vegetables (page 24)

Egg Rolls (page 30) and
Crab Rangoon (page 36)

Buttermilk Fried Chicken (page 40)
and Classic French Fries (page 22)

Old-Fashioned Cake
Donuts (page 48)

Crunchy Granola Cups with Yogurt and Fruit (page 56)

Portobello and Prosciutto Air-Fried Eggs
(page 60) and Spicy-Sweet Bacon (page 57)

Lemon Raspberry Dutch Baby (variation, page 72)

Chocolate Croissant Donuts (page 78)

# Crispy, Crunchy Cheese Ravioli

~~~~~~~~~~~~~~~~~~~~~~~~~~~~~~~~~~~~~~~~~~~~~~~~~~

**Cheese ravioli are excellent in the air fryer. The crunch of the coated pasta dough perfectly complements the creamy interiors. Combined with warmed Easy Marinara Sauce (page 255) for dipping, they make a very easy but very impressive appetizer.**

**Makes 8 pieces**

**Tip**
Two large egg whites can be used in place of the whole egg.

• *Preheat air fryer to 390°F (200°C)*

| | | |
|---|---|---|
| ⅔ cup | all-purpose flour | 150 mL |
| ⅔ cup | panko (Japanese bread crumbs) | 150 mL |
| 1 | large egg | 1 |
| 1 tbsp | water | 15 mL |
| 8 | 1½-inch (4 cm) wide frozen cheese-stuffed ravioli (do not thaw) | 8 |
| | Nonstick cooking spray | |

1. Place flour in a large sealable plastic bag.

2. Spread panko in a shallow dish.

3. In another shallow dish, whisk egg and water until blended.

4. Add ravioli to flour, seal bag and toss until coated. Working with 1 ravioli at a time, remove from flour, shaking off excess. Dip in egg mixture, shaking off excess, then dredge in panko, pressing gently to adhere. As they are dredged, place ravioli in air fryer basket, leaving space in between. Spray with cooking spray. Discard any excess flour, egg mixture and panko.

5. Air-fry for 14 to 19 minutes or until golden brown. Serve immediately.

# Air-Fried Mac and Cheese Minis

Fried — or, in this case, air-fried — macaroni and cheese is one of those state fair foods that sound faintly ridiculous until you try it. Then you wonder why you never had it before.

**Makes about 30 minis**

## Tips

The macaroni takes longer to cook than the package recommends because the cooking process starts with cold milk and broth rather than boiling water.

The eggs can be replaced by 4 large egg whites. In step 5, whisk the egg whites until slightly frothy.

• Large baking sheet, lined with parchment paper

| | | |
|---|---|---:|
| 8 oz | elbow macaroni (uncooked) | 250 g |
| 1 cup | milk | 250 mL |
| 1 cup | ready-to-use chicken broth | 250 mL |
| 4 oz | brick-style cream cheese, cut into small pieces | 125 g |
| 1½ cups | shredded sharp (old) Cheddar cheese | 375 mL |
| 1½ tsp | Dijon mustard | 7 mL |
| | Salt and freshly ground black pepper | |
| 1½ cups | panko (Japanese bread crumbs) | 375 mL |
| 2 | large eggs | 2 |
| | Nonstick cooking spray | |

1. In a medium saucepan, combine macaroni, milk and broth. Bring to a boil over medium-high heat. Boil, stirring occasionally, for 14 to 16 minutes or until liquid has reduced and thickened to a sauce-like consistency and pasta is tender. Stir in cream cheese, Cheddar and mustard until melted and smooth. Season to taste with salt and pepper. Let cool for 30 minutes.

2. Scoop out 2-tbsp (30 mL) portions of cooled mac and cheese onto prepared baking sheet. Cover loosely with plastic wrap and refrigerate for at least 2 hours, until firm, or for up to 24 hours.

3. Preheat air fryer to 390°F (200°C).

## Variation

*Bacon Mac and Cheese Minis:* Add ¼ cup (60 mL) chopped cooked bacon along with the cheeses in step 1.

**4.** Spread panko in a shallow dish.

**5.** In another shallow dish, whisk eggs until blended.

**6.** Working with 1 mac and cheese portion at a time, dip in egg, shaking off excess, then dredge in panko, pressing gently to adhere. As they are dredged, place 6 mac and cheese portions in air fryer basket, leaving space in between. Spray with cooking spray. (Keep the remaining portions in the refrigerator until ready to coat and air-fry.)

**7.** Air-fry for 7 to 10 minutes or until golden brown. Serve immediately.

**8.** Repeat steps 6 and 7 with the remaining mac and cheese pieces. Discard any excess eggs and panko.

# Hoisin Shrimp Wontons

Hoisin takes something familiar, like shrimp, and gives it a deep, nuanced flavor that is not specifically Asian so much as it is global. Good luck eating only one.

**Makes
12 wontons**

## Variation

*Barbecue Shrimp Wontons:* Replace the hoisin sauce with an equal amount of barbecue sauce.

• *Preheat air fryer to 350°F (180°C)*

| | | |
|---|---|---|
| 12 | jumbo shrimp, peeled and deveined, tails on | 12 |
| 1/3 cup | hoisin sauce | 75 mL |
| 2 | green onions | 2 |
| 12 | 2-inch (5 cm) square wonton wrappers | 12 |
| | Nonstick cooking spray | |

1. In a medium bowl, gently toss together shrimp and hoisin sauce until coated.

2. Cut each green onion lengthwise into thin strips, then cut the strips crosswise into 2-inch (5 cm) lengths.

3. Place wonton wrappers on work surface. Place green onions in center of each wrapper so that they lie in a diagonal from one corner to another. Place 1 shrimp on top. Fold opposite corners across the filling to create a triangle, tucking corners in to secure.

4. Spray half of the wontons with cooking spray and place in air fryer basket, leaving space in between (refrigerate the remaining wontons). Air-fry for 10 to 13 minutes or until golden brown. Serve immediately. Repeat with the remaining wontons.

# Chicken and Black Bean Nacho Bites

Leftover chicken is ideal for these incredibly delicious and decadent-tasting handheld nacho bites, but you can use finely chopped steak, pork or whatever meat you have left over from yesterday's dinner.

## Makes 20 pieces

### Variation

*Black Bean Nacho Bites:* Omit the chicken and increase the beans to 1 cup (250 mL).

• *Preheat air fryer to 350°F (180°C)*

| | | |
|---|---|---|
| ¾ cup | finely chopped cooked chicken | 175 mL |
| ⅓ cup | rinsed drained canned black beans, coarsely mashed | 75 mL |
| ⅓ cup | shredded Monterey Jack or pepper Jack cheese | 75 mL |
| ¼ cup | thick and chunky salsa | 60 mL |
| 20 | 2-inch (5 cm) square wonton wrappers | 20 |
| 1 | large egg, beaten | 1 |
| | Nonstick cooking spray | |

1. In a medium bowl, stir together chicken, beans, cheese and salsa until combined.

2. Place wonton wrappers on work surface. Spoon 2 tsp (10 mL) chicken mixture into center of each wrapper. Using a brush or fingertip, brush edges of each wrapper with egg. Fold opposite corners across the filling to create a triangle. Press edges together to seal.

3. Spray 7 wontons with cooking spray and place in air fryer basket, leaving space in between (refrigerate the remaining wontons). Air-fry for 10 to 13 minutes or until golden brown. Serve immediately. Repeat with the remaining wontons.

# Cheddar Bacon Croquettes

Happiness is having a fresh batch of crispy-gooey Cheddar bacon croquettes and a select group of friends with whom you can share. The recipe requires a few more steps than others, but it's a project that can easily fit into your cooking repertoire.

**Makes
8 croquettes**

### Variation

*Gluten-Free Cheddar Bacon Croquettes:* Replace the all-purpose flour with an all-purpose gluten-free flour blend, and replace the panko with an equal amount of crushed gluten-free corn flakes cereal.

- *Baking sheet, lined with parchment paper*

| | | |
|---|---|---|
| 8 oz | sharp (old) Cheddar cheese | 250 g |
| 8 | bacon slices (not thick-cut) | 8 |
| 1 cup | all-purpose flour | 250 mL |
| 1/2 cup | panko (Japanese bread crumbs) | 125 mL |
| 2 | large eggs | 2 |
| | Nonstick cooking spray | |

1. Cut cheese into 8 blocks of equal size. Wrap 1 slice of bacon around each cheese piece, enclosing most of the cheese. Place wrapped cheese pieces on prepared baking sheet and place in the freezer for 15 minutes (no longer).

2. Preheat air fryer to 390°F (200°C).

3. Place flour in a large sealable plastic bag.

4. Spread panko in a shallow dish.

5. In another shallow dish, whisk eggs until blended.

6. Add wrapped cheese pieces to flour, seal bag and toss until coated. Working with 1 cheese piece at a time, remove from flour, shaking off excess. Dip in egg, shaking off excess, then dredge in panko, pressing gently to adhere. As they are dredged, place cheese pieces in air fryer basket, leaving space in between. Spray with cooking spray. Discard any excess flour, egg and panko.

7. Air-fry for 5 to 8 minutes or until golden brown. Serve immediately.

# Stuffed Mushrooms with Bacon and Herbs

**Mushrooms in general are great for stuffing. A stuffing made of bacon and basil is perhaps the best of all.**

### Makes about 10 mushrooms

### Variation

*Gluten-Free Stuffed Mushrooms:* Replace the panko with an equal amount of crushed gluten-free corn flakes cereal.

- *Preheat air fryer to 390°F (200°C)*
- *Food processor*

| | | |
|---|---|---|
| 8 oz | medium-large cremini mushrooms (about 10) | 250 g |
| 1 | slice bacon, cooked and crumbled | 1 |
| 1 | green onion, roughly chopped | 1 |
| ½ cup | panko (Japanese bread crumbs) | 125 mL |
| ¼ cup | loosely packed fresh basil leaves | 60 mL |
| 2 tsp | olive oil | 10 mL |
| | Salt and freshly cracked black pepper | |
| | Nonstick cooking spray | |

1. Remove mushroom stems and set the caps aside.

2. In food processor, combine mushroom stems, bacon, green onion, panko, basil and oil. Pulse until finely ground. Season to taste with salt and pepper.

3. Place mushroom caps, hollow side up, on work surface. Divide filling evenly among mushrooms, mounding it in the center of each. Spray with cooking spray.

4. Place mushrooms in air fryer basket. Air-fry for 9 to 12 minute or until filling is golden brown and mushrooms are tender. Serve immediately.

# Corn Dog Minis

It's time to think outside the frozen-food box. These corn dog minis may not look like what is on offer in the frozen foods section, but the taste will win over one and all.

## Storage Tip

Store the cooled corn dog minis in an airtight container in the refrigerator for up to 3 days or in the freezer for up to 3 months. Let thaw in the refrigerator for 3 to 4 hours, then microwave on Medium (50%) for 30 to 60 seconds.

## Variation

*Gluten-Free Corn Dog Minis:* Replace the all-purpose flour with an all-purpose gluten-free flour blend and check the label on the wieners to make sure they are gluten-free.

- *Preheat air fryer to 360°F (180°C)*
- *16 miniature foil or paper muffin cup liners*

| | | |
|---|---|---|
| ⅓ cup | all-purpose flour | 75 mL |
| ⅓ cup | yellow cornmeal | 75 mL |
| ¼ tsp | baking soda | 1 mL |
| ⅛ tsp | salt | 0.5 mL |
| 1 tbsp | granulated sugar | 15 mL |
| 1 | large egg | 1 |
| ⅓ cup | buttermilk | 75 mL |
| 2 tbsp | unsalted butter, melted | 30 mL |
| 2 | all-beef hot dog wieners, each cut crosswise into 4 pieces | 2 |
| | Nonstick cooking spray | |

1. Place one muffin cup liner inside another. Repeat to create 8 doubled liners.

2. In a medium bowl, whisk together flour, cornmeal, baking soda and salt.

3. In a small bowl, whisk together sugar, egg, buttermilk and butter.

4. Add the egg mixture to the flour mixture and stir until just blended.

5. Scoop 1 heaping tbsp (15 mL) batter into each doubled liner. Place 1 hot dog piece, cut side up, in the center of each. Spray lightly with cooking spray.

6. Place filled liners in air fryer basket, spacing them evenly. Air-fry for 6 to 9 minutes or until golden brown. Transfer to a wire rack and let cool for at least 5 minutes. Serve warm.

# Air-Fried Sesame Edamame

I first had fried edamame as an appetizer at a very fancy restaurant for an exorbitant price. Then I found out that they couldn't be simpler to make, especially in an air fryer. The fact that they are so inexpensive to make at home adds to the pleasure of the preparation.

## Makes 6 servings

### Storage Tip

Store air-fried edamame in an airtight container at room temperature for up to 2 weeks.

- *Preheat air fryer to 390°F (200°C)*

| | | |
|---|---|---|
| 1½ cups | frozen shelled edamame, thawed | 375 mL |
| ⅛ tsp | salt | 0.5 mL |
| ⅛ tsp | freshly ground black pepper | 0.5 mL |
| 1½ tsp | toasted (dark) sesame oil | 7 mL |

1. In a medium bowl, combine edamame, salt, pepper and oil.

2. Transfer edamame to air fryer basket. Air-fry for 8 to 10 minutes, shaking basket once halfway through, until crisp and dry. Transfer edamame to a large plate, spread in a single layer and let cool completely.

# Wonton Chips with Hot and Light Artichoke Dip

Wonton chips plus artichoke dip equals an outstanding appetizer, substantial yet special. Adding to the appeal of the combination, the chips can be prepared and stored in an airtight container up to 1 day ahead of serving. The dip can also be assembled and refrigerated up to the point of air-frying, then covered and refrigerated up to 1 day ahead.

### Makes 4 servings

### Tips

You can use 1¼ cups (300 mL) drained canned artichoke hearts from a 15-oz (425 mL) can in place of the frozen artichoke hearts.

If you prefer, you can use regular mayonnaise and cream cheese in place of reduced-fat.

For a milder dip, omit the hot pepper sauce.

- Preheat air fryer to 390°F (200°C)
- Two ¾-cup (175 mL) ramekins, sprayed with nonstick cooking spray

### Wonton Chips

| 12 | 3½-inch (9 cm) square wonton wrappers | 12 |
| | Nonstick cooking spray | |
| | Salt | |

### Hot and Light Artichoke Dip

| 1 | clove garlic, minced | 1 |
| ¼ cup | reduced-fat brick-style cream cheese, softened | 60 mL |
| ¼ cup | reduced-fat mayonnaise | 60 mL |
| 2 tbsp | freshly grated Parmesan cheese | 30 mL |
| 1 tsp | freshly squeezed lemon juice | 5 mL |
| ½ tsp | hot pepper sauce | 2 mL |
| 1 | package (9 oz/255 g) frozen artichoke hearts, thawed and chopped | 1 |
| | Salt | |

1. *Chips:* Cut wonton wrappers in half diagonally. Spray with cooking spray and sprinkle with salt.

2. Place as many triangles in air fryer basket as will fit in a single layer. Air-fry for 3 to 5 minutes or until golden brown. Transfer chips to a wire rack and let cool completely. Repeat with the remaining triangles.

## Variation

*Wonton Chips with Hot and Light Spinach Dip:* Replace the artichoke hearts with a 9-oz (256 g) box of frozen chopped spinach, thawed and excess liquid squeezed out.

**3.** Reduce air fryer temperature to 350°F (180°C).

**4.** *Dip:* In a medium bowl, stir together garlic, cream cheese, mayonnaise, Parmesan, lemon juice and hot pepper sauce until blended and smooth. Stir in artichoke hearts. Season to taste with salt. Spoon dip into prepared ramekins.

**5.** Place ramekins in air fryer basket. Air-fry for 23 to 28 minutes or until dip is hot and beginning to brown.

**6.** Serve dip warm, with wonton chips.

# Pappadums

Pappadums are crisp lentil wafers served with a wide range of Indian foods. Their great appeal lies in their light-as-air crispiness, which is typically achieved through quick deep-frying. Air-frying works every bit as well.

## Makes 6 servings

**Tip**

Look for ready-to-cook pappadums in packages (containing anywhere from 6 to 12 uncooked pappadums) at Asian supermarkets and in the international foods section of well-stocked grocery stores.

• Preheat air fryer to 390°F (200°C)

| | | |
|---|---|---|
| 6 | ready-to-cook pappadums | 6 |
| | Nonstick cooking spray | |

1. Lightly spray both sides of 1 pappadum with cooking spray.

2. Place sprayed pappadum in air fryer basket. Air-fry for 20 to 40 seconds or until it begins to blister and puff (check often, as they scorch easily). Turn pappadum over and air-fry for 10 to 30 seconds or until blistered and puffed. Carefully transfer pappadum to a wire rack and let cool completely.

3. Repeat steps 1 and 2 with each remaining pappadum.

# Garlicky Pita Chips

The distinct flavor of garlic turns whole wheat pitas into an additive snack, ideal for scooping up especially thick dips and spreads. If you prefer, regular pitas can be used in place of whole wheat.

**Makes 4 servings**

## Storage Tip

Store pita chips in an airtight container at room temperature for up to 2 weeks.

## Variations

*Cinnamon-Sugar Pita Chips:* Replace the garlic powder and salt with a mixture of 1 tbsp (15 mL) granulated sugar and ¾ tsp (3 mL) ground cinnamon.

*Herbed Pita Chips:* Reduce the garlic powder to ½ tsp (2 mL) and sprinkle the pitas with 1 tsp (5 mL) dried Italian herb seasoning.

• *Preheat air fryer to 390°F (200°C)*

| 2 | 6-inch (15 cm) whole wheat pitas | 2 |
| | Nonstick cooking spray (preferably olive oil) | |
| 1 tsp | garlic powder | 5 mL |
| ⅛ tsp | salt | 0.5 mL |

1. Spray one side of each pita with cooking spray. Sprinkle each with half the garlic powder and salt. Cut each pita into 8 wedges of equal size.

2. Place half the pita wedges in air fryer basket. Air-fry for 4 to 7 minutes, shaking basket once halfway through, until golden. Transfer pita chips to a large plate, spread in a single layer and let cool completely. Repeat with the remaining pita wedges.

# Chipotle Tortilla Chips

**The smoky-spicy flavor of chipotle adds a south-of-the-border note to these light and healthy tortilla chips.**

## Makes 4 servings

**Tip**

For plain tortilla chips, omit the chile powder.

**Storage Tip**

Store tortilla chips in an airtight container at room temperature for up to 2 weeks.

• *Preheat air fryer to 350°F (180°C)*

| | | |
|---|---|---|
| 3 | 6-inch (15 cm) corn tortillas | 3 |
| | Nonstick cooking spray | |
| 1 tsp | chipotle chile powder | 5 mL |
| 1/8 tsp | salt | 0.5 mL |

1. Spray one side of each tortilla with cooking spray. Sprinkle evenly with chile powder and salt. Cut each tortilla into 8 wedges of equal size.

2. Arrange half the tortilla wedges in air fryer basket. Air-fry for 7 to 10 minutes, shaking basket once halfway through, until golden. Transfer tortilla chips to a large plate, spread in a single layer and let cool completely. Repeat with the remaining tortilla wedges.

# Crunchy Bowtie Chips

Caution: may require a double batch. These easy-to-prepare pasta chips are sure to please a crowd, not to mention your wallet. The flavorful crumb coating requires only ingredients you almost certainly have on hand.

**Tip**

For less spicy bowtie chips, omit the black pepper.

**Storage Tip**

Store bowtie chips in an airtight container at room temperature for up to 2 weeks.

**Variation**

*Pesto Bowtie Chips:* Replace the milk and olive oil with 2 tbsp (30 mL) pesto, and reduce the salt to 1/4 tsp (1 mL).

| | | |
|---|---|---|
| 8 oz | bowtie (farfalle) pasta (uncooked) | 250 g |
| 1/4 cup | all-purpose flour | 60 mL |
| 1 | large egg | 1 |
| 1 tbsp | olive oil | 15 mL |
| 1 tbsp | milk | 15 mL |
| 3/4 tsp | salt | 3 mL |
| 1/4 tsp | freshly ground black pepper | 1 mL |
| 3/4 cup | dry bread crumbs with Italian seasoning | 175 mL |
| 1/2 cup | freshly grated Parmesan cheese | 125 mL |
| | Nonstick cooking spray | |

1. Cook pasta according to package directions. Drain and rinse under cold water until cool. Transfer to a medium bowl, sprinkle with flour and stir to combine.

2. Preheat air fryer to 350°F (180°C).

3. In a small bowl, whisk together egg, oil, milk, salt and pepper until blended. Pour over pasta and stir until coated. Add bread crumbs and Parmesan, stirring until coated.

4. Place as many bowties in air fryer basket as will fit in a single layer. Spray with cooking spray. Air-fry for 7 to 10 minutes, shaking basket once halfway through, until golden. Transfer bowtie chips to a wire rack and let cool completely. Repeat with the remaining bowties.

# Cinnamon Apple Chips

I like these simple, delicate apple chips topped with a pleasant cinnamon-sugar crunch just as they are, but you could easily substitute any sweet spice — cardamom, ginger, allspice — you have in your pantry.

**Makes 4 servings**

**Storage Tip**

Store apple chips in an airtight container at room temperature for up to 1 week.

**Variation**

*Pear Chips:* Use 2 medium Bosc pears, halved and cored, in place of the apples.

• *Preheat air fryer to 390°F (200°C)*

| | | |
|---|---|---|
| 2 | large tart-sweet apples (such as Braeburn, Gala or Pippin), halved and cored | 2 |
| 1½ tbsp | granulated sugar | 22 mL |
| ½ tsp | ground cinnamon | 2 mL |
| Pinch | salt | Pinch |
| | Nonstick cooking spray | |

1. Using a very sharp knife or a mandoline, cut apples into ⅛-inch (3 mm) thick slices.

2. In a small bowl, combine sugar, cinnamon and salt.

3. Arrange one-quarter of the apple slices in a single layer on work surface. Spray with cooking spray and sprinkle with some of the sugar mixture.

4. Place apple slices in air fryer basket (it is okay if they overlap slightly). Air-fry for 6 to 9 minutes, shaking basket once halfway through, until slices appear dry and are pale golden brown. Transfer chips to a wire rack and let cool completely.

5. Repeat steps 3 and 4 with the remaining apple slices and sugar mixture.

# Jerk-Seasoned Plantain Chips

Plantains are firm and starchy, but easy to slice for homemade chips. Tossing the slices with jerk seasoning evokes the warm beaches of Jamaica.

## Makes 4 servings

### Tips

Make sure the plantain slices are of even thickness, or some will be overdone before others are ready.

It's okay for the plantain slices to overlap slightly in the bottom of the basket.

Check the chips frequently as they air-fry; they can quickly turn from golden brown to burned.

### Storage Tip

Store plantain chips in an airtight container at room temperature for up to 1 week.

• Preheat air fryer to 360°F (180°C)

| | | |
|---|---|---|
| 2 | green plantains, peeled | 2 |
| 1 tbsp | olive oil | 15 mL |
| 1 tsp | jerk seasoning | 5 mL |
| $\frac{1}{4}$ tsp | salt | 1 mL |

1. Using a very sharp knife or a mandoline, cut plantains into $\frac{1}{16}$-inch (2 mm) thick slices.

2. In a large bowl, toss together plantains, oil, jerk seasoning and salt until plantains are coated.

3. Place as many plantain slices in air fryer basket as will fit in a single layer. Air-fry for 21 to 25 minutes, shaking basket once halfway through, until edges are golden brown. Transfer chips to a wire rack and let cool completely (they will crisp more as they cool). Repeat with the remaining plantain slices.

# No-Kettle Potato Chips

Freshly ground black pepper is more distinctive with a minimalist recipe like these chips, so be sure not to use pre-ground. And while these homemade chips are great alongside homemade dips, they also shine when eaten solo.

## Tips

Make sure the potato slices are of even thickness, or some will be overdone before others are ready.

It's okay for the potato slices to overlap slightly in the bottom of the basket.

Check the chips frequently as they air-fry; they can quickly turn from golden brown to burned.

## Storage Tip

Store potato chips in an airtight container at room temperature for up to 1 week.

| 2 | medium russet potatoes, peeled | 2 |
| | Ice water | |
| 2 tsp | olive oil | 10 mL |
| $\frac{1}{2}$ tsp | salt | 2 mL |
| | Freshly ground black pepper | |

1. Using a very sharp knife or a mandoline, cut potatoes into $\frac{1}{16}$-inch (2 mm) thick slices. Place potatoes in a large bowl of ice water for 30 minutes to remove excess starch.

2. Preheat air fryer to 330°F (160°C).

3. Drain about half the potatoes, then pat dry with paper towels. (Keep the remaining potatoes in ice water.) In a medium bowl, toss together drained potatoes, half the oil, half the salt and a pinch of pepper until potatoes are coated.

4. Place coated potatoes in air fryer basket. Air-fry for 25 to 30 minutes, shaking basket two or three times, until edges are golden brown and chips appear crisp. Transfer chips to a wire rack and let cool completely (they will crisp more as they cool).

5. Repeat steps 3 and 4 with the remaining potatoes, oil and salt and a pinch of pepper.

# Sweet Potato Chips

Unless it's the holiday cooking season, sweet potatoes are easy to overlook as an anytime chip option. These faintly sweet and smoky chips will broaden your horizons.

## Makes 6 servings

### Tips

Make sure the sweet potato slices are of even thickness, or some will be overdone before others are ready.

It's okay for the sweet potato slices to overlap slightly in the bottom of the basket.

Check the chips frequently as they air-fry; they can quickly turn from golden brown to burned.

### Storage Tip

Store sweet potato chips in an airtight container at room temperature for up to 1 week.

• *Preheat air fryer to 390°F (200°C)*

| 2 | medium-large sweet potatoes, peeled | 2 |
| 1 tbsp | olive oil | 15 mL |
| 1 tbsp | packed light brown sugar | 15 mL |
| 1 tsp | garlic powder | 5 mL |
| ½ tsp | ground cumin | 2 mL |
| ½ tsp | salt | 2 mL |

1. Using a very sharp knife or a mandoline, cut sweet potatoes into $\frac{1}{16}$-inch (2 mm) thick slices.

2. In a large bowl, toss together sweet potatoes, oil, brown sugar, garlic powder, cumin and salt until sweet potatoes are coated.

3. Place as many sweet potato slices in air fryer basket as will fit in a single layer. Air-fry for 9 to 13 minutes, shaking basket once halfway through, until edges are golden brown. Transfer chips to a wire rack and let cool completely (they will crisp more as they cool). Repeat with the remaining sweet potatoes.

# Chili-Garlic Yucca Chips

If you already love potato and tortilla chips, why not give yucca chips a try?

## Makes 4 servings

### Tips

Make sure the yucca slices are of even thickness, or some will be overdone before others are ready.

It's okay for the yucca slices to overlap slightly in the bottom of the basket.

Check the chips frequently as they air-fry; they can quickly turn from golden brown to burned.

### Storage Tip

Store yucca chips in an airtight container at room temperature for up to 1 week.

| | | |
|---|---|---|
| 2 | medium yucca roots, peeled | 2 |
| 1 tbsp | olive oil | 15 mL |
| 1 tsp | chili powder | 5 mL |
| 1 tsp | garlic powder | 5 mL |
| $1/2$ tsp | ground cumin | 2 mL |
| $1/2$ tsp | salt | 2 mL |

1. Using a very sharp knife or a mandoline, cut yucca into $1/16$-inch (2 mm) thick slices (about 2 cups/500 mL).

2. In a large bowl, toss together yucca, oil, chili powder, garlic powder, cumin and salt until yucca slices are coated. Let stand for 20 minutes.

3. Meanwhile, preheat air fryer to 360°F (180°C).

4. Place as many yucca slices in air fryer basket as will fit in a single layer. Air-fry for 21 to 25 minutes, shaking basket once halfway through, until edges are golden brown. Transfer chips to a wire rack and let cool completely (they will crisp more as they cool). Repeat with the remaining yucca slices.

# Parmesan Zucchini Chips

Unlike many versions of chips, which are mostly about the crunch and the salt, these delicate zucchini crisps have a fresh, straightforward flavor. They are best eaten soon after making them, which should not be a problem.

**Makes 4 servings**

## Tip
These chips are best eaten immediately after cooking.

## Variation
*Gluten-Free Zucchini Chips:* Replace the bread crumbs with an equal amount of crushed gluten-free corn flakes cereal.

| | | |
|---|---|---|
| 2 | medium zucchini | 2 |
| 1 tbsp | salt | 15 mL |
| 2/3 cup | dry bread crumbs with Italian seasoning | 150 mL |
| 3/4 cup | finely grated Parmesan cheese | 175 mL |
| 1 | large egg | 1 |
| 2 tbsp | milk | 30 mL |
| | Nonstick cooking spray | |

1. Using a very sharp knife or a mandoline, cut zucchini into $1/8$-inch (3 mm) thick slices. Place slices in a colander and sprinkle with salt. Let stand for 30 minutes to drain.

2. Preheat air fryer to 390°F (200°C).

3. In a shallow dish, combine bread crumbs and Parmesan.

4. In another shallow dish, whisk egg and milk until blended.

5. Rinse one-quarter of the zucchini slices to remove excess salt, then pat dry with paper towels. Working with 1 slice at a time, dip in egg mixture, shaking off excess, then dredge in bread crumb mixture, pressing gently to adhere. As they are dredged, arrange zucchini slices in a single layer in air fryer basket (it is okay if they overlap slightly). Spray with cooking spray.

6. Air-fry for 7 to 10 minutes or until golden brown and crisp. Transfer chips to a wire rack to cool slightly.

7. Repeat steps 5 and 6 with the remaining zucchini slices, egg mixture and bread crumb mixture. Discard any excess egg mixture and bread crumb mixture.

# Tuscan Eggplant Chips

Eggplant and Parmesan cheese have a real affinity — they're both beloved ingredients in Italian cuisine, after all. Here, they come together in enticing herb-scented chips.

**Makes 6 servings**

**Tip**

These chips are best eaten immediately after cooking.

- *Large baking sheet, lined with parchment paper*

| | | |
|---|---|---|
| 1 | large eggplant, peeled | 1 |
| 1 tbsp | salt | 15 mL |
| 2 cups | panko (Japanese bread crumbs) | 500 mL |
| ¾ cup | finely grated Parmesan cheese | 175 mL |
| 2 tsp | dried Italian seasoning | 10 mL |
| 1 | large egg | 1 |
| 2 tbsp | water | 30 mL |
| | Nonstick cooking spray | |

1. Cut eggplant lengthwise into quarters. Cut each quarter crosswise into very thin slices. Place slices in a colander and sprinkle with salt. Let stand for 30 minutes to drain.

2. Rinse eggplant slices to remove excess salt, then pat dry with paper towels. Place slices in a single layer on prepared baking sheet and place in the freezer for 30 minutes (no longer).

3. Preheat air fryer to 390°F (200°C).

4. In a shallow dish, combine panko, Parmesan and Italian seasoning.

5. In another shallow dish, whisk together egg and water until blended.

## Variation

*Gluten-Free Eggplant Chips:* Replace the panko with an equal amount of crushed gluten-free corn flakes cereal.

6. Working with 1 eggplant slice at a time, dip in egg mixture, shaking off excess, then dredge in panko mixture, pressing gently to adhere. As they are dredged, place as many eggplant slices in air fryer basket as will fit in a single layer. Spray with cooking spray. (Return the remaining eggplant slices to the freezer until ready to coat and air-fry.)

7. Air-fry for 4 to 7 minutes or until golden brown. Transfer chips to a wire rack to cool slightly.

8. Repeat steps 6 and 7 with the remaining eggplant slices, egg mixture and panko mixture. Discard any excess egg mixture and panko mixture.

# Crispy Kale Chips

You can never have enough chips — at least, you can't when they are made with kale. Regardless of your feeling about greens in general, kale chips in particular are thoroughly addictive. Go ahead, eat your fill!

## Makes 4 servings

### Tips

The key to really crisp kale chips is super-dry leaves. Be sure to pat the leaves completely dry before air-frying. Or, if you have a salad spinner, spin the leaves to remove the excess moisture after rinsing.

The chips lose their crunch after a couple of hours, so, for the best texture, eat them soon after making them.

• Preheat air fryer to 390°F (200°C)

| | | |
|---|---|---|
| 1 lb | kale, rinsed and patted dry | 500 g |
| | Nonstick cooking spray (preferably olive oil) | |
| ¼ tsp | salt | 1 mL |

1. Remove tough stems and center ribs from kale, then tear leaves into roughly 3-inch (7.5 cm) pieces.

2. Arrange one-quarter of the kale pieces in a single layer on work surface. Spray with cooking spray and sprinkle with some of the salt.

3. Place kale leaves in air fryer basket (it is okay if they overlap slightly). Air-fry for 4 to 6 minutes, shaking basket once halfway through, until edges are browned and leaves are crispy. Transfer chips to a wire rack and let cool completely.

4. Repeat steps 2 and 3 with the remaining kale leaves.

# Sweet and Spicy Nuts

Coating nuts with a spicy-sweet coating and air-frying them to golden-brown, toasty perfection gives them undeniable verve.

**Makes about 1½ cups (375 mL)**

## Tip

For the nuts, try a mix of almonds, pecans, walnuts and cashews.

## Storage Tip

Store air-fried nuts in an airtight container at room temperature for up to 2 weeks.

- *Preheat air fryer to 330°F (160°C)*
- *Fine-mesh sieve*

| | | |
|---|---|---|
| 1 tbsp | granulated sugar | 15 mL |
| ½ tsp | ground coriander | 2 mL |
| ¼ tsp | salt | 1 mL |
| ⅛ tsp | cayenne pepper | 0.5 mL |
| 1 | large egg white, at room temperature | 1 |
| 1½ cups | mixed raw nuts | 375 mL |

1. In a small cup, whisk together sugar, coriander, salt and cayenne.

2. In a medium bowl, whisk egg white until light and frothy. Add nuts and toss until evenly coated with egg white. Transfer nuts to the fine-mesh sieve to drain off excess egg white.

3. Return nuts to bowl and sprinkle with sugar mixture, tossing to coat.

4. Spread nuts in a single layer in air fryer basket. Air-fry for 16 to 20 minutes, shaking basket once or twice, until deep golden brown and dry-looking. Transfer nuts to a large plate lined with parchment paper and let cool completely.

# Tamari Almonds

A trio of everyday ingredients — tamari, vegetable oil and brown sugar — will quickly enliven the almonds that have been parked in your pantry.

**Makes about 1¹⁄₂ cups (375 mL)**

**Tip**

An equal amount of pecan or walnut halves can be used in place of the almonds.

**Storage Tip**

Store air-fried almonds in an airtight container at room temperature for up to 2 weeks.

- Preheat air fryer to 330°F (160°C)

| 1¹⁄₂ cups | raw almonds | 375 mL |
| 1 tbsp | tamari or soy sauce | 15 mL |
| 1 tsp | vegetable oil | 5 mL |
| 1 tsp | packed light brown sugar | 5 mL |

1. In a medium bowl, toss together almonds, tamari, oil and brown sugar until almonds are evenly coated.

2. Spread almonds in a single layer in air fryer basket. Air-fry for 16 to 20 minutes, shaking basket once or twice, until deep golden brown and dry-looking. Transfer almonds to a large plate lined with parchment paper and let cool completely.

# Spicy, Crispy Roasted Chickpeas

~~~~~~~~~~~~~~~~~~~~~~~~~~~~~~~~~~~~~~~~~~~~~~~~~~~~~~~~~~~~~~~~~~~~

**With a hint of oil, a sprinkle of spice and a blast of heat, canned chickpeas transform into a tasty nibble akin to roasted nuts.**

## Makes 4 servings

**Tip**
You can use an equal amount of chili powder (any variety) in place of the paprika.

**Storage Tip**
Store air-fried chickpeas in an airtight container at room temperature for up to 2 weeks.

• *Preheat air fryer to 390°F (200°C)*

| | | |
|---|---|---|
| 1 | can (14 to 19 oz/398 to 540 mL) chickpeas, drained, rinsed and patted dry | 1 |
| 1 tbsp | olive oil | 15 mL |
| 1 tsp | smoked paprika (sweet or hot) | 5 mL |
| ¾ tsp | salt | 3 mL |
| ¼ tsp | ground cumin | 1 mL |

**1.** In a large bowl, combine chickpeas, oil, paprika, salt and cumin.

**2.** Spread half the chickpeas in air fryer basket. Air-fry for 7 to 10 minutes, shaking basket once or twice, until deep golden brown and crisp-looking. Transfer chickpeas to a large plate lined with parchment paper and let cool completely. Repeat with the remaining chickpeas.

# Entrées

# Pan Pizza Margherita

You may end up deleting the number for your favorite pizza delivery joint once you make this air fryer pizza. The intense heat of the air fryer yields a crust that is light and crisp, akin to brick oven–style pizza.

**Makes 2 servings**

### Variation

*Pepperoni Pizza:* Omit the olive oil, tomatoes and basil. In step 2, spread 2 tbsp (30 mL) marinara sauce over the pressed-out dough. Top with the cheeses and 6 to 8 slices of regular or turkey pepperoni.

- Preheat air fryer to 390°F (200°C)
- 6-inch (15 cm) round metal cake pan, sprayed with nonstick cooking spray

|  | All-purpose flour |  |
|---|---|---|
| 8 oz | fresh or thawed frozen pizza dough | 250 g |
| 2 tsp | extra virgin olive oil | 10 mL |
| 2 | plum (Roma) tomatoes, thinly sliced horizontally | 2 |
| 3 oz | fresh mozzarella cheese in water, drained and diced | 90 g |
| ¼ cup | freshly grated Parmesan cheese | 60 mL |
| ¼ cup | loosely packed fresh basil leaves, torn | 60 mL |

1. On a lightly floured work surface, cut dough in half.

2. Press half of dough into bottom and sides of prepared pan. Drizzle with half the oil and top with half each of the tomatoes, mozzarella and Parmesan.

3. Place pan in air fryer basket. Air-fry for 10 to 12 minutes or until crust is golden brown. Using a spatula, slide pizza out of pan onto a wire rack and let cool for 5 minutes before serving topped with basil.

4. Repeat steps 2 and 3 with the remaining dough, oil, tomatoes, cheeses and basil.

# Black Bean Quesadillas

As the quesadillas cook, the tortillas become golden and toasty while inside, pepper Jack cheese, black beans and cilantro coalesce into a rich, gooey concoction.

**Makes 2 servings**

**Tip**

An equal amount of Cheddar or Monterey Jack cheese can be used in place of the pepper Jack cheese.

- *Preheat air fryer to 390°F (200°C)*

| 4 | 6-inch (15 cm) flour tortillas | 4 |
| 2 cups | shredded pepper Jack cheese | 500 mL |
| 1 cup | rinsed drained canned black beans | 250 mL |
| 2 tbsp | chopped fresh cilantro (optional) | 30 mL |
| | Nonstick cooking spray | |

**Suggested Accompaniments**

Guacamole

Salsa

Sour cream or plain Greek-style yogurt

1. Place 2 tortillas on a work surface. Divide cheese, beans and cilantro (if using) evenly between tortillas, distributing to cover. Top with the remaining tortillas, pressing down gently. Spray lightly with cooking spray.

2. Place 1 quesadilla in air fryer basket. Air-fry for 7 to 10 minutes or until cheese is melted and tortillas are golden brown. Transfer to cutting board and let cool for 2 to 3 minutes, then cut into quarters. Repeat with the remaining quesadilla. Serve with any of the suggested accompaniments, as desired.

# Black Bean Burgers with Sriracha Mayonnaise

This is by far my most popular burger recipe among my circle of friends, appealing to both vegetarians and meat-eaters. The Sriracha Mayonnaise could not be easier, and once you try it, you'll understand why I included it as an integral part of the recipe instead of merely a suggestion.

## Makes 2 servings

**Tip**

If you can only find larger 19-oz (540 mL) cans of beans, you will need about 1½ cups (375 mL) drained.

- Preheat air fryer to 390°F (200°C)
- Food processor

| | | |
|---|---|---|
| 2 | cloves garlic, coarsely chopped | 2 |
| ⅓ cup | coarsely chopped green onions | 75 mL |
| 1 | can (14 to 15 oz/398 to 425 mL) black beans, drained and rinsed, divided | 1 |
| 1 | large egg | 1 |
| 2 tsp | Worcestershire sauce | 10 mL |
| ¼ tsp | salt | 1 mL |
| ½ cup | panko (Japanese bread crumbs) | 125 mL |
| 2 | hamburger buns, split and toasted | 2 |
| | Nonstick cooking spray | |
| | Sriracha Mayonnaise (page 278) | |

### Suggested Toppings

Sliced tomatoes
Lettuce or spinach leaves
Thinly sliced Cheddar or Swiss cheese

1. In food processor, combine garlic, green onions, half the beans, egg, Worcestershire sauce and salt; pulse until a chunky purée forms.

2. Transfer purée to a medium bowl and stir in the remaining beans and panko. Form into two ¾-inch (2 cm) thick patties.

## Variation

For vegan burgers, use 3 tbsp (45 mL) vegan mayonnaise alternative in place of the egg.

3. Spray both sides of patties with cooking spray and place in air fryer basket, spacing them evenly. Air-fry for 8 minutes. Using a spatula, turn patties over. Air-fry for 4 to 6 minutes or until crispy on the outside and hot in the center.

4. Transfer patties to bottom halves of buns and top with Sriracha Mayonnaise and any of the suggested toppings, as desired. Cover with top halves of buns, pressing down gently.

# Eggplant Parmesan Boats

This recipe is a light, fresh and fast adaptation of one of my favorite Italian dishes, eggplant Parmesan. Traditional versions can be a caloric colossus, but this delicious riff qualifies as spa cuisine.

## Makes 2 servings

**Tip**
Regular mozzarella (not packed in water) may be used in place of the water-packed mozzarella.

• *Preheat air fryer to 390°F (200°C)*

| | | |
|---|---|---|
| 1 | Japanese or small Italian eggplant (about 8 oz/250 g), trimmed and cut in half lengthwise | 1 |
| ¼ tsp | salt | 1 mL |
| 2 tbsp | dry bread crumbs with Italian seasoning | 30 mL |
| | Nonstick cooking spray | |
| ¼ cup | marinara sauce | 60 mL |
| 2 tbsp | freshly grated Parmesan cheese | 30 mL |
| 1 | ball (about 4 oz/125 g) fresh mozzarella in water, drained and sliced | 1 |
| 6 | fresh basil leaves, thinly sliced | 6 |

1. Sprinkle cut sides of eggplant halves with salt and sprinkle each half with 1 tbsp (15 mL) bread crumbs. Spray with cooking spray.

2. Place eggplant halves, cut side up, in air fryer basket, spacing them evenly. Air-fry for 10 minutes.

3. Spread half the marinara sauce over each eggplant half and sprinkle with half the Parmesan. Top with mozzarella, dividing equally. Air-fry for 5 to 8 minutes or until cheese is melted. Top with basil.

# Chickpea and Bulgur–Stuffed Peppers

The best qualities of stuffed peppers shine in this simple vegetarian rendition: sweet, tender bell peppers and earthy bulgur meld with herbs and spices to form a satisfying, cohesive whole.

**Makes 2 servings**

## Tips

An equal amount of white beans (such as Great Northern or cannellini) can be used in place of the chickpeas.

Other dried fruits, such as chopped apricots, cherries or cranberries, can be used in place of the raisins.

When lining the basket with foil in step 1, be sure to leave at least 1/2 inch (1 cm) between the foil and the inside edge of the basket.

## Variation

*Southwestern Stuffed Peppers:* Replace the parsley with an equal amount of cilantro leaves and the chickpeas with an equal amount of black beans. Replace the raisins with 1/2 cup (125 mL) thawed frozen corn kernels and replace the cinnamon with 1 tsp (5 mL) chile powder.

• Preheat air fryer to 360°F (180°C)

| | | |
|---|---|---|
| 1/2 cup | fine or medium bulgur | 125 mL |
| 1 cup | boiling water | 250 mL |
| 2 | medium red or green bell peppers | 2 |
| 1 cup | packed fresh flat-leaf (Italian) parsley leaves, chopped | 250 mL |
| 1 cup | rinsed drained canned chickpeas, coarsely chopped | 250 mL |
| 1/3 cup | raisins, coarsely chopped | 75 mL |
| 1 tsp | dried cumin | 5 mL |
| 1/2 tsp | ground cinnamon | 2 mL |
| 1/4 tsp | salt | 1 mL |
| 1 tbsp | extra virgin olive oil | 15 mL |

1. In a medium bowl, combine bulgur and boiling water. Let stand for about 30 minutes or until water is absorbed.

2. Meanwhile, cut tops off bell peppers, setting the tops aside. Pull out and discard seeds and membranes.

3. Place peppers and their tops in air fryer basket, spacing them evenly. Air-fry for 10 minutes. Transfer peppers and tops to a plate and let cool.

4. To the bulgur, add parsley, chickpeas, raisins, cumin, cinnamon, salt and oil, stirring until blended. Spoon bulgur mixture into bell peppers, dividing equally.

5. Place a piece of foil in bottom of air fryer basket (see tip, at left). Place stuffed peppers on foil and place tops beside peppers. Air-fry for 10 to 14 minutes or until peppers are soft and filling is warmed through. Serve, replacing the tops on each stuffed pepper.

# Air-Fried Falafel

**Better than anything you can make from a mix, these falafel are light, fresh and flavorful.**

## Makes 4 servings

### Tips

Do not substitute canned chickpeas for the soaked dried chickpeas; if you do, the texture will be very mushy and the mixture will be too loose to form into patties.

Air fryers become very hot, especially when heated to maximum temperature. Use oven pads or mitts when touching the appliance and when opening and closing the basket.

### Storage Tip

Prepare the patties through step 3 and place on a baking sheet lined with parchment paper. Freeze until firm, then transfer patties to an airtight container or sealable freezer bag and freeze for up to 3 months. Thaw at room temperature for 2 hours, then air-fry as directed.

• *Food processor*

| | | |
|---|---|---|
| 1 cup | dried chickpeas | 250 mL |
| 3 | cloves garlic | 3 |
| 1 cup | packed fresh flat-leaf (Italian) parsley leaves | 250 mL |
| 2/3 cup | coarsely chopped red onion | 150 mL |
| 1 1/2 tsp | ground cumin | 7 mL |
| 3/4 tsp | salt | 3 mL |
| 1/4 tsp | freshly ground black pepper | 1 mL |
| 1 tbsp | olive oil | 15 mL |

### Suggested Accompaniments

Warm pitas

Sliced cucumber

Sliced tomatoes

Plain Greek yogurt

Lemon wedges

1. Pick through chickpeas and remove any stones and discolored peas. Place chickpeas in a medium bowl and add enough water to cover by about 2 inches (5 cm). Cover bowl and let soak at room temperature overnight. Drain well.

2. Preheat air fryer to 390°F (200°C).

3. In food processor, combine chickpeas, garlic, parsley, onion, cumin, salt, pepper and oil; process until smooth. Form into about 12 patties that are 1/2 inch (1 cm) thick and 2 inches (5 cm) in diameter.

4. Place 3 to 4 patties in air fryer basket, spacing them evenly. Air-fry for 6 minutes. Open basket and, using a spatula, carefully turn patties over. Air-fry for 5 to 7 minutes or until falafel are browned. Repeat with the remaining patties. Serve warm, with any of the suggested accompaniments, as desired.

# Crisp Air-Fried Tofu

This is one of my favorite ways to eat tofu. Toss some with your favorite sauce, add it to your favorite salad for a tremendous protein boost, or serve it as an appetizer along with one of the dips or sauces in the final chapter of the book.

## Makes 4 servings

### Tips

It is imperative to use tofu labeled "extra-firm." Anything less than extra-firm (including tofu labeled "firm") contains too much water and will explode in the microwave.

If you prefer, you can drain tofu the traditional way (as opposed to the quick method in step 1). Wrap the block of tofu in four or five layers of paper towels. Place on a dinner plate. Cover with a second dinner plate. Place two or three heavy cans on top. Let drain for 30 minutes. Remove cans, plates and paper towels. Repeat process once more. Cut tofu into 1-inch (2.5 cm) cubes.

### Storage Tip

Store cooled tofu cubes in an airtight container in the refrigerator for up to 5 days.

- Preheat air fryer to 390°F (200°C)

| 1 lb | extra-firm tofu, packing water poured off | 500 g |
| | Nonstick cooking spray | |
| | Salt and freshly ground black pepper | |

1. Cut tofu into 1-inch (2.5 cm) cubes and place in a single layer on a microwave-safe plate. Microwave on High for 2 minutes. Stir tofu gently. Microwave on High for 1 to 2 minutes or until surface of tofu appears dry.

2. Spray tofu cubes with cooking spray and season with salt and pepper.

3. Arrange tofu in a single layer in air fryer basket. Air-fry for 5 minutes, then shake the basket. Air-fry for another 5 minutes, then shake the basket again. Air-fry for 2 to 5 minutes or until tofu is golden brown and crispy.

# Fish Sticks

Fresh and crispy-edged, these are not your typical frozen fish sticks. You can assemble and cook them in minutes, then serve with lemon wedges, a dollop of ketchup or the sauce of your choice.

## Makes 2 servings

### Tip

Sea bass, halibut or any other firm white fish fillets may be used in place of the cod.

### Variation

Gluten-Free Fish Sticks: Replace the bread crumbs with an equal amount of crushed gluten-free corn flakes cereal.

• Preheat air fryer to 390°F (200°C)

| | | |
|---|---|---|
| 1 cup | plain dry bread crumbs | 250 mL |
| 2 tsp | Old Bay or other seafood seasoning | 10 mL |
| 1 | large egg | 1 |
| 1 tbsp | water | 15 mL |
| 12 oz | skinless Pacific cod fillets, cut into 3-inch (7.5 cm) strips | 375 g |
| | Nonstick cooking spray | |

1. In a shallow dish, combine bread crumbs and Old Bay seasoning.

2. In another shallow dish, beat egg and water until blended.

3. Dip fish strips in egg mixture, shaking off excess, then in bread crumb mixture, pressing to adhere and shaking off excess. Discard any excess egg mixture and bread crumb mixture.

4. Place strips in a single layer in air fryer basket, spacing them evenly. Spray with cooking spray. Air-fry for 8 to 12 minutes, turning once halfway through, until coating is golden brown and fish is opaque and flakes easily when tested with a fork.

# Potato Chip–Crusted Cod Fillets

Think of these fillets as fish and chips, all in one — vinegar included!
Packed with flavor, it's a quick fix for a busy weeknight.

## Makes 2 servings

### Tips

Sea bass, halibut or any other firm white fish fillets may be used in place of the cod.

An equal amount of plain salted kettle-style potato chips can be used in place of the salt and vinegar chips.

• *Preheat air fryer to 390°F (200°C)*

| | | |
|---|---|---|
| 2 tsp | mayonnaise | 10 mL |
| 2 | skinless cod fillets (each about 6 oz/175 g) | 2 |
| | Salt and freshly cracked black pepper | |
| 1 cup | salt and vinegar kettle-style potato chips, finely crushed | 250 mL |
| | Nonstick cooking spray | |
| | Buttermilk Ranch Dressing (page 275) | |

1. Spread 1 tsp (5 mL) mayonnaise over top of each fish fillet. Season with salt and pepper. Gently press half the crushed potato chips evenly on top of each fillet.

2. Place fillets in air fryer basket, spacing them evenly. Spray with cooking spray. Air-fry for 7 to 10 minutes or until fish is opaque and flakes easily when tested with a fork. Serve with Buttermilk Ranch Dressing.

# Lemon Thyme Halibut

Mild, firm, versatile halibut has a characteristically fresh flavor of the sea. A quick vinaigrette of lemon, olive oil and thyme enhances the flavor without masking it.

## Makes 2 servings

### Tips

Sea bass, cod or any other firm white fish fillets may be used in place of the halibut.

You can use 1/4 tsp (1 mL) dried thyme in place of fresh.

• Preheat air fryer to 390°F (200°C)

| | | |
|---|---|---|
| 3/4 tsp | minced fresh thyme | 3 mL |
| 1/8 tsp | granulated sugar | 0.5 mL |
| 1 tsp | finely grated lemon zest | 5 mL |
| 1 tbsp | freshly squeezed lemon juice | 15 mL |
| 4 tsp | extra virgin olive oil, divided | 20 mL |
| | Salt and freshly cracked black pepper | |
| 2 | skinless Pacific halibut fillets (each about 6 oz/175 g) | 2 |
| 1 tbsp | chopped fresh flat-leaf (Italian) parsley (optional) | 15 mL |

1. In a small bowl, whisk together thyme, sugar, lemon zest, lemon juice and 3 tsp (15 mL) oil. Season to taste with salt and pepper.

2. Brush fish fillets with the remaining oil and season with salt.

3. Place fillets in air fryer basket, spacing them evenly. Air-fry for 6 to 9 minutes or until fish is opaque and flakes easily when tested with a fork. Serve drizzled with lemon thyme vinaigrette and sprinkled with parsley (if using).

# Hawaiian Barbecue Salmon

An adaptation of a favorite dish available on all of the Hawaiian islands as a component of ready-to-go lunch plates, these delicious fillets are incredibly moist and juicy.

**Makes 2 servings**

## Tips

An equal amount of lemon zest and juice can be used in place of the lime zest and juice.

An equal amount of chile powder can be used in place of the cumin.

For a more pronounced ginger flavor, omit the cumin and increase the ground ginger to ¾ tsp (3 mL).

| | | |
|---|---|---|
| 3 tbsp | pineapple juice | 45 mL |
| 1 tbsp | freshly squeezed lime juice | 15 mL |
| 2 | skinless salmon fillets (each about 6 oz/175 g) | 2 |
| 1 tbsp | packed light brown sugar | 15 mL |
| 2 tsp | chili powder | 10 mL |
| 1 tsp | finely grated lime zest | 5 mL |
| ½ tsp | ground cumin | 2 mL |
| ¼ tsp | salt | 1 mL |
| ⅛ tsp | ground ginger | 0.5 mL |
| | Nonstick cooking spray | |
| | Lime wedges (optional) | |

1. In a medium sealable plastic bag, combine pineapple juice and lime juice. Add salmon fillets, seal bag and refrigerate for 1 hour, turning once.

2. Preheat air fryer to 390°F (200°C).

3. In a small bowl, stir together brown sugar, chili powder, lime zest, cumin, salt and ginger.

4. Remove fillets from bag and discard marinade. Rub brown sugar mixture over top and sides of fish.

5. Place fillets in air fryer basket, spacing them evenly. Spray with cooking spray. Air-fry for 6 to 9 minutes or until fish is opaque and flakes easily when tested with a fork. Serve with lime wedges, if desired.

# Cornmeal-Crusted Tilapia with Watermelon Salsa

Crunchy, spicy, zesty and slightly sweet all at once, this easy entrée will make tilapia your new favorite fish.

## Makes 2 servings

### Tips

An equal amount of chili powder can be used in place of the cumin.

Other mild, lean white fish, such as orange roughy, snapper, cod, tilefish or striped bass, may be used in place of the tilapia.

• *Preheat air fryer to 360°F (180°C)*

**Watermelon Salsa**

| | | |
|---|---|---|
| 1 cup | diced seedless watermelon (¼-inch/0.5 cm dice) | 250 mL |
| 2 tbsp | chopped red onion | 30 mL |
| 1 tbsp | chopped fresh cilantro | 15 mL |
| ¼ tsp | salt | 1 mL |
| Pinch | cayenne pepper | Pinch |
| 2 tsp | freshly squeezed lime juice | 10 mL |
| 1 tsp | liquid honey | 5 mL |

**Fish**

| | | |
|---|---|---|
| 2 tbsp | yellow cornmeal | 30 mL |
| 2 tbsp | all-purpose flour | 30 mL |
| 1 tsp | ground cumin | 5 mL |
| ¼ tsp | salt | 1 mL |
| 1 | large egg | 1 |
| 2 | skinless farmed tilapia fillets (each about 6 oz/175 g) | 2 |
| | Nonstick cooking spray | |

1. *Salsa:* In a small bowl, combine watermelon, onion, cilantro, salt, cayenne, lime juice and honey. Cover and refrigerate until ready to use.

2. *Fish:* In a shallow dish, stir together cornmeal, flour, cumin and salt.

3. In a separate shallow dish, whisk egg until blended.

## Variation

*Gluten-Free Cornmeal-Crusted Tilapia:* Replace the all-purpose flour with an all-purpose gluten-free flour blend.

4. Working with 1 fillet at a time, dip in egg, shaking off excess, then dredge in cornmeal mixture until coated, shaking off excess. As they are dredged, place fillets in air fryer basket, spacing them evenly. Spray with cooking spray. Discard any excess egg and cornmeal mixture.

5. Air-fry for 9 to 13 minutes or until crust is golden brown and fish flakes easily when tested with a fork. Serve with salsa.

# Salmon Glazed with Orange Marmalade and Soy

A trio of humble ingredients — soy sauce, orange marmalade and garlic — melds into the ideal glaze for salmon fillets, as rich as it is succulent.

## Makes 2 servings

### Tips

An equal amount of apricot preserves or liquid honey can be used in place of the orange marmalade.

Air fryers become very hot, especially when heated to maximum temperature. Use oven pads or mitts when touching the appliance and when opening and closing the basket.

• *Preheat air fryer to 390°F (200°C)*

|  | Nonstick cooking spray | |
|---|---|---|
| 1 | clove garlic, minced | 1 |
| 2 tbsp | orange marmalade | 30 mL |
| 1 tsp | soy sauce | 5 mL |
|  | Salt and freshly cracked black pepper | |
| 2 | skinless salmon fillets (each about 6 oz/175 g) | 2 |
| 2 tbsp | thinly sliced green onions | 30 mL |

1. Tear a piece of foil large enough to cover the bottom of the air fryer basket with ½ inch (1 cm) between the foil and the inside edge of the basket. Spray foil with cooking spray.

2. In a small bowl, stir together garlic, marmalade and soy sauce.

3. Season salmon fillets with salt and pepper and place on prepared foil. Brush with half the marmalade glaze.

4. Place foil with fillets in air fryer basket. Air-fry for 3 minutes. Open basket and brush fish with the remaining glaze. Air-fry for 3 to 6 minutes or until fish is opaque and flakes easily when tested with a fork. Serve sprinkled with green onions.

# Classic Salmon Cakes

Warm up on a chilly evening with a batch of these salmon cakes, made with fresh lemon, green onions and the convenience of canned salmon.

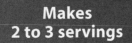

**Makes
2 to 3 servings**

## Tip

Two large egg whites can be used in place of the whole egg.

## Variation

*Gluten-Free Salmon Cakes:* Replace the panko with an equal amount of crushed gluten-free corn flakes cereal.

• *Preheat air fryer to 360°F (180°C)*

| | | |
|---|---|---|
| ⅔ cup | panko (Japanese bread crumbs) | 150 mL |
| 3 tbsp | finely chopped green onions | 45 mL |
| ½ tsp | Old Bay or other seafood seasoning | 2 mL |
| ¼ tsp | freshly ground black pepper | 1 mL |
| ¼ tsp | salt | 1 mL |
| 1 | large egg, beaten | 1 |
| 2 tbsp | mayonnaise | 30 mL |
| 2 tsp | freshly squeezed lemon juice | 10 mL |
| 1 tsp | Dijon mustard | 5 mL |
| 1 | can (15 oz/425 g) wild Alaskan salmon, drained and flaked (skin removed, if necessary) | 1 |
| | Nonstick cooking spray | |
| | Buttermilk Dill Dressing (variation, page 275) | |

1. In a large bowl, combine panko, green onions, Old Bay seasoning, pepper, salt, egg, mayonnaise, lemon juice and mustard. Add salmon, stirring until just combined. Form into six ¾-inch (2 cm) thick patties.

2. Place 3 patties in air fryer basket, leaving space in between. Spray with cooking spray. Air-fry for 4 minutes. Open basket and, using a spatula, carefully turn patties over. Air-fry for 4 to 7 minutes or until golden brown. Serve immediately with Buttermilk Dill Dressing. Repeat with the remaining patties.

# Mediterranean Tuna Cakes

**More convenient and frugal than crab cakes, these flavor-packed tuna cakes are as suitable for weeknight fare as they are for special occasions.**

### Makes
### 2 to 3 servings

### Tip
Two large egg whites can be used in place of the whole egg.

### Variation
*Gluten-Free Tuna Cakes:* Replace the bread crumbs with an equal amount of crushed gluten-free corn flakes cereal.

• *Preheat air fryer to 360°F (180°C)*

| | | |
|---|---|---|
| ½ cup | dry bread crumbs with Italian seasoning | 125 mL |
| ⅓ cup | chopped drained roasted red bell peppers | 75 mL |
| 3 tbsp | finely chopped green onions | 45 mL |
| 1½ tsp | finely grated lemon zest | 7 mL |
| 1 tsp | dried basil | 5 mL |
| ¼ tsp | salt | 1 mL |
| ⅛ tsp | freshly cracked black pepper | 0.5 mL |
| 1 | large egg, beaten | 1 |
| 2 tbsp | mayonnaise | 30 mL |
| 2 | cans (each 6 oz/170 g) water-packed tuna, drained | 2 |
| | Nonstick cooking spray | |
| | Lemon Herb Aïoli (page 276) | |

1. In a medium bowl, gently combine bread crumbs, roasted peppers, green onions, lemon zest, basil, salt, pepper, egg and mayonnaise. Gently stir in tuna. Form into six ¾-inch (2 cm) thick patties.

2. Place 3 patties in air fryer basket, leaving space in between. Spray with cooking spray. Air-fry for 4 minutes. Open basket and, using a spatula, carefully turn patties over. Air-fry for 4 to 7 minutes or until golden brown. Serve immediately with Lemon Herb Aïoli. Repeat with the remaining patties.

# Maryland Crab Cakes

These refined — but easy to assemble — crab cakes evoke the famous flavors of Maryland's Eastern Shore.

## Makes 2 servings

### Tip

Air fryers become very hot. Use oven pads or mitts when touching the appliance and when opening and closing the basket.

### Variation

*Gluten-Free Crab Cakes:* Replace the panko with an equal amount of crushed gluten-free corn flakes cereal.

- • *Preheat air fryer to 375°F (180°C)*

| | | |
|---|---|---|
| 1 | large egg white | 1 |
| ¾ tsp | Old Bay or other seafood seasoning | 3 mL |
| ⅛ tsp | salt | 0.5 mL |
| 2 tbsp | mayonnaise | 30 mL |
| 1 tsp | freshly squeezed lemon juice | 5 mL |
| ¾ tsp | Dijon mustard | 3 mL |
| ½ tsp | Worcestershire sauce | 2 mL |
| 8 oz | backfin (lump) crabmeat, cooked fresh or canned, drained and picked over | 250 g |
| ⅔ cup | panko (Japanese bread crumbs), divided | 150 mL |
| | Nonstick cooking spray | |
| | Spicy Mustard Sauce (page 257) | |
| | Chopped fresh parsley leaves (optional) | |

1. In a medium bowl, whisk together egg white, Old Bay seasoning, salt, mayonnaise, lemon juice, mustard and Worcestershire sauce until well blended. Gently stir in crab until well combined, being careful not to overmix (maintain some of the lumps).

2. Sprinkle half the panko over crab mixture and mix in gently but thoroughly (do not mash). Form into four 1-inch (2.5 cm) thick patties.

3. Place the remaining panko in a small dish. Dredge patties in panko, pressing gently to adhere. As they are dredged, place patties in air fryer basket, spacing evenly. Spray with cooking spray. Discard any excess panko.

4. Air-fry for 5 minutes. Open basket and, using a spatula, carefully turn patties over. Air-fry for 5 to 7 minutes or until golden brown. Serve immediately with Spicy Mustard Sauce. Sprinkle with parsley, if desired.

# Crispy Cajun Oysters with Spicy Cocktail Sauce

Oysters from my neighboring state (Louisiana) are plentiful, but it's not always convenient to light a fire to roast them (a favorite Cajun method). So I set about adapting my favorite spicy oyster recipe to the air fryer. I hope you are as pleased with the results as I am.

## Makes 2 servings

### Tip

Air fryers become very hot, especially when heated to maximum temperature. Use oven pads or mitts when touching the appliance and when opening and closing the basket.

### Variation

*Gluten-Free Crispy Cajun Oysters:* Replace the bread crumbs with an equal amount of crushed gluten-free corn flakes cereal.

• Preheat air fryer to 390°F (200°C)

| | | |
|---|---|---|
| ¼ cup | yellow cornmeal | 60 mL |
| ¼ cup | plain dry bread crumbs | 60 mL |
| 1 tsp | paprika | 5 mL |
| ½ tsp | salt | 2 mL |
| ¼ tsp | cayenne pepper | 1 mL |
| ¼ tsp | freshly ground black pepper | 1 mL |
| 16 | shucked medium oysters, drained well | 16 |
| | Nonstick cooking spray | |
| | Spicy Cocktail Sauce (page 256) | |
| | Lemon wedges (optional) | |

1. In a medium bowl, whisk together cornmeal, bread crumbs, paprika, salt, cayenne and black pepper.

2. Add half the oysters to the cornmeal mixture, gently tossing to coat.

3. Place coated oysters in air fryer basket, leaving space in between. Spray with cooking spray. Air-fry for 4 minutes. Open basket and, using tongs or a spatula, carefully turn oysters over. Air-fry for 4 to 7 minutes or until golden brown. Serve immediately with Spicy Cocktail Sauce and lemon wedges (if using).

4. Repeat steps 2 and 3 with the remaining oysters and cornmeal mixture. Discard any excess cornmeal mixture.

Blooming Onion with
Creamy Chipotle Dip (page 90)

Peppered Goat Cheese Poppers
with Honey (page 94)

Wonton Chips with Hot and Light
Artichoke Dip (page 106)

*Clockwise from left:*
Chili-Garlic Yucca Chips (page 116),
No-Kettle Potato Chips (page 114)
and Sweet Potato Chips (page 115)

Black Bean Burgers with
Sriracha Mayonnaise (page 128)

Air-Fried Falafel (page 132)

Cornmeal-Crusted Tilapia with
Watermelon Salsa (page 138)

Maple, Cranberry and Sausage–Stuffed
Acorn Squash (page 164)

# Blackened Sea Scallops

This spicy treatment for sea scallops comes courtesy of my New Orleans (born and raised) neighbor. Sea scallops are available all year, but like all shellfish, they are best when they are super-fresh.

## Makes 2 servings

### Tip

Two large egg whites can be used in place of the whole egg.

### Variation

*Gluten-Free Blackened Sea Scallops:* Replace the bread crumbs with an equal amount of crushed gluten-free corn flakes cereal.

• *Preheat air fryer to 390°F (200°C)*

| | | |
|---|---|---|
| 1/2 cup | dry bread crumbs with Italian seasoning | 125 mL |
| 3 tbsp | freshly grated Parmesan cheese | 45 mL |
| 2 tbsp | yellow cornmeal | 30 mL |
| 1/2 tsp | paprika | 2 mL |
| 1/4 tsp | dried thyme | 1 mL |
| 1/4 tsp | garlic powder | 1 mL |
| 1/4 tsp | freshly ground black pepper | 1 mL |
| 1 | large egg | 1 |
| 1 tbsp | hot pepper sauce (such as Tabasco) | 15 mL |
| 12 oz | large sea scallops, side muscles removed | 375 g |
| | Nonstick cooking spray | |
| | Rémoulade (page 279) | |

1. In a shallow dish, combine bread crumbs, Parmesan, cornmeal, paprika, thyme, garlic powder and black pepper.

2. In another shallow dish, whisk together egg and hot pepper sauce.

3. Working with 1 scallop at a time, dip in egg mixture, shaking off excess, then dredge in bread crumb mixture until coated, shaking off excess. As they are dredged, place half the scallops in air fryer basket, leaving space in between, and spray with cooking spray.

4. Air-fry for 5 to 8 minutes or until golden brown. Serve immediately with Rémoulade.

5. Repeat steps 3 and 4 with the remaining scallops, egg mixture and bread crumb mixture. Discard any excess egg mixture and bread crumb mixture.

# New Orleans BBQ Shrimp

Any true seafood aficionado knows the difference between good-tasting and great-tasting shrimp. This Louisiana standard — made with humble ingredients and the freshest shrimp you can get your hands on — falls into the latter camp.

**Makes 2 servings**

**Tip**

An equal amount of packed brown sugar or liquid honey can be used in place of the granulated sugar.

• *Preheat air fryer to 390°F (200°C)*

| | | |
|---|---|---|
| 1 tsp | granulated sugar | 5 mL |
| ¼ tsp | salt | 1 mL |
| 1 tbsp | unsalted butter, melted | 15 mL |
| 2 tsp | hot pepper sauce (such as Tabasco) | 10 mL |
| 2 tsp | freshly squeezed lemon juice | 10 mL |
| 8 oz | large shrimp, peeled and deveined | 250 g |
| | Chopped fresh parsley (optional) | |

1. In a medium bowl, combine sugar, salt, butter, hot pepper sauce and lemon juice. Reserve 1 tbsp (15 mL) sauce. Add shrimp to the remaining sauce and toss to coat.

2. Arrange shrimp in a single layer in air fryer basket. Air-fry for 4 to 7 minutes, shaking basket once, until shrimp are pink, firm and opaque.

3. Transfer shrimp to a clean medium bowl and toss with the reserved sauce. Serve immediately.

# Beer-Battered Shrimp with Horseradish Sauce

Featuring a beer batter, salty-sweet shrimp and a tangy sauce alongside, this recipe has all the bases covered.

**Makes 4 servings**

### Variation

*Gluten-Free Beer-Battered Shrimp:* Use gluten-free beer, replace the all-purpose flour with an all-purpose gluten-free flour blend, and replace the panko with an equal amount of crushed gluten-free corn flakes cereal.

| | | |
|---|---|---|
| ¾ cup | all-purpose flour | 175 mL |
| ¼ cup | cornstarch | 60 mL |
| ¼ tsp | salt | 1 mL |
| ¼ tsp | freshly cracked black pepper | 1 mL |
| 1 | large egg, lightly beaten | 1 |
| ¾ cup | beer, chilled | 175 mL |
| 1½ cups | panko (Japanese bread crumbs) | 375 mL |
| 1 lb | large shrimp, peeled and deveined | 500 g |
| | Nonstick cooking spray | |
| | Horseradish Sauce (page 253) | |

1. In a medium bowl, whisk together flour, cornstarch, salt and pepper. Whisk in egg and beer until blended and smooth. Cover loosely with plastic wrap and refrigerate for 30 minutes to thicken.

2. Preheat air fryer to 390°F (200°C).

3. Spread panko in a shallow dish.

4. Working with 1 shrimp at a time, dip in batter, shaking off excess, then dredge in panko, gently pressing to adhere. As they are dredged, place 5 to 6 shrimp in air fryer basket, leaving space in between. Spray with cooking spray.

5. Air-fry for 5 to 8 minutes or until golden brown. Serve immediately with Horseradish Sauce.

6. Repeat steps 4 and 5 with the remaining shrimp, batter and panko. Discard excess batter and panko.

# Fritto Misto

~~~~~~~~~~~~~~~~~~~~~~~~~~~~~~~~~~~~~~~~~~~~~~~~~~~~~~~~~~~~~~~~~~~~~

**This version may not be strictly traditional, but a light batter, delicate panko crumbs and a varied mix of vegetables and seafood bring the flavors of fritto misto together in a satisfying way.**

## Makes 4 servings

### Tips

Two large egg whites can be used in place of the whole egg.

Eight slender stalks of asparagus, trimmed, can be used in place of the green beans.

For best results, air-fry different types and sizes of seafood and vegetables individually to ensure even cooking.

| | | |
|---|---|---|
| ⅔ cup | all-purpose flour | 150 mL |
| ⅓ cup | cornstarch | 75 mL |
| ¼ tsp | salt | 1 mL |
| ¼ tsp | freshly cracked black pepper | 1 mL |
| 1 | large egg, lightly beaten | 1 |
| ¾ cup | club soda, chilled | 175 mL |
| 8 oz | cleaned squid | 250 g |
| 2 cups | panko (Japanese bread crumbs) | 500 mL |
| 8 oz | large shrimp, peeled and deveined | 250 g |
| 12 | mushrooms, trimmed | 12 |
| 8 | green beans, trimmed | 8 |
| 1 | small red bell pepper, cut into ¼-inch (0.5 cm) thick strips | 1 |
| | Nonstick cooking spray | |
| | Lemon wedges | |

1. In a medium bowl, whisk together flour, cornstarch, salt and pepper. Whisk in egg and club soda until blended and smooth. Cover loosely with plastic wrap and refrigerate for 30 minutes to thicken.

2. Meanwhile, separate the squids' tentacles from their bodies (if not done already). Slice the bodies into ½-inch (1 cm) rings and cut the tentacles in half if they are large. Rinse squid in a colander and drain.

3. Preheat air fryer to 390°F (200°C).

4. Spread panko in a shallow dish.

## Variation

*Gluten-Free Fritto Misto:* Replace the flour with an all-purpose gluten-free flour blend, and replace the panko with an equal amount of crushed gluten-free corn flakes cereal.

**5.** Working with 1 piece of seafood or vegetable at a time, dip squid, shrimp, mushrooms, green beans and red pepper strips in batter, shaking off excess, then dredge in panko, gently pressing to adhere. As they are dredged, place 5 to 6 pieces in air fryer basket, leaving space in between. Spray with cooking spray.

**6.** Air-fry for 5 to 8 minutes or until golden brown. Serve immediately with lemon wedges.

**7.** Repeat steps 5 and 6 with the remaining seafood, vegetables, batter and panko. Discard any excess batter and panko.

# Spicy, Crispy Drumsticks

You can never pass up a chicken drumstick, especially when it's perked up with a peppery Parmesan and cornflake crust and cooked to perfection in your air fryer.

**Makes 2 servings**

### Tips

An equal amount of plain yogurt (not Greek-style) can be used in place of the buttermilk.

The corn flakes cereal can be replaced with an equal amount of panko (Japanese bread crumbs).

| | | |
|---|---|---|
| 4 | chicken drumsticks (about 1 lb/500 g total), skin removed | 4 |
| ½ tsp | salt, divided | 2 mL |
| ½ cup | buttermilk | 125 mL |
| 1 tsp | hot pepper sauce (such as Tabasco) | 5 mL |
| 1½ cups | corn flakes cereal, crushed | 375 mL |
| ⅓ cup | freshly grated Parmesan cheese | 75 mL |
| ¼ tsp | freshly ground black pepper | 1 mL |
| | Nonstick cooking spray | |

1. In a medium sealable plastic bag, combine drumsticks, half the salt, buttermilk and hot pepper sauce. Seal bag and refrigerate for 1 hour, turning once.

2. Preheat air fryer to 390°F (200°C).

3. In a shallow dish, stir together corn flakes, Parmesan, the remaining salt and black pepper.

4. Remove drumsticks from bag and discard marinade. Working with 1 drumstick at a time, dredge in corn flakes mixture until coated, shaking off excess. As they are dredged, place drumsticks in air fryer basket, spacing them evenly. Spray with cooking spray. Discard any excess corn flakes mixture.

5. Air-fry for 10 minutes. Open basket and, using tongs, turn drumsticks over. Air-fry for 10 minutes. Reduce air fryer temperature to 300°F (150°C) and air-fry for 5 to 10 minutes or until an instant-read thermometer inserted in the thickest part of a drumstick registers 165°F (74°C).

# BBQ Chicken Thighs

It's dinnertime, so here's what's on the menu: barbecue. Specifically, two-ingredient barbecue chicken thighs, cooked to perfection without fuss or muss in the air fryer. Happy eating.

## Makes 2 servings

### Tips

Choose a barbecue sauce that is free of corn syrup and preservatives and has a short list of all-natural ingredients.

Air fryers become very hot. Use oven pads or mitts when touching the appliance and when opening and closing the basket.

• *Preheat air fryer to 370°F (180°C)*

| 4 | small bone-in skin-on chicken thighs (about 1 lb/500 total), patted dry | 4 |
| | Salt and freshly cracked black pepper | |
| ½ cup | barbecue sauce | 125 mL |

1. Season chicken thighs on both sides with salt and pepper. Place chicken, skin side down, in air fryer basket, spacing them evenly. Air-fry for 15 minutes.

2. Open basket and brush chicken generously with barbecue sauce. Air-fry for 5 minutes.

3. Open basket and brush the tops of the chicken with more sauce. Air-fry for 5 to 10 minutes or until an instant-read thermometer inserted in the thickest part of a thigh registers 165°F (74°C).

# Crispy Coconut Chicken Thighs

**Marinated in a fragrant and flavorful combination of coconut milk, lime and hot pepper sauce, chicken thighs take on the exotic flavors of the Caribbean.**

## Makes 2 servings

### Variation

*Gluten-Free Crispy Coconut Chicken Thighs:* Replace the panko with crushed gluten-free corn flakes cereal.

| | | |
|---|---|---|
| 2 | boneless skinless chicken thighs (each about 5 oz/150 g) | 2 |
| ½ cup | full-fat coconut milk | 125 mL |
| 2 tsp | freshly squeezed lime juice | 10 mL |
| 2 tsp | hot pepper sauce (such as Tabasco) | 10 mL |
| ½ cup | panko (Japanese bread crumbs) | 125 mL |
| ¼ cup | flaked sweetened coconut | 60 mL |
| ¼ tsp | salt | 1 mL |
| ⅛ tsp | freshly ground black pepper | 0.5 mL |
| | Nonstick cooking spray | |

1. In a large sealable plastic bag, combine chicken, coconut milk, lime juice and hot pepper sauce. Seal bag and refrigerate for 1 hour, turning once.

2. Preheat air fryer to 390°F (200°C).

3. In a shallow dish, stir together panko, coconut, salt and black pepper.

4. Remove chicken from bag and discard marinade. Working with 1 thigh at a time, dredge in panko mixture, pressing gently to adhere. As they are dredged, spray both sides of thighs with cooking spray and place in air fryer basket, spacing them evenly. Discard any excess panko mixture.

5. Air-fry for 10 to 14 minutes or until coating is golden brown and an instant-read thermometer inserted in the thickest part of a thigh registers 165°F (74°C).

# Rosemary Walnut Air-Fried Chicken

Chicken cutlets are one of the fastest and easiest chicken options to prepare, but this jazzed-up rosemary and walnut rendition shows that they need not be bland.

**Makes 2 servings**

## Tips

You can use ¼ tsp (1 mL) dried rosemary, crumbled, in place of the fresh rosemary.

An equal amount of pecans can be used in place of the walnuts.

• *Preheat air fryer to 380°F (190°C)*

| | | |
|---|---|---|
| ⅓ cup | panko (Japanese bread crumbs) | 75 mL |
| ⅓ cup | finely chopped walnuts | 75 mL |
| 2 tbsp | freshly grated Parmesan cheese | 30 mL |
| ½ tsp | minced fresh rosemary | 2 mL |
| ⅛ tsp | salt | 0.5 mL |
| ⅛ tsp | freshly ground black pepper | 0.5 mL |
| 3 tbsp | buttermilk | 45 mL |
| 1 tbsp | Dijon mustard | 15 mL |
| 2 | chicken cutlets (each about 6 oz/175 g) | 2 |
| | Nonstick cooking spray | |

1. In a shallow dish, stir together panko, walnuts, Parmesan, rosemary, salt and pepper.

2. In another shallow dish, whisk together buttermilk and mustard.

3. Working with 1 cutlet at a time, dip in buttermilk mixture, then dredge in panko mixture until coated, shaking off excess. As they are dredged, spray both sides of cutlets with cooking spray and place in air fryer basket, spacing them evenly. Discard any excess buttermilk mixture and panko mixture.

4. Air-fry for 4 minutes. Open basket and, using a spatula, turn cutlets over. Air-fry for 2 to 4 minutes or until crust is golden brown and chicken is no longer pink inside.

# Crunchy Honey Mustard Chicken Strips

With grown-up flavors of mustard, yogurt and onion, and not too much sweetness from the honey, these chicken strips put to rest this dish's reputation as kids' cuisine.

**Makes 4 servings**

## Tips

An equal amount of finely chopped almonds can be used in place of the pecans.

For spicier chicken strips, replace the Dijon mustard with an equal amount of hot mustard.

Air fryers become very hot. Use oven pads or mitts when touching the appliance and when opening and closing the basket.

• Preheat air fryer to 360°F (180°C)

| | | |
|---|---|---|
| ⅔ cup | pecan halves, finely chopped | 150 mL |
| ½ cup | panko (Japanese bread crumbs) | 125 mL |
| 1 tsp | onion powder | 5 mL |
| 2 tbsp | mayonnaise | 30 mL |
| 2 tbsp | plain Greek-style yogurt | 30 mL |
| 2 tbsp | Dijon mustard | 30 mL |
| 2 tbsp | liquid honey | 30 mL |
| 1 lb | boneless skinless chicken breasts, cut into 1-inch (2.5 cm) strips | 500 g |
| | Salt and freshly ground black pepper | |
| | Nonstick cooking spray | |
| 2 tbsp | chopped fresh parsley (optional) | 30 mL |

1. In a shallow dish, stir together pecans, panko and onion powder.

2. In a separate shallow dish, whisk together mayonnaise, yogurt, mustard and honey.

3. Season chicken with salt and pepper. Working with 1 chicken strip at a time, dip in honey mustard, then dredge in pecan mixture, pressing gently to adhere. As they are dredged, spray both sides of 4 to 5 strips with cooking spray and place in air fryer basket, spacing them evenly.

## Variation

*Gluten-Free Honey Mustard Chicken Strips:* Replace the panko with an equal amount of crushed gluten-free corn flakes cereal.

4. Air-fry for 8 minutes. Open basket and, using tongs, turn strips over. Air-fry for 5 to 8 minutes or until crust is golden brown and chicken is no longer pink inside. Serve immediately, sprinkled with parsley, if desired.

5. Repeat steps 3 and 4 with the remaining chicken strips, honey mustard and pecan mixture. Discard any excess honey mustard and pecan mixture.

# Pecan Chicken Tenders

Paprika plays a stealth role in these easy chicken tenders, adding a subtle and distinctive zest that complements the sweetness of the pecans.

## Makes 4 servings

### Variation

*Gluten-Free Pecan Chicken Tenders:* Replace the panko with an equal amount of crushed gluten-free corn flakes cereal, and replace the all-purpose flour with an all-purpose gluten-free flour blend.

• *Preheat air fryer to 360°F (180°C)*

| | | |
|---|---|---|
| ¼ cup | all-purpose flour | 60 mL |
| 1 cup | panko (Japanese bread crumbs) | 250 mL |
| ½ cup | pecan halves, finely ground | 125 mL |
| 1½ tsp | paprika | 7 mL |
| ¼ tsp | salt | 1 mL |
| ⅛ tsp | freshly cracked black pepper | 0.5 mL |
| 1 | large egg white | 1 |
| 1 lb | chicken tenders, patted dry | 500 g |
| | Nonstick cooking spray | |

1. Place flour in a shallow dish.

2. In another shallow dish, stir together panko, pecans, paprika, salt and pepper.

3. In a third shallow dish, whisk egg white with a fork until foamy.

4. Working with 1 chicken tender at a time, dredge in flour, shaking off excess. Dip in egg white, shaking off excess, then dredge in panko mixture, pressing gently to adhere. As they are dredged, spray both sides of half the tenders with cooking spray and arrange in air fryer basket, spacing them evenly.

5. Air-fry for 11 to 15 minutes or until crust is golden brown and chicken is no longer pink inside.

6. Repeat steps 4 and 5 with the remaining tenders, flour, egg white and panko mixture. Discard any excess flour, egg white and panko mixture.

# Chicken Parmesan Sliders

These sliders are at once grown-up and adorable. Fresh basil leaves add a fresh and aromatic element to each bite.

## Makes 2 servings

### Tips

Choose a marinara sauce that is free of corn syrup and preservatives and has a short list of all-natural ingredients.

An equal amount of ground turkey breast can be used in place of the ground chicken breast.

• *Preheat air fryer to 390°F (200°C)*

| | | |
|---|---|---|
| 12 oz | ground chicken breast | 375 g |
| 1/2 cup | freshly grated Parmesan cheese | 125 mL |
| 1/8 tsp | salt | 0.5 mL |
| 1/8 tsp | freshly cracked black pepper | 0.5 mL |
| 1/2 cup | marinara sauce, divided | 125 mL |
| 4 | slider buns, split | 4 |
| 4 | slices water-packed mozzarella cheese | 4 |
| 8 | fresh basil leaves | 8 |

1. In a medium bowl, combine chicken, Parmesan, salt, pepper and half the marinara sauce until blended (be careful not to overmix or compact mixture). Form into 4 small patties, each about 1/2 inch (1 cm) thick.

2. Arrange patties in air fryer basket, spacing them evenly. Air-fry for 8 to 12 minutes or until patties are no longer pink inside and an instant-read thermometer inserted horizontally in the center of a patty registers 165°F (74°C).

3. Spread top halves of buns with the remaining marinara sauce. Transfer patties to bottom halves and top with mozzarella and basil. Cover with top halves, pressing down gently.

# Spicy Chinese Chicken Wings

The spirit of Chinese cooking comes alive in this wings recipe, which balances the contrasting tastes of sweet, salty, sour and piquant in harmony.

**Makes 2 servings**

## Variations

*Gluten-Free Spicy Chinese Chicken Wings:* Replace the all-purpose flour with an all-purpose gluten-free flour blend.

*Lemon Honey Chicken Wings:* Reduce the black pepper to ⅛ tsp (0.5 mL) and replace the sauce from step 3 with Lemon Honey Wing Sauce (page 259).

• Preheat air fryer to 360°F (180°C)

| | | |
|---|---|---|
| ½ cup | all-purpose flour | 125 mL |
| 3 tbsp | cornstarch | 45 mL |
| ½ tsp | salt | 2 mL |
| ¼ tsp | freshly ground black pepper | 1 mL |
| 6 | chicken wings, tips removed and wings cut into drumettes and flats | 6 |
| | Nonstick cooking spray | |
| 3 | cloves garlic, minced | 3 |
| ¼ tsp | ground ginger | 1 mL |
| 2 tbsp | soy sauce | 30 mL |
| 1½ tsp | toasted (dark) sesame oil | 7 mL |
| 1 tbsp | liquid honey | 15 mL |
| 1 tsp | apple cider vinegar or white vinegar | 5 mL |
| ½ tsp | hot pepper sauce (such as Tabasco) | 2 mL |

1. In a large sealable plastic bag, combine flour, cornstarch, salt and black pepper. Add chicken wings, seal bag and shake to coat. Remove wings, shaking off excess flour mixture.

2. Place chicken wings in a single layer in air fryer basket. Spray with cooking spray. Air-fry for 24 to 28 minutes, opening basket twice to turn wings with tongs, until coating is browned and crisp and juices run clear when chicken is pierced.

## Variations

*Spicy Apricot Chicken Wings:* Replace the sauce from step 3 with Spicy Apricot Wing Sauce (page 259).

*Barbecue Chicken Wings:* Replace the sauce from step 3 with 3 tbsp (45 mL) barbecue sauce.

**3.** Meanwhile, in a small saucepan set over medium heat, combine garlic, ginger, soy sauce, sesame oil, honey, vinegar and hot pepper sauce. Cook, stirring, until just starting to bubble. Remove from heat.

**4.** Transfer wings to a medium bowl. Add sauce and toss to coat. Serve immediately.

# Crispy California Turkey Burgers

~~~~~~~~~~~~~~~~~~~~~~~~~~~~~~~~~~~~~~~~~~~~~~~

**Lean ground turkey, shredded zucchini and a hint of cumin give these burgers their fresh and earthy California vibe, but if you want to make them extra-authentic, be sure to pile on additional veggies from the list of suggested toppings.**

## Makes 2 servings

### Tips

An equal amount of finely shredded carrot can be used in place of the zucchini.

Air fryers become very hot. Use oven pads or mitts when touching the appliance and when opening and closing the basket.

• *Preheat air fryer to 360°F (180°C)*

| | | |
|---|---|---|
| 12 oz | lean ground turkey | 375 g |
| 1/3 cup | finely shredded zucchini | 75 mL |
| 1/2 tsp | ground cumin | 2 mL |
| | Salt and freshly ground black pepper | |
| 1/4 cup | all-purpose flour | 60 mL |
| 2/3 cup | panko (Japanese bread crumbs) | 150 mL |
| 1 | large egg | 1 |
| | Nonstick cooking spray | |
| 2 | hamburger buns or soft sandwich rolls, split | 2 |

### Suggested Toppings

Guacamole or sliced avocado
Thinly sliced Swiss cheese
Spinach leaves
Sliced tomatoes

1. In a large bowl, combine turkey, zucchini, cumin, 1/4 tsp (1 mL) salt and 1/8 tsp (0.5 mL) pepper until blended. Form into two 3/4-inch (2 cm) thick patties.

2. In a shallow plate, combine flour and 1/4 tsp (1 mL) salt.

3. Place panko in another shallow plate.

4. In a third plate, whisk egg until blended.

## Variation

*Gluten-Free California Turkey Burgers:* Replace the panko with an equal amount of crushed gluten-free corn flakes cereal and use gluten-free hamburger buns.

5. Working with 1 patty at a time, coat patty in flour, dip in egg, shaking off excess, then dredge in panko, pressing gently to adhere. As they are dredged, spray both sides of patties with cooking spray and place in air fryer basket, spacing them evenly. Discard any excess flour, egg and panko.

6. Air-fry for 8 minutes. Open basket and, using a spatula, carefully turn patties over. Air-fry for 7 to 10 minutes or until coating is crisp and an instant-read thermometer inserted horizontally in the center of a patty registers 165°F (74°C).

7. Transfer patties to bottom halves of buns and layer with any of the suggested toppings, as desired. Cover with top halves of buns, pressing down gently.

# Portobello Pepperoni Pizzas

Portobello mushrooms do double duty in these easy pizzas, adding their rich meaty flavor while also serving as a crust.

## Makes 2 servings

### Tip
Regular or soy pepperoni can be used in place of the turkey pepperoni.

### Variation
Use an equal amount of basil pesto in place of the marinara sauce.

• *Preheat air fryer to 380°F (180°C)*

| | | |
|---|---|---|
| 2 | medium portobello mushrooms | 2 |
| | Nonstick cooking spray | |
| 1 cup | shredded Italian cheese blend | 250 mL |
| 2/3 cup | drained roasted red bell peppers, coarsely chopped | 150 mL |
| 2 tbsp | marinara sauce | 30 mL |
| 1 oz | turkey pepperoni slices | 30 g |

1. Remove stems from mushrooms. Chop stems and set aside. Using a spoon, gently scoop out black gills on underside of mushroom caps. Discard gills. Spray mushroom caps with cooking spray.

2. Place mushroom caps, hollow side down, in air fryer basket, spacing them evenly. Air-fry for 8 to 10 minutes or until softened.

3. Meanwhile, in a medium bowl, combine chopped mushroom stems, cheese blend and roasted peppers.

4. Open air fryer basket and turn mushroom caps over. Fill caps with marinara sauce and cheese mixture. Top with pepperoni. Air-fry for 3 to 6 minutes or until filling is melted and bubbly.

# Sausage Meatballs with Marinara Sauce

My best friend's grandmother makes crave-worthy sausage meatballs, but when pressed for the recipe, everything is approximate. ("About this much sausage, a little bit of bread crumbs, a good amount of garlic...") My lightened version isn't hers, but it is darn good, and, for convenience sake, I am providing the exact measurements!

## Makes 4 servings

### Tip
Regular (pork) Italian sausage can be used in place of the Italian turkey sausage.

### Variation
*Gluten-Free Sausage Meatballs:* Replace the panko with an equal amount of crushed gluten-free corn flakes cereal.

• *Preheat air fryer to 360°F (180°C)*

| | | |
|---|---|---:|
| ¾ cup | packed fresh flat-leaf (Italian) parsley leaves, chopped, divided | 175 mL |
| 1 lb | Italian turkey sausage (bulk or casings removed) | 500 g |
| 3 | cloves garlic, minced | 3 |
| ½ cup | panko (Japanese bread crumbs) | 125 mL |
| 1 | large egg | 1 |
| | Easy Marinara Sauce (page 255) | |
| ½ cup | freshly grated Parmesan cheese | 125 mL |

1. Reserve 1 tbsp (15 mL) chopped parsley. In a large bowl, combine the remaining parsley, sausage, garlic, panko and egg until just combined (be careful not to overmix). Form into 1½-inch (4 cm) meatballs.

2. Arrange half the meatballs in air fryer basket, spacing them evenly. Air-fry for 9 to 13 minutes or until meatballs are browned and no longer pink inside. Repeat with the remaining meatballs.

3. Divide meatballs among serving plates and spoon Easy Marinara Sauce over top. Sprinkle with Parmesan and the reserved parsley.

# Maple, Cranberry and Sausage–Stuffed Acorn Squash

Although delicious when made exactly as written, this autumnal squash dish has lots of room for personal interpretation. For example, use your preferred dried fruit (perhaps cherries or currants), try rosemary in place of thyme, and swap out the pecans with walnuts.

**Makes 2 servings**

**Tip**
An equal amount of dried cherries or currants can be used in place of the cranberries.

• *Preheat air fryer to 360°F (180°C)*

| | | |
|---|---|---|
| 1 | small acorn squash (about 1¼ lbs/ 625 g), halved lengthwise and seeds removed | 1 |
| | Nonstick cooking spray | |
| | Salt and freshly ground black pepper | |
| 4 oz | turkey or pork sausage (bulk or casings removed) | 125 g |
| 1 | small tart-sweet apple, peeled and chopped | 1 |
| ¼ cup | chopped onion | 60 mL |
| ¼ cup | dried cranberries | 60 mL |
| ¼ tsp | dried thyme | 1 mL |
| 2 tbsp | chopped pecans | 30 mL |
| 1 tbsp | pure maple syrup | 15 mL |

1. Spray insides of squash with cooking spray. Season with ¼ tsp (1 mL) each salt and pepper.

2. Place squash halves, cut side up, in air fryer basket, spacing them evenly. Air-fry for 30 to 35 minutes or until squash is tender.

## Tip

If the two squash halves will not fit side by side in the air fryer, air-fry one half at a time. Reheat the filling and fill the second squash half just before air-frying.

3. Meanwhile, in a large nonstick skillet, cook sausage over medium-high heat, breaking it up with the back of a spoon, for 5 to 7 minutes or until no longer pink. Drain off and discard fat. Add apple, onion, cranberries and thyme to the skillet; cook, stirring, for 7 to 8 minutes or until apples are tender. Stir in pecans and season to taste with salt and pepper.

4. Open air fryer basket and fill squash halves with sausage mixture. Drizzle each with maple syrup. Air-fry for 5 to 7 minutes or until filling is golden.

# Italian Sausages, Peppers and Onions

For some of us, the combination of Italian sausages, peppers and onions is already close to perfection, and it tastes even better when simply prepared. It doesn't get much simpler than my air fryer rendition. Don't skip the fresh rosemary — it adds just the right amount of something new.

## Makes 2 servings

### Tip
You can substitute ½ tsp (2 mL) dried rosemary, crumbled, or dried Italian seasoning for the fresh rosemary.

### Variation
*Italian Sausage and Pepper Subs:* Serve the sausage, peppers and onions on 2 split soft Italian sub rolls.

• Preheat air fryer to 360°F (180°C)

| | | |
|---|---|---|
| 1 | large red, orange, yellow or green bell pepper | 1 |
| 1 | small onion | 1 |
| 1 tbsp | olive oil | 15 mL |
| 1 tsp | chopped fresh rosemary | 5 mL |
| ¼ tsp | salt | 1 mL |
| ¼ tsp | freshly cracked black pepper | 1 mL |
| 2 | sweet or hot Italian sausages (about 8 oz/250 g total) | 2 |

1. Cut bell pepper in half lengthwise. Remove ribs, seeds and stem, then cut each half lengthwise into 6 wedges. Cut onion in half lengthwise, then cut each half into 6 wedges.

2. In a medium bowl, toss together bell pepper, onion, oil, rosemary, salt and pepper.

3. Spread pepper mixture in a single layer in air fryer basket. Nestle sausages among the vegetables, spacing evenly. Air-fry for 20 minutes. Open basket and stir vegetables and sausages. Air-fry for 10 to 15 minutes or until sausages are lightly browned and juices run clear when sausages are pierced.

# Parmesan Pork Chops

With flavorful doses of Parmesan cheese and dried basil, these easy, elegant pork chops will knock deep-fried versions off their pedestal.

## Makes 2 servings

### Tip

Air fryers become very hot. Use oven pads or mitts when touching the appliance and when opening and closing the basket.

### Variation

*Gluten-Free Parmesan Pork Chops:* Replace the bread crumbs with an equal amount of crushed gluten-free corn flakes cereal. If desired, add 1/8 tsp (0.5 mL) dried Italian seasoning to the corn flakes.

• *Preheat air fryer to 360°F (180°C)*

| | | |
|---|---|---|
| 2 | boneless center-cut loin pork chops (each about 4 oz/125 g) | 2 |
| 1/4 cup | dry bread crumbs with Italian seasoning | 60 mL |
| 3 tbsp | freshly grated Parmesan cheese | 45 mL |
| 1 tsp | dried basil | 5 mL |
| 1/8 tsp | salt | 0.5 mL |
| 1/8 tsp | freshly ground black pepper | 0.5 mL |
| 1 | large egg | 1 |
| | Nonstick cooking spray | |
| 1 tbsp | chopped fresh flat-leaf (Italian) parsley | 15 mL |
| | Lemon wedges | |

1. Place pork chops between two double layers of plastic wrap. Using a mallet or rolling pin, pound pork chops to 1/4-inch (0.5 cm) thickness. Unwrap chops.

2. In a shallow dish, stir together bread crumbs, Parmesan, basil, salt and pepper.

3. In another shallow dish, whisk egg until blended

4. Working with 1 chop at a time, dip in egg, shaking off excess, then dredge in bread crumb mixture until coated, shaking off excess. As they are dredged, spray both sides of chops with cooking spray and place in air fryer basket, spacing them evenly. Discard any excess egg and bread crumb mixture.

5. Air-fry for 3 minutes. Open basket and, using a spatula, carefully turn chops over. Air-fry for 2 to 4 minutes or until crust is golden brown and just a hint of pink remains inside pork. Serve sprinkled with parsley, with lemon wedges on the side.

# Air Fryer Fajitas

Ready your air fryer. These fajitas capture the south-of-the-border flavors of Mexico with exemplary ease. Be extravagant or sparing with the suggested accompaniments; whatever you decide will be the right choice.

## Makes 2 servings

### Tip

To warm the tortillas, completely enclose them in foil. Place in the preheated air fryer before cooking the fajitas and air-fry for 5 minutes. Remove from air fryer but keep wrapped in foil until ready to use.

### Variation

An equal weight of boneless skinless chicken breasts or thighs can be used in place of the pork tenderloin.

• Preheat air fryer to 390°F (200°C)

| | | |
|---|---|---|
| 1 tsp | chipotle chile powder | 5 mL |
| ¾ tsp | ground cumin | 3 mL |
| ¼ tsp | salt | 1 mL |
| 1 tbsp | vegetable oil | 15 mL |
| 8 oz | pork tenderloin, trimmed, patted dry and cut into 3- by ½-inch (7.5 by 1 cm) strips | 250 g |
| 1 | large red or green bell pepper | 1 |
| 1 | small onion, halved lengthwise, then sliced | 1 |
| 4 | 6-inch (15 cm) flour or corn tortillas, warmed | 4 |

### Suggested Accompaniments

Lime wedges

Sour cream or plain Greek yogurt

Fresh cilantro leaves

Queso fresco or mild feta cheese, crumbled

Hot pepper sauce

Guacamole or diced avocado

1. In a medium bowl, stir together chile powder, cumin, salt and oil until blended. Add pork, bell pepper and onion, tossing until coated.

2. Spread pork mixture evenly in air fryer basket. Air-fry for 5 minutes, then shake basket. Air-fry for another 5 minutes, then shake basket again. Air-fry for 3 to 6 minutes or until vegetables are tender-crisp and just a hint of pink remains inside pork.

3. Divide pork mixture among serving plates and serve with warm tortillas and any of the suggested accompaniments, as desired.

# Chicken Air-Fried Steak with Redeye Gravy

This very Southern dish is typically labor-intensive, but not so here. Ready-to-use cube steaks need little more than some Worcestershire sauce and a two-step egg and flour coating before hitting the air fryer. Redeye gravy is often served with ham steaks, but it's a winning partner with beef steaks, too.

## Makes 2 servings

### Tip

Minute steaks can be used in place of the cube steaks. Place steaks between two double layers of plastic wrap. Using a mallet or rolling pin, pound steaks to 1/4-inch (0.5 cm) thickness. Proceed with step 1.

### Variation

*Gluten-Free Chicken Air-Fried Steak:* Replace the all-purpose flour with an all-purpose gluten-free flour blend.

• Preheat air fryer to 360°F (180°C)

| 2 | cube steaks (each about 4 oz/125 g) | 2 |
| 2 tsp | Worcestershire sauce | 10 mL |
| 1/3 cup | all-purpose flour | 75 mL |
| 1/4 tsp | salt | 1 mL |
| 1/4 tsp | freshly ground black pepper | 1 mL |
| 1/8 tsp | baking powder | 0.5 mL |
| 1 | large egg | 1 |
| 2 tbsp | buttermilk | 30 mL |
| | Nonstick cooking spray | |
| | Redeye Gravy (page 254) | |

1. Place steaks on a plate and brush both sides of steaks with Worcestershire sauce.

2. In a shallow dish, stir together flour, salt, pepper and baking powder.

3. In another shallow dish, whisk together egg and buttermilk.

4. Working with 1 steak at a time, dip in egg mixture, shaking off excess, then dredge in flour mixture until coated, shaking off excess. As they are dredged, spray both sides of steaks with cooking spray and place in air fryer basket, spacing them evenly. Discard any excess egg mixture and flour mixture.

5. Air-fry for 3 minutes. Open basket and, using a spatula, turn steaks over. Air-fry for 2 to 4 minutes or until crust is golden brown. Serve with gravy.

# Skirt Steak
# with Romesco Sauce

**Romesco sauce is a boldly flavored bell pepper sauce from the northeast region of Spain. Simply seasoned skirt steak is an appropriate showcase.**

## Makes 4 servings

### Tip
An equal amount of melted unsalted butter can be used in place of the olive oil.

• *Preheat air fryer to 390°F (200°C)*

| | | |
|---|---|---|
| 1 lb | beef skirt steak, trimmed and patted dry | 500 g |
| 1 tbsp | olive oil | 15 mL |
| ½ tsp | salt | 2 mL |
| ¼ tsp | freshly cracked black pepper | 1 mL |
| | Romesco Sauce (page 258) | |

1. Rub steak all over with oil, salt and pepper. Cut into 4 pieces of equal size.

2. Place 2 steak pieces in air fryer basket, spacing them evenly. Air-fry for 8 to 12 minutes for medium-rare to medium, or to desired doneness. Transfer steak to a cutting board and tent with foil. Let rest for 10 minutes. Repeat with the remaining steak pieces.

3. Cut steak across the grain into ¼-inch (0.5 cm) slices. Divide among serving plates and serve with Romesco Sauce.

# Steak Tacos with Mango Avocado Salsa

These laid-back tacos — spicy steak, mango, avocado — conjure vacations along the Mexican Riviera. The simple salsa is also great as an accompaniment for chips.

## Makes 2 servings

### Tips

An equal amount of pimentón (smoked paprika) or ground cumin can be used in place of the chipotle chile powder.

To warm the tortillas, completely enclose them in foil. Place in the preheated air fryer before cooking the tacos and air-fry for 5 minutes. Remove from air fryer but keep wrapped in foil until ready to use.

• *Preheat air fryer to 390°F (200°C)*

| | | |
|---|---|---|
| 8 oz | boneless beef strip loin (top loin) or top sirloin steak, trimmed and patted dry | 250 g |
| 2 tsp | vegetable oil | 10 mL |
| ¾ tsp | chipotle chile powder | 3 mL |
| ¼ tsp | salt | 1 mL |
| 4 | 6-inch (15 cm) flour or corn tortillas, warmed | 4 |
| | Mango Avocado Salsa (page 261) | |

### Suggested Accompaniments

Crumbled queso fresco or mild feta cheese

Sour cream or plain Greek yogurt

1. Rub steak all over with oil, chile powder and salt. Cut into 2 pieces of equal size.

2. Place steak pieces in air fryer basket, spacing them evenly. Air-fry for 8 to 12 minutes for medium-rare to medium, or to desired doneness. Transfer steak to a cutting board and tent with foil. Let rest for 10 minutes.

3. Cut steak across the grain into ¼-inch (0.5 cm) slices. Fill tortillas with steak and top with salsa and any of the suggested accompaniments, as desired.

# Beef Burgers Deluxe

The glory of a good burger is all in the details: choosing good ground beef, cooking to the perfect degree of doneness and accessorizing with your favorite toppers. The air fryer makes the cooking part a breeze. And as for the addition of fish sauce to the patties, it adds an extra layer of umami flavor, as well as saltiness, without imparting a specific Asian or fish flavor.

## Makes 2 servings

### Tip
Air fryers become very hot, especially when heated to maximum temperature. Use oven pads or mitts when touching the appliance and when opening and closing the basket.

### Variation
Substitute ground turkey or lean ground pork for the beef.

• Preheat air fryer to 390°F (200°C)

| | | |
|---|---|---|
| 12 oz | extra-lean ground beef | 375 g |
| 2 | cloves garlic, mashed | 2 |
| 1/8 tsp | salt | 0.5 mL |
| 1/8 tsp | freshly ground black pepper | 0.5 mL |
| 1 tbsp | Asian fish sauce or soy sauce | 15 mL |
| 1 tbsp | olive oil | 15 mL |
| 2 | hamburger buns, split and toasted | 2 |
| 2 | butter or romaine lettuce leaves | 2 |
| 2 | large tomato slices | 2 |

**Suggested Toppings**

Sliced avocado

Mayonnaise

Thinly sliced cheese (such as provolone, Swiss or Munster)

Thinly sliced red onion

1. In a large bowl, gently combine beef, garlic, salt, pepper, fish sauce and oil. Form into two 3/4-inch (2 cm) thick patties.

2. Place patties in air fryer basket, spacing them evenly. Air-fry for 6 minutes. Open basket and, using a spatula, carefully turn patties over. Air-fry for 5 to 7 minutes or until patties are no longer pink inside and an instant-read thermometer inserted horizontally in the center of a patty registers 165°F (74°C).

3. Transfer patties to bottom halves of buns and top with lettuce, tomato and any of the suggested toppings, as desired. Cover with top halves of buns, pressing down gently.

# Mini Italian Meatloaves

Despite a minimal number of ingredients, these meatloaves resonate with deep flavor. Leftovers (rare, but possible) make a great sandwich the next day.

## Makes 2 servings

**Tip**

Choose a marinara sauce that is free of corn syrup and preservatives and has a short list of all-natural ingredients.

• *Preheat air fryer to 360°F (180°C)*

| | | |
|---|---|---|
| 12 oz | extra-lean ground beef | 375 g |
| 1/4 cup | finely chopped onion | 60 mL |
| 3 tbsp | quick-cooking rolled oats | 45 mL |
| 2 tbsp | chopped fresh flat-leaf (Italian) parsley | 30 mL |
| 1 tsp | dried Italian seasoning | 5 mL |
| 1/4 tsp | salt | 1 mL |
| 1/8 tsp | freshly cracked black pepper | 0.5 mL |
| 5 tbsp | marinara sauce, divided | 75 mL |

1. In a medium bowl, combine beef, onion, oats, parsley, Italian seasoning, salt, pepper and 4 tbsp (60 mL) marinara sauce until blended. Form into 2 small loaves, each about 4$\frac{1}{2}$ by 2$\frac{1}{2}$ inches (11 by 6 cm).

2. Place meatloaves in air fryer basket, spacing them evenly. Brush tops with the remaining marinara sauce. Air-fry for 16 to 21 minutes or until an instant-read thermometer inserted in the center of the meatloaves registers 165°F (74°C).

# Hoisin Meatballs

Ever-popular meatballs get extra pep from garlic, ginger and green onions, not to mention a slathering of sweet and zesty hoisin glaze.

## Makes 4 servings

### Tip
Lean ground turkey or pork can be used in place of the beef.

### Variation
*Gluten-Free Hoisin Meatballs:* Replace the panko with an equal amount of crushed gluten-free corn flakes cereal.

• Preheat air fryer to 360°F (180°C)

| | | |
|---|---|---|
| 1 | large egg | 1 |
| 1 lb | lean ground beef | 500 g |
| 2 | cloves garlic, minced | 2 |
| ½ cup | panko (Japanese bread crumbs) | 125 mL |
| ⅓ cup | finely chopped green onions | 75 mL |
| 1 tsp | ground ginger | 5 mL |
| ¾ tsp | salt | 3 mL |
| ⅛ tsp | freshly cracked black pepper | 0.5 mL |
| | Hoisin Glaze (page 260) | |

**Suggested Garnishes**
Thinly sliced green onions
Toasted sesame seeds

1. In a large bowl, beat egg. Add beef, garlic, panko, green onions, ginger, salt and pepper, mixing until just combined (be careful not to overmix). Form into 1½-inch (4 cm) meatballs.

2. Arrange half the meatballs in air fryer basket, spacing them evenly. Air-fry for 9 to 13 minutes or until meatballs are browned and no longer pink inside. Repeat with the remaining meatballs.

3. Divide meatballs among serving plates and spoon Hoisin Glaze over top. Sprinkle with suggested garnishes, as desired.

# Garlicky Lamb Chops with Mint Chimichurri

> The rich flavor of lamb stands up well to strong flavors, like garlic and fresh mint.

**Makes 2 servings**

**Tip**

You can use ½ tsp (2 mL) garlic powder in place of the garlic clove.

- Preheat air fryer to 390°F (200°C)

| | | |
|---|---|---|
| 1 | clove garlic, mashed | 1 |
| ¼ tsp | salt | 1 mL |
| ⅛ tsp | freshly cracked black pepper | 0.5 mL |
| 1 tbsp | olive oil | 15 mL |
| 4 | small lamb chops (each about 3 oz/90 g), trimmed and patted dry | 4 |
| | Mint Chimichurri (page 262) | |

1. In a small bowl or cup, combine garlic, salt, pepper and oil. Brush one side of each lamb chop with oil mixture.

2. Arrange chops, oiled side up, in air fryer basket, spacing them evenly. Air-fry for 8 to 11 minutes for medium-rare, or to desired doneness. Serve with Mint Chimichurri.

# Curried Lamb Samosas

Talk about pastries with bravado. The bold flavors start with lean ground lamb seasoned with curry and cumin and enriched with green onions and currants. Then come the delicate layers of puff pastry, encasing all. If you think more is more, make the suggested accompaniments mandatory.

**Makes 9 samosas**

**Tip**
Lean ground turkey or beef can be used in place of the lamb.

| | | |
|---|---|---|
| 1 lb | lean ground lamb | 500 g |
| 1/2 cup | finely chopped green onions | 125 mL |
| 1/3 cup | dried currants | 75 mL |
| 1 tsp | curry powder | 5 mL |
| 1/2 tsp | ground cumin | 2 mL |
| 1/2 tsp | salt | 2 mL |
| 1/4 tsp | freshly ground black pepper | 1 mL |
| | All-purpose flour | |
| 1 | sheet frozen puff pastry (half a 17.3-oz/490 g package), thawed | 1 |
| 1 | large egg, lightly beaten | 1 |

*Suggested Accompaniments*
Plain yogurt
Mango chutney

1. In a medium bowl, combine lamb, green onions, currants, curry powder, cumin, salt and pepper until blended.

2. On a lightly floured surface, roll out puff pastry into a 12-inch (30 cm) square. Cut into 9 equal squares. Brush edges of each pastry square with some of the egg.

## Tip

An equal amount of raisins, coarsely chopped, can be used in place of the currants.

3. Spoon one-ninth of the lamb mixture into the center of each square. Fold each square over on the diagonal, pressing edges together to seal. Transfer to a plate and brush with the remaining egg. Cover loosely and refrigerate for at least 30 minutes or for up to 2 hours.

4. Preheat air fryer to 390°F (200°C).

5. Place 5 samosas in air fryer basket, spacing them evenly. Air-fry for 9 to 13 minutes or until pastry is deep golden brown and lamb is no longer pink. Transfer samosas to a wire rack and let cool for 5 minutes. Repeat with the remaining samosas. Serve with any of the suggested accompaniments, as desired.

# Vegetables
# and Sides

# Seasoned Curly Fries

A homemade riff on a fast-food favorite, these curlicue potatoes will disappear as fast as you make them.

## Tips

An equal amount of table salt can be used in place of the seasoning salt.

Use oven pads or mitts when shaking the basket.

- *Vegetable spiralizer*

| | | |
|---|---|---:|
| 1 | large russet potato (14 to 16 oz/420 to 500 g), peeled | 1 |
| | Hot (not boiling) water | |
| 1 tbsp | vegetable oil | 15 mL |
| ½ tsp | seasoning salt | 2 mL |
| ⅛ tsp | cayenne pepper | 0.5 mL |

1. Spiral potato through the large holes of the spiralizer, using kitchen shears to cut the curls after every 3 or 5 rotations. Place spirals in a large bowl and add enough hot water to cover. Let stand for 10 minutes. Drain, pat dry and return to dry bowl. Add oil, seasoning salt and cayenne, tossing to coat.

2. Preheat air fryer to 360°F (180°C).

3. Place half the potatoes in a single layer in air fryer basket. Air-fry for 5 minutes, then shake the basket. Increase temperature to 390°F (200°C) and air-fry for 10 to 14 minutes, shaking the basket two more times, until potatoes are golden brown. Serve immediately. Repeat with the remaining potatoes.

# Roasted Red Potatoes

A flurry of chopped herbs adds freshness and verve to these crispy-creamy potatoes.

## Makes 2 servings

### Tips

Small gold-fleshed potatoes can be used in place of the red-skinned potatoes.

An equal amount of packed fresh cilantro or basil, chopped, can be used in place of the parsley.

• *Preheat air fryer to 360°F (180°C)*

| 1 lb | small red-skinned potatoes, quartered lengthwise | 500 g |
| 1 tbsp | olive oil | 15 mL |
| ½ tsp | salt | 2 mL |
| ⅛ tsp | freshly cracked black pepper | 0.5 mL |
| ¼ cup | packed fresh parsley, chopped (optional) | 60 mL |

1. In a medium bowl, toss potatoes with oil, salt and pepper.

2. Spread potatoes in air fryer basket. Air-fry for 10 minutes, then shake the basket. Increase temperature to 390°F (200°C) and air-fry for 5 minutes, then shake the basket again. Air-fry for 4 to 8 minutes or until potatoes are golden brown and fork-tender. Serve immediately, sprinkled with parsley, if desired.

# Warm German Potato Salad

Everything old is new again: classic German potato salad gets a svelte makeover with the assistance of an air fryer. Restrained amounts of mustard, vinegar and chives complement the potatoes without overwhelming them.

## Makes 2 servings

**Tips**

Gold-fleshed potatoes can be used in place of the red-skinned potatoes.

An equal amount of chopped green onions can be used in place of the chives.

• *Preheat air fryer to 360°F (180°C)*

| | | |
|---|---|---|
| 12 oz | red-skinned potatoes, cut into 1-inch (2.5 cm) pieces | 375 g |
| 4 tsp | olive oil, divided | 20 mL |
| | Salt and freshly cracked black pepper | |
| ½ tsp | granulated sugar | 2 mL |
| 1 tbsp | red wine vinegar | 15 mL |
| 1 tsp | whole-grain Dijon mustard | 5 mL |
| 1 tbsp | minced fresh chives | 15 mL |

**1.** In a medium bowl, toss potatoes with 1 tsp (5 mL) oil. Season with salt and pepper, tossing to coat.

**2.** Spread potatoes in air fryer basket. Air-fry for 10 minutes, shaking the basket halfway through. Increase temperature to 390°F (200°C). Air-fry for 10 to 15 minutes, shaking the basket twice, until potatoes are golden brown and fork-tender.

**3.** Meanwhile, in a small bowl, whisk together sugar, vinegar, mustard and the remaining oil. Season to taste with salt and pepper.

**4.** Transfer potatoes to a medium bowl and let cool for 15 minutes. Drizzle potatoes with dressing and sprinkle with chives, gently tossing to combine.

# Hasselback Potatoes

If you are weary of mashed and roasted russet potatoes, try hot-rodding them with this recipe. With a bit of slicing, some melted butter and a Parmesan–bread crumb topping, you'll have a spectacular side in no time.

## Makes 2 servings

### Variation

*Gluten-Free Hasselback Potatoes:* Replace the bread crumbs with an equal amount of crushed gluten-free corn flakes cereal.

• *Preheat air fryer to 390°F (200°C)*

| | | |
|---|---|---|
| 2 | russet or gold-fleshed potatoes (each about 6 oz/175 g), peeled | 2 |
| 1 tbsp | unsalted butter, melted | 15 mL |
| | Salt and freshly cracked black pepper | |
| 1 tbsp | plain dry bread crumbs | 15 mL |
| 1 tbsp | finely grated Parmesan cheese | 15 mL |
| | Nonstick cooking spray | |

1. Slice each potato crosswise at $\frac{1}{8}$-inch (3 mm) intervals, cutting to within $\frac{1}{4}$ inch (0.5 cm) of the bottom. Brush with butter and season with salt and pepper.

2. Place potatoes, cut side up, in air fryer basket. Air-fry for 20 minutes.

3. Meanwhile, in a small cup, combine bread crumbs and Parmesan.

4. Open air fryer basket and sprinkle bread crumb mixture over potatoes. Spray with cooking spray. Air-fry for 5 to 7 minutes or until potatoes are tender and bread crumbs are golden brown. Serve immediately.

# Crispy Potato Wedges

In an uncertain world, everyone needs a truly excellent potato dish, one that will never fail you. This is it. These wedges go with just about anything, year-round, so it is a good idea to keep a couple of russet potatoes on hand at all times.

**Makes 2 servings**

## Tips

Gold-fleshed potatoes can be used in place of the russet potatoes.

Use oven pads or mitts when shaking the basket.

## Variation

*Spanish Potato Wedges:* Replace the paprika with an equal amount of smoked paprika (sweet or hot).

| 2 | russet potatoes (each about 8 oz/250 g), scrubbed and rinsed | 2 |
| 1 tsp | paprika | 5 mL |
| ¾ tsp | granulated sugar | 3 mL |
| ½ tsp | salt | 2 mL |
| ⅛ tsp | freshly ground black pepper | 0.5 mL |
| | Nonstick cooking spray | |

1. Place potatoes in a medium saucepan and add enough water to cover by 1 inch (2.5 cm). Bring to a boil over medium-high heat. Boil for 35 to 40 minutes or until fork-tender. Drain potatoes, transfer to a plate and let stand until cool enough to handle.

2. Preheat air fryer to 390°F (200°C).

3. In a small cup, combine paprika, sugar, salt and pepper.

4. Cut cooled potatoes into quarters. Generously spray potatoes with cooking spray and sprinkle with paprika mixture.

5. Arrange potatoes in air fryer basket, leaving space in between. Air-fry for 12 to 15 minutes, gently shaking the basket after 8 minutes, until potatoes are golden brown. Serve immediately.

# Sweet Potato Fries

Sweet potato fries are a surprise to the uninitiated at the dinner table — and no one will miss the marshmallows. Nothing more than a shake of salt is needed to complement the natural sweetness of the potatoes, but if you want a bit of spice, try the variation.

## Makes 2 servings

### Tip

Be sure to watch the sweet potatoes closely so they do not burn.

### Variation

*Spicy Sweet Potato Fries:* Add ¼ tsp (1 mL) chipotle chile powder and ¼ tsp (1 mL) ground cumin with the salt in step 1.

| 2 | sweet potatoes (each about 8 oz/250 g), peeled and cut into 3-inch (7.5 cm) long by ¼-inch (0.5 cm) thick sticks | 2 |
| 1 tbsp | vegetable oil | 15 mL |
| ½ tsp | salt | 2 mL |

1. Place sweet potatoes in a large bowl and add enough water to cover. Let stand for 30 minutes. Drain, pat dry and return to dry bowl. Add oil and salt, tossing to coat.

2. Preheat air fryer to 330°F (160°C).

3. Spread half the sweet potatoes in a single layer in air fryer basket. Air-fry for 5 minutes, then shake the basket. Increase temperature to 390°F (200°C) and air-fry for 13 to 17 minutes, shaking the basket twice, until sweet potatoes are golden brown. Serve immediately. Repeat with the remaining sweet potatoes.

# Cheddar and Bacon Mashed Potato Balls

Much like loaded baked potatoes, these air-fried potato balls are stuffed with all sorts of good things, including bacon, cheese and chives.

**Makes about 24 balls**

## Tips

An equal amount of chopped green onions can be used in place of the chives.

An equal amount of crumbled blue cheese can be used in place of the Cheddar.

### Filling

| | | |
|---|---|---|
| 3 | russet potatoes (each about 8 oz/250 g), scrubbed and rinsed | 3 |
| 1 | large egg, lightly beaten | 1 |
| 1 cup | shredded sharp (old) Cheddar cheese | 250 mL |
| 1/3 cup | crumbled cooked bacon | 75 mL |
| 3 tbsp | minced fresh chives | 45 mL |
| 3 tbsp | all-purpose flour | 45 mL |
| 1/2 tsp | salt | 2 mL |
| 1/4 tsp | freshly ground black pepper | 1 mL |

### Coating

| | | |
|---|---|---|
| 3/4 cup | all-purpose flour | 175 mL |
| 3/4 cup | plain dry bread crumbs | 175 mL |
| 2 | large eggs | 2 |
| | Nonstick cooking spray | |

1. *Filling:* Place potatoes in a medium saucepan and add enough water to cover by 1 inch (2.5 cm). Bring to a boil over medium-high heat. Boil for 15 to 20 minutes or until fork-tender. Drain potatoes, transfer to a large bowl and let cool completely.

2. Finely mash potatoes. Add egg, cheese, bacon, chives, flour, salt and pepper, stirring until completely blended. Form potato mixture into 1½-inch (4 cm) balls. Set aside 8 potato balls. Loosely cover and refrigerate the remaining balls until ready to coat and air-fry.

3. Preheat air fryer to 390°F (200°C).

## Variation

*Gluten-Free Cheddar and Bacon Mashed Potato Balls:* Replace the all-purpose flour with an all-purpose gluten-free flour blend, and replace the bread crumbs with an equal amount of crushed gluten-free corn flakes cereal.

4. *Coating:* Spread flour in a shallow dish.

5. Spread bread crumbs in another shallow dish.

6. In a third shallow dish, whisk eggs until blended.

7. Working with 1 potato ball at a time, roll in flour to coat, dip in egg, shaking off excess, then roll in bread crumbs, pressing gently to adhere. As they are coated, spray balls all over with cooking spray and place in a single layer in air fryer basket, leaving space in between.

8. Air-fry for 6 to 9 minutes or until coating is golden brown and insides are hot. Serve immediately.

9. Repeat steps 7 and 8 with the remaining potato balls, flour, egg and bread crumbs. Discard any excess flour, egg and bread crumbs.

# Rosemary Butternut Squash

Roasted butternut squash is a modern classic, made even simpler by the air fryer. Rosemary and a hint of brown sugar interact beautifully with the crisp-and-soft smoothness of the squash.

## Makes 2 servings

### Tips

An equal amount of dried rubbed sage or dried thyme can be used in place of the rosemary.

Use oven pads or mitts when shaking the basket.

• *Preheat air fryer to 390°F (200°C)*

| | | |
|---|---|---|
| 1 | small butternut squash (about 1 lb/500 g), peeled and cut into ¾-inch (2 cm) cubes | 1 |
| 1 tbsp | olive oil | 15 mL |
| 1½ tsp | dried rosemary, crumbled | 7 mL |
| 1½ tsp | packed light brown sugar | 7 mL |
| ½ tsp | salt | 2 mL |
| ⅛ tsp | freshly cracked black pepper | 0.5 mL |

1. In a large bowl, toss together squash, oil, rosemary, brown sugar, salt and pepper until coated.

2. Transfer squash to air fryer basket. Air-fry for 15 to 20 minutes, shaking the basket at least twice, until squash is browned and tender. Serve immediately.

# Avocado Fries

Crunchy and creamy, these avocado fries are the best of both worlds. Be sure to choose avocados that are ripe but not at all mushy so that they can stand up to the air-frying.

## Makes 4 servings

### Variation

*Gluten-Free Avocado Fries:* Replace the all-purpose flour with an all-purpose gluten-free flour blend, and replace the panko with an equal amount of crushed gluten-free corn flakes cereal.

• Preheat air fryer to 390°F (200°C)

| | | |
|---|---|---|
| 2 | firm-ripe Hass avocados | 2 |
| ½ cup | all-purpose flour | 125 mL |
| 1 tsp | ground cumin | 5 mL |
| ½ tsp | chili powder | 2 mL |
| ½ tsp | salt | 2 mL |
| 1 cup | panko (Japanese bread crumbs) | 250 mL |
| 2 | large eggs | 2 |
| 1 tbsp | water | 15 mL |
| | Nonstick cooking spray | |

1. Peel, halve and pit avocados. Cut each avocado half lengthwise into 4 slices.

2. In a large sealable plastic bag, gently shake together flour, cumin, chili powder and salt. Add avocado slices and very gently toss until coated.

3. Place panko in a shallow dish.

4. In another shallow dish, whisk eggs and water until blended.

5. Working with 1 avocado slice at a time, remove from flour mixture, shaking off excess. Dip in egg mixture, shaking off excess, then dredge in panko, pressing gently to adhere. As they are dredged, place 6 to 8 slices (depending on size) in air fryer basket, leaving space in between. Spray with cooking spray.

6. Air-fry for 5 minutes, then gently shake the basket. Air-fry for 2 to 6 minutes or until coating is golden brown. Serve immediately.

7. Repeat steps 5 and 6 with the remaining avocado slices, egg mixture and panko. Discard any excess flour mixture, egg mixture and panko.

# Lemon Pepper Asparagus Fries

*These are unique fries: crispy and crunchy on the outside, as great fries should be, but positively juicy inside, as only great asparagus can be. One pound (500 g) is enough for four people, but in my experience, it is easy for just two people to polish off that much with ease.*

## Makes 4 servings

**Tip**
Use oven pads or mitts when shaking the basket.

**Variation**
*Gluten-Free Lemon Pepper Asparagus Fries:* Replace the all-purpose flour with an all-purpose gluten-free flour blend, and replace the panko with an equal amount of crushed gluten-free corn flakes cereal.

• *Preheat air fryer to 390°F (200°C)*

| | | |
|---|---|---|
| ½ cup | all-purpose flour | 125 mL |
| 1 tbsp | finely grated lemon zest | 15 mL |
| ½ tsp | salt | 2 mL |
| ½ tsp | freshly cracked black pepper | 2 mL |
| 1 lb | asparagus, trimmed | 500 g |
| 1 cup | panko (Japanese bread crumbs) | 250 mL |
| ½ cup | freshly grated Parmesan cheese | 125 mL |
| 2 | large eggs | 2 |
| | Nonstick cooking spray | |

1. In a large sealable plastic bag, gently shake together flour, lemon zest, salt and pepper. Add asparagus and toss until coated.

2. In a shallow dish, combine panko and Parmesan cheese.

3. In another shallow dish, whisk eggs.

4. Working with 1 asparagus spear at a time, remove from flour mixture, shaking off excess. Dip in egg, shaking off excess, then dredge in panko mixture, pressing gently to adhere. As they are dredged, place 6 to 10 spears (depending on size) in air fryer basket, leaving space in between. Spray with cooking spray.

## Variation

*Green Bean Fries:* Omit the lemon zest and reduce the pepper to $\frac{1}{8}$ tsp (0.5 mL). Use 12 oz (375 g) green beans, trimmed, in place of the asparagus.

**5.** Air-fry for 5 minutes, then gently shake the basket. Air-fry for 2 to 6 minutes or until coating is golden brown. Serve immediately.

**6.** Repeat steps 4 and 5 with the remaining asparagus spears, egg and panko mixture. Discard any excess flour mixture, egg and panko mixture.

# Garlicky "Fried" Broccoli Rabe

If you've only steamed or sautéed broccoli rabe, this recipe will be a revelation. The high heat of the air fryer renders the stems and florets tender, while the leaves become crispy-crunchy around the edges.

**Makes 4 servings**

### Tips

For a milder dish, omit both the garlic and the hot pepper flakes.

Use oven pads or mitts when shaking the basket.

*• Preheat air fryer to 390°F (200°C)*

| | | |
|---|---|---|
| 1 lb | broccoli rabe, tough, fibrous stems removed (keep tender stems) | 500 g |
| 2 | cloves garlic, minced | 2 |
| 1 tbsp | olive oil | 15 mL |
| ¼ tsp | salt | 1 mL |
| ⅛ tsp | hot pepper flakes | 0.5 mL |

1. In a large bowl, toss together broccoli rabe, garlic, oil, salt and hot pepper flakes.

2. Transfer broccoli rabe mixture to air fryer basket. Air-fry for 9 to 12 minutes, shaking the basket every 5 minutes, until broccoli rabe stems are tender and leaves are crisp. Serve immediately.

Hoisin Meatballs (page 174)

Garlicky Lamb Chops with
Mint Chimichurri (page 175)

Cauliflower Crispers (page 195)
and Blistered Edamame (page 196)

Air-Fried Ratatouille (page 204)

Toffee Apple Hand Pies (page 216)

Molten Chocolate Cakes (page 222)

Air-Fried Chocolate Crème-Filled Cookies (page 232)
and Air-Fried Candy Bars (page 241)

Caramel Corn (page 247)

# Garlicky Brussels Sprouts

If you think you don't like Brussels sprouts, this recipe will change your mind. Cooking them in the air fryer gives them a nutty, toasty flavor that is irresistible, even to the most hardened skeptics.

## Makes 2 servings

### Tips

For a milder dish, omit the garlic and the vinegar.

If the Brussels sprouts are particularly large, quarter them lengthwise.

• Preheat air fryer to 390°F (200°C)

| | | |
|---|---|---|
| 12 oz | Brussels sprouts, trimmed and halved lengthwise | 375 g |
| 2 tsp | olive oil | 10 mL |
| ¼ tsp | salt | 1 mL |
| ⅛ tsp | freshly cracked black pepper | 0.5 mL |
| 2 | cloves garlic, roughly chopped | 2 |
| 2 tsp | balsamic vinegar | 10 mL |

1. In a medium bowl, toss together Brussels sprouts, oil, salt and pepper.

2. Transfer sprouts to air fryer basket. Air-fry for 10 minutes. Open basket, stir sprouts and sprinkle with garlic. Air-fry for 10 to 15 minutes, shaking the basket twice, until sprouts are browned and tender. Serve immediately, drizzled with vinegar.

# Air-Roasted Baby Carrots with Fresh Dill

> Here, air-roasting allows baby carrots to escape their kid-food cliché and find new expression as a grown-up, dill-scented side dish.

**Makes 4 servings**

**Tips**

An equal amount of mint, cilantro or flat-leaf (Italian) parsley can be used in place of the dill.

Use oven pads or mitts when shaking the basket.

• *Preheat air fryer to 390°F (200°C)*

| | | |
|---|---|---|
| 1 | package (1 lb/500 g) baby carrots | 1 |
| 2 tsp | olive oil | 10 mL |
| ½ tsp | salt | 2 mL |
| ⅛ tsp | freshly cracked black pepper | 0.5 mL |
| 2 tbsp | chopped fresh dill | 30 mL |

1. In a medium bowl, toss together carrots, oil, salt and pepper.

2. Transfer carrots to air fryer basket. Air-fry for 17 to 22 minutes, shaking the basket every 5 minutes, until carrots are fork-tender. Serve immediately, sprinkled with dill.

# Cauliflower Crispers

The intense, even temperature of the air fryer browns cauliflower to perfection, bringing out its natural sugars. Olive oil, salt and pepper are the only adornments needed to take it over the top.

**Makes 2 servings**

**Variation**

Replace the cauliflower with an equal amount of broccoli florets, cut in the same manner.

• Preheat air fryer to 390°F (200°C)

| | | |
|---|---|---|
| 1½ cups | cauliflower florets, cut into ½-inch (1 cm) thick slices | 375 mL |
| 1 tbsp | olive oil | 15 mL |
| ⅛ tsp | salt | 0.5 ml |
| Pinch | freshly ground black pepper | Pinch |

1. In a medium bowl, gently toss together cauliflower, oil, salt and pepper.

2. Spread half the cauliflower in a single layer in air fryer basket. Air-fry for 5 to 6 minutes, gently shaking the basket halfway through, until golden brown. Serve immediately. Repeat with the remaining cauliflower.

# Blistered Edamame

Buttery and rich in protein, these zesty edamame make it easy to understand their popularity at sushi restaurants and beyond.

**Makes 4 servings**

## Tips

Do not eat the edamame pods, only the beans inside the pods.

Use oven pads or mitts when shaking the basket.

- Preheat air fryer to 390°F (200°C)

| | | |
|---|---|---|
| 1 | package (10 oz/300 g) frozen edamame in their pods, thawed | 1 |
| 2 tsp | vegetable oil | 10 mL |
| ¼ tsp | garlic powder | 1 mL |
| ¼ tsp | salt | 1 mL |
| Pinch | cayenne pepper | Pinch |
| | Lime wedges | |

1. Pat edamame dry with paper towels and place in a medium bowl. Add oil, garlic powder, salt and cayenne, tossing to coat.

2. Transfer edamame to air fryer basket. Air-fry for 12 to 15 minutes, shaking the basket every 5 minutes, until edamame have blistered (dark) spots. Serve immediately with lime wedges.

# Portobello Mushroom Fries

Portobello mushrooms have a meaty earthiness that is best accentuated in straightforward form, such as these crave-worthy fries.

## Makes 4 servings

### Variation

*Gluten-Free Portobello Fries:* Replace the all-purpose flour with an all-purpose gluten-free flour blend, and replace the bread crumbs with an equal amount of crushed gluten-free corn flakes cereal.

• *Preheat air fryer to 390°F (200°C)*

| | | |
|---|---|---|
| 2 | large portobello mushrooms | 2 |
| | Nonstick cooking spray | |
| ½ cup | all-purpose flour | 125 mL |
| ¾ tsp | dried oregano | 3 mL |
| ½ tsp | salt | 2 mL |
| ½ cup | dry bread crumbs with Italian seasoning | 125 mL |
| ½ cup | freshly grated Parmesan cheese | 125 mL |
| 2 | large eggs | 2 |

1. Remove stems from mushrooms and reserve for another use. Using a spoon, gently scoop out and discard black gills on underside of mushroom caps. Cut each mushroom cap into ½-inch (1 cm) wide strips. Spray strips all over with cooking spray.

2. In a large sealable plastic bag, gently shake together flour, oregano and salt. Add mushrooms and toss until coated.

3. In a shallow dish, combine bread crumbs and Parmesan.

4. In another shallow dish, whisk eggs until blended.

5. Working with 1 mushroom piece at a time, remove from flour mixture, shaking off excess. Dip in egg, shaking off excess, then dredge in bread crumb mixture, pressing gently to adhere. As they are dredged, place 6 to 10 pieces (depending on size) in air fryer basket, leaving space in between. Spray with cooking spray.

6. Air-fry for 5 minutes, then gently shake the basket. Air-fry for 1 to 5 minutes or until coating is golden brown. Serve immediately.

7. Repeat steps 5 and 6 with the remaining mushroom pieces, egg and bread crumb mixture. Discard any excess flour mixture, egg and bread crumb mixture.

# Southern Air-Fried Okra

Stewed okra is an acquired taste, but air-fried okra is something else entirely. It has a crisp and wonderful seared texture and is never gooey.

## Makes 2 servings

### Variation

*Gluten-Free Air-Fried Okra:* Replace the bread crumbs with an equal amount of crushed gluten-free corn flakes cereal, and replace the all-purpose flour with an all-purpose gluten-free flour blend.

| | | |
|---|---|---|
| 1 | clove garlic, minced | 1 |
| 1/4 tsp | salt | 1 mL |
| 1/3 cup | buttermilk | 75 mL |
| 1 tsp | hot pepper sauce (such as Tabasco) | 5 mL |
| 8 oz | okra, trimmed and halved lengthwise | 250 g |
| 1/4 cup | yellow cornmeal | 60 mL |
| 1/4 cup | plain dry bread crumbs | 60 mL |
| 1 tbsp | all-purpose flour | 15 mL |
| | Nonstick cooking spray | |

1. In a medium bowl, whisk together garlic, salt, buttermilk and hot pepper sauce. Add okra, gently tossing to combine. Let stand for 15 minutes, then drain off and discard excess buttermilk mixture.

2. Preheat air fryer to 390°F (200°C).

3. In a large sealable plastic bag, combine cornmeal, bread crumbs and flour. Add okra and toss until coated.

4. One at a time, remove okra pieces from cornmeal mixture, shaking off excess, and place in air fryer basket, leaving space in between. Spray with cooking spray.

5. Air-fry for 8 to 12 minutes, shaking the basket twice, until coating is golden brown. Serve immediately.

6. Repeat steps 4 and 5 with the remaining okra. Discard any excess cornmeal mixture.

# Parsnip Fries

Move over, potatoes — parsnips are ready for their turn in the fryer. Creamy white parsnips (they look like white carrots) have a mild, pleasantly sweet flavor that, when given the french fry treatment, tastes delightfully new.

## Makes 2 servings

**Tip**
Use oven pads or mitts when shaking the basket.

*Variation*
An equal amount of carrots can be used in place of the parsnips.

• *Preheat air fryer to 390°F (200°C)*

| | | |
|---|---|---|
| 1 lb | parsnips, cut into 3-inch (7.5 cm) long by ¼-inch (0.5 cm) thick sticks | 500 g |
| 1 tbsp | olive oil | 15 mL |
| ¼ tsp | salt | 1 mL |
| ⅛ tsp | freshly ground black pepper | 0.5 mL |
| 1 tbsp | chopped fresh flat-leaf (Italian) parsley | 15 mL |

1. In a large bowl, toss together parsnips, oil, salt and pepper.

2. Spread half the parsnips in a single layer in air fryer basket. Air-fry for 5 minutes, then shake the basket. Air-fry for 4 to 8 minutes or until parsnips are golden brown. Serve immediately, sprinkled with parsley. Repeat with the remaining parsnips.

# Shishito Peppers with Sea Salt

Fiercely fresh shishito peppers are irresistible when flash-cooked in the air fryer and adorned with nothing more than olive oil and a sprinkle of salt. The flavor is typically very mild, but every once in a while you'll get one with a hit of heat, which only adds to the thrill of eating them.

**Makes 2 to 3 servings**

## Tips

An equal amount of Padrón peppers can be used in place of the shishito peppers.

Table salt can be used in place of the flaky sea salt.

• *Preheat air fryer to 390°F (200°C)*

| | | |
|---|---|---|
| 8 oz | shishito peppers | 250 g |
| 2 tsp | olive oil | 10 mL |
| | Flaky sea salt | |

1. In a medium bowl, toss together peppers and oil.

2. Transfer peppers to air fryer basket. Air-fry for 7 to 12 minutes, shaking the basket every 3 minutes, until skins are blistered and flesh is softened. Serve immediately, sprinkled with sea salt.

# Air-Fried Green Tomatoes

Unadorned, über-ripe summer tomatoes have their place, but snagging a few while they are still green, dressing them up in a crispy coating and air-frying them until golden brown is an enticing alternative.

## Makes 4 servings

### Tip

Regular firm-ripe red tomatoes can be used in place of the green tomatoes.

### Variation

*Gluten-Free Air-Fried Green Tomatoes:* Replace the all-purpose flour with an all-purpose gluten-free flour blend, and replace the panko with an equal amount of crushed gluten-free corn flakes cereal.

• *Preheat air fryer to 390°F (200°C)*

| | | |
|---|---|---|
| 2 | large green tomatoes | 2 |
| 2/3 cup | all-purpose flour | 150 mL |
| 1/4 tsp | salt | 1 mL |
| 1/8 tsp | freshly ground black pepper | 0.5 mL |
| 1 1/4 cups | panko (Japanese bread crumbs) | 300 mL |
| 2 | large eggs | 2 |
| 3 tbsp | buttermilk | 45 mL |
| | Nonstick cooking spray | |

1. Cut tomatoes into 1/4-inch (0.5 cm) thick slices. Blot cut sides with paper towels to absorb excess liquid.

2. In a shallow dish, stir together flour, salt and pepper.

3. Spread panko in another shallow dish.

4. In a third shallow dish, whisk together eggs and buttermilk until blended.

5. Working with 1 tomato slice at a time, dredge in flour mixture, shaking off excess. Dip in egg mixture, shaking off excess, then dredge in panko, pressing gently to adhere. Spray both sides with cooking spray. As they are sprayed, place 3 slices flat in air fryer basket, spacing them evenly.

6. Air-fry for 5 to 8 minutes or until tomatoes are softened and coating is golden brown. Serve immediately.

7. Repeat steps 5 and 6 with the remaining tomato slices, flour mixture, egg mixture and panko. Discard any excess flour mixture, egg mixture and panko.

# Parmesan Zucchini Fries

Zucchini and Parmesan cheese have a real affinity. Here, they come together in a minimalist recipe that highlights the delicate flavor of the former and the nutty, umami flavor of the latter.

**Makes 2 servings**

## Tips

Serve with Lemon Herb Aïoli (page 276), if desired.

Use oven pads or mitts when shaking the basket.

## Variation

*Gluten-Free Parmesan Zucchini Fries:* Replace the panko with an equal amount of crushed gluten-free corn flakes cereal.

| 2 | zucchini (about 1 lb/500 g total), trimmed | 2 |
|---|---|---|
| | Salt | |
| ¾ cup | panko (Japanese bread crumbs) | 175 mL |
| ½ cup | freshly grated Parmesan cheese | 125 mL |
| | Nonstick cooking spray | |

1. Cut each zucchini lengthwise into ½-inch (1 cm) slices. Cut each slice lengthwise into ½-inch (1 cm) strips, then cut the strips crosswise in half. Sprinkle with salt and let stand at room temperature for 10 minutes. Blot zucchini with paper towels to remove any excess moisture.

2. Preheat air fryer to 390°F (200°C).

3. In a shallow dish, combine panko and Parmesan.

4. Working with 1 zucchini strip at a time, spray with cooking spray, then dredge in panko mixture, pressing gently to adhere. As they are dredged, place 6 to 8 zucchini strips in air fryer basket, leaving space in between. Spray with cooking spray.

5. Air-fry for 5 minutes, then gently shake the basket. Air-fry for 2 to 5 minutes or until coating is golden brown. Serve immediately.

6. Repeat steps 4 and 5 with the remaining zucchini strips and panko mixture. Discard any excess panko mixture.

# Herb-Stuffed Zucchini

Packed with a simple stuffing of tomatoes, walnuts and herbs, this easy and elegant zucchini dish evokes summer.

## Makes 2 servings

### Tip

Look for zucchini that are about 5 to 6 inches (12.5 to 15 cm) long and about 1½ inches (4 cm) wide.

### Variation

*Gluten-Free Herb-Stuffed Zucchini:* Replace the panko with an equal amount of crushed gluten-free corn flakes cereal.

• *Preheat air fryer to 390°F (200°C)*

| | | |
|---|---|---|
| 2 | small zucchini (see tip, at left), halved lengthwise | 2 |
| | Salt and freshly cracked black pepper | |
| 1 | clove garlic, minced | 1 |
| ¼ cup | chopped fresh tomatoes | 60 mL |
| ¼ cup | panko (Japanese bread crumbs) | 60 mL |
| 2 tbsp | fresh parsley or basil leaves, chopped | 30 mL |
| 1 tbsp | finely chopped walnuts | 15 mL |
| 1 tbsp | olive oil | 15 mL |
| | Nonstick cooking spray | |

1. Using a metal spoon, scoop and scrape out seeds from each zucchini half; discard seeds. Sprinkle cut sides with salt and pepper.

2. In a small bowl, combine garlic, tomatoes, panko, parsley, walnuts and oil until blended. Season to taste with salt and pepper. Pack into hollowed-out zucchini, dividing equally. Spray with cooking spray.

3. Place zucchini halves, stuffing side up, in air fryer basket, spacing them evenly. Air-fry for 15 to 20 minutes or until zucchini are tender and topping is golden brown. Serve immediately.

# Air-Fried Ratatouille

Ratatouille is a late-summer recipe with multiple charms. Air-frying makes the whole process a breeze and also cooks the dish perfectly without losing the essential texture and flavors of the individual vegetables. The dish is less stewy and more salad-like than a typical ratatouille, but with its concentrated flavor and fresh texture, along with a kick of garlic, it may soon become your favorite.

**Makes 4 servings**

## Tips

One medium plum (Roma) tomato, diced, may be used in place of the cherry tomatoes.

An equal amount of fresh flat-leaf (Italian) parsley leaves can be used in place of the basil.

• *Preheat air fryer to 360°F (180°C)*

| | | |
|---|---|---|
| 8 | cherry or grape tomatoes | 8 |
| 2 | cloves garlic, minced | 2 |
| 1 | small red bell pepper, cut into ½-inch (1 cm) pieces | 1 |
| 1½ cups | cubed eggplant (½-inch/1 cm cubes) | 375 mL |
| ½ cup | cubed zucchini (½-inch/1 cm cubes) | 125 mL |
| ⅓ cup | coarsely chopped onion | 75 mL |
| 2 tsp | olive oil | 10 mL |
| ¼ tsp | salt | 1 mL |
| ⅛ tsp | freshly cracked black pepper | 0.5 mL |
| ¼ cup | chopped fresh basil | 60 mL |
| 2 tbsp | freshly grated Parmesan cheese | 30 mL |

1. In a large bowl, toss together tomatoes, garlic, red pepper, eggplant, zucchini, onion, oil, salt and pepper until coated.

2. Transfer vegetables to air fryer basket. Air-fry for 13 to 17 minutes, shaking the basket every 5 minutes, until vegetables are tender. Serve sprinkled with basil and Parmesan.

# Polenta Fries

If you have yet to discover the ready-to-use rolls of polenta at the supermarket, now is the time, and this is the recipe. Crispy on the outside and creamy on the inside, the fries they yield will both surprise and delight.

**Makes 4 servings**

### Tips

An equal amount of Romano or Asiago cheese can be used in place of the Parmesan cheese. Alternatively, the fries can be served without the Parmesan and parsley.

Use oven pads or mitts when shaking the basket.

- *Preheat air fryer to 390°F (200°C)*

| | | |
|---|---|---|
| 1 | roll (17 oz/482 g) prepared plain polenta | 1 |
| | Nonstick cooking spray | |
| 1/4 tsp | salt | 1 mL |
| 2/3 cup | freshly grated Parmesan cheese | 150 mL |
| 1 tbsp | chopped fresh flat-leaf (Italian) parsley or basil | 15 mL |

1. Cut polenta lengthwise into 1/2-inch (1 cm) slices. Cut each slice lengthwise into 2- by 1/2-inch (5 by 1 cm) pieces.

2. Spray half the fries with cooking spray; refrigerate the remaining fries. Place sprayed fries in a single layer in air fryer basket, leaving space in between (it is okay if some overlap slightly).

3. Air-fry for 4 minutes, then gently shake the basket. Air-fry for 2 to 4 minutes or until fries are golden brown. Serve immediately, sprinkled with half each of the salt, Parmesan and parsley.

4. Repeat steps 2 and 3 with the remaining polenta fries, salt, Parmesan and parsley.

# Provençal Chickpea Fries

Chickpea flour, a naturally gluten-free flour made from dried chickpeas, is gaining popularity in North America, but it is already a much-loved ingredient in multiple Mediterranean countries. In the south of France, it is most often used to make *socca*, a simple and versatile flatbread, and *panisses*, which are chickpea flour fries. They are traditionally served with a sprinkle of sea salt and lemon wedges, but I can attest that they are great dunked in ketchup, too.

## Makes 2 servings

### Tip

Chickpea flour goes by many names, including garbanzo bean flour, besan, gram flour and ceci flour. Look for it in the healthy foods section of well-stocked grocery stores, natural foods stores, Southeast Asian grocery stores and some Italian food stores.

• 9- by 5-inch (23 by 12.5 cm) loaf pan, sprayed with nonstick cooking spray

| | | |
|---|---|---|
| 1 | small clove garlic, grated | 1 |
| ½ cup | chickpea flour | 125 mL |
| ¼ tsp | salt | 1 mL |
| Pinch | cayenne pepper | Pinch |
| ¾ cup | water | 175 mL |
| 2 tsp | olive oil | 10 mL |
| | Nonstick cooking spray | |

**Suggested Accompaniments**

Sea salt

Lemon wedges

1. In a small saucepan, whisk together garlic, chickpea flour, salt, cayenne, water and oil. Cook, whisking, over medium heat for 7 to 8 minutes or until mixture is bubbling and very thick but still pourable.

2. Pour chickpea flour mixture into prepared pan, smoothing top. Place plastic wrap directly on surface of chickpea flour mixture and refrigerate for 3 to 4 hours or until cold and completely set.

3. Preheat air fryer to 390°F (200°C).

## Tips

For milder fries, omit the garlic and cayenne pepper.

You can use ¼ tsp (1 mL) garlic powder in place of the garlic clove.

The fries can be made through step 2 up to 2 days in advance.

Use oven pads or mitts when shaking the basket.

4. Invert pan onto a cutting board (the chickpea flour mixture will slide right out). Cut into 3- by ½-inch (7.5 by 1 cm) pieces.

5. Spray half the fries with cooking spray; refrigerate the remaining fries. Place sprayed fries in a single layer in air fryer basket, leaving space in between.

6. Air-fry for 12 minutes, then gently shake the basket. Air-fry for 6 to 11 minutes or until fries are golden brown and crispy. Serve immediately with sea salt and lemon wedges, as desired.

7. Repeat steps 5 and 6 with the remaining fries.

# Double Corn Fritters

Cornmeal plus corn kernels may sound obvious, but delectable combinations often are. Need proof? Make these easy fritters, pronto.

**Makes 2 servings**

**Tip**

An equal amount of finely chopped green onions can be used in place of the chives.

**Variation**

*Gluten-Free Double Corn Fritters:* Replace the all-purpose flour with an all-purpose gluten-free flour blend.

| | | |
|---|---|---|
| ⅓ cup | all-purpose flour | 75 mL |
| ¼ cup | yellow cornmeal | 60 mL |
| ¼ tsp | baking powder | 1 mL |
| ¼ tsp | salt | 1 mL |
| Pinch | cayenne pepper | Pinch |
| 1 | large egg, lightly beaten | 1 |
| 2 tbsp | milk | 30 mL |
| 1 tbsp | unsalted butter, melted | 15 mL |
| 1 cup | fresh or thawed frozen corn kernels | 250 mL |
| 2 tbsp | freshly grated Parmesan cheese | 30 mL |
| 1 tbsp | minced fresh chives | 15 mL |
| | Nonstick cooking spray | |

1. In a medium bowl, whisk together flour, cornmeal, baking powder, salt and cayenne. Add egg, milk and butter, stirring just until blended. Add corn, Parmesan and chives, stirring just until blended. Let stand for 10 minutes to thicken.

2. Preheat air fryer to 390°F (200°C).

3. Form 2 tbsp (30 mL) dough into a ball and flatten slightly with your palms. Make 4 more flattened balls. Spray both sides of fritters with cooking spray and place in air fryer basket, spacing them evenly.

4. Air-fry for 8 to 11 minutes or until fritters are golden brown and set at the center. Serve immediately.

5. Repeat steps 3 and 4 with the remaining dough.

# Quick Cornbread Stuffing

This scrumptious, simple-to-make stuffing is as variable as the Turkey Day original, making it a go-to side dish all year round.

## Tips

Look for packages (14 to 16 oz/398 to 500 g) of cornbread stuffing in the bread section of the supermarket.

An equal amount of torn crusty, rustic-style bread or dry crumbled cornbread can be used in place of the cornbread stuffing.

Use oven pads or mitts when shaking the basket.

• Preheat air fryer to 390°F (200°C)

| | | |
|---|---|---|
| 1 | small tart-sweet apple (such as Gala, Braeburn or Golden Delicious), peeled and very coarsely chopped | 1 |
| 1 | small onion, coarsely chopped | 1 |
| ½ cup | chopped celery | 125 mL |
| 1 tsp | poultry seasoning | 5 mL |
| 1 tbsp | unsalted butter | 15 mL |
| 3½ cups | plain dry cornbread stuffing (see tips, at left) | 875 mL |
| ⅔ cup | ready-to-use chicken or vegetable broth | 150 mL |
| | Salt and freshly cracked black pepper | |
| | Nonstick cooking spray | |

### Suggested Stir-Ins

| | | |
|---|---|---|
| ¼ cup | dried cranberries, chopped | 60 mL |
| ¼ cup | chopped fresh flat-leaf (Italian) parsley | 60 mL |

1. In a medium bowl, toss together apple, onion, celery, poultry seasoning and butter.

2. Transfer apple mixture to air fryer basket. Air-fry for 15 minutes.

3. Meanwhile, in the same bowl (no need to clean it), combine cornbread stuffing and broth. Season with salt and pepper. Let stand for 10 minutes.

4. Open air fryer basket and add stuffing mixture, stirring to combine. Spray with cooking spray. Air-fry for 20 to 25 minutes, shaking the basket every 10 minutes, until stuffing is golden brown. If desired, stir in cranberries and/or parsley.

# Desserts

~~~~~~~~~~~~~~~~~~~~~~~~~~~~~~~~~~~~~~~~~~~

# Cranberry Maple Air-Baked Apples

Maple syrup adds sophisticated notes to this old-fashioned dessert. It is especially great in autumn, when apples are at their peak.

**Makes 2 servings**

## Tips

You can toast the pecans in the air fryer before cooking the apples. Preheat the air fryer to 360°F (180°C) and spread the pecans in the unsprayed cake pan. Place pan in air fryer basket and air-fry for 3 to 6 minutes or until golden brown and fragrant. Transfer pecans to a small plate to cool, increase air fryer temperature to 390°F (200°C) and proceed with step 1.

Other varieties of dried fruit, such as cherries, blueberries or raisins, may be used in place of the cranberries.

## Storage Tip

Store the cooled apples, loosely covered in foil or plastic wrap, in the refrigerator for up to 1 day. Serve cold, or warm in the microwave on Medium-High (70%) for about 1 minute.

- Preheat air fryer to 390°F (200°C)
- 6-inch (15 cm) round metal cake pan, sprayed with nonstick cooking spray

| | | |
|---|---|---|
| 2 | small tart-sweet apples (such as Braeburn, Gala or Fuji), cored | 2 |
| 2 tbsp | dried cranberries, roughly chopped | 30 mL |
| 2 tbsp | chopped toasted pecans (see tip, at left) | 30 mL |
| 3 tbsp | crushed gingersnap cookies | 45 mL |
| 2 tbsp | pure maple syrup | 30 mL |
| | Nonstick cooking spray | |
| 2 tbsp | vanilla-flavored Greek yogurt | 30 mL |

1. Using a vegetable peeler, peel off top 1 inch (2.5 cm) of apples. Place apples, top side up, in prepared cake pan.

2. In a small bowl, combine cranberries, pecans and gingersnaps. Stuff cranberry mixture into apple cavities. Drizzle 1 tbsp (15 mL) maple syrup over each apple. Spray with cooking spray.

3. Place pan in air fryer basket. Air-fry for 35 to 40 minutes, occasionally opening basket to spoon accumulated juices over apples, until apples are tender.

4. Transfer apples to a plate and pour pan juices over top. Serve each apple dolloped with 1 tbsp (15 mL) yogurt.

# Bananas Foster

A favorite New Orleans dessert, bananas Foster was created at Brennan's restaurant in the French Quarter in the 1950s. It was named for a regular customer, Dick Foster. It never fails to please, including this lightened air fryer interpretation.

**Makes 2 servings**

## Tips

For the best flavor, choose a banana that is firm but has some light spotting on the peel (indicating ripeness).

To make the bananas without alcohol, omit the rum and increase the total amount of orange juice to 1 tbsp (15 mL). If desired, add ¼ tsp (1 mL) rum extract or vanilla extract.

- *Preheat oven to 390°F (200°C)*
- *6-inch (15 cm) round metal cake pan, sprayed with nonstick cooking spray*

| | | |
|---|---|---|
| 1 | large banana, peeled and sliced crosswise | 1 |
| 1 tbsp | packed brown sugar | 15 mL |
| ⅛ tsp | ground cinnamon | 0.5 mL |
| Pinch | salt | Pinch |
| 2 tsp | unsalted butter, cut into small pieces | 10 mL |
| 1 tsp | orange juice | 5 mL |
| 2 tsp | rum or brandy | 10 mL |

### Suggested Accompaniments

Chopped toasted pecans
Light or regular vanilla ice cream

1. Place banana slices in a single layer in prepared cake pan. Sprinkle with brown sugar, cinnamon, salt, butter and orange juice.

2. Place pan in air fryer basket. Air-fry for 5 to 9 minutes or until bananas are brown and sugar is melted and bubbly. Remove pan from air fryer and gently stir in rum. Serve with any of the suggested accompaniments, as desired.

# Raspberry Crumbles

Minimal preparation plus a short time in the air fryer yields two perfect crumbles that showcase raspberries in an understated but glorious way.

## Makes 2 servings

### Tips

An equal amount of blueberries or blackberries, or a mix of several berries, can be used in place of the raspberries.

The raspberry mixture and the flour mixture can each be prepared up to 1 day ahead and stored in the refrigerator in separate airtight containers. When ready to air-fry, proceed with steps 3 and 4, increasing the cooking time by 2 to 3 minutes.

- Preheat air fryer to 360°F (180°C)
- Two ³⁄₄-cup (175 mL) ramekins, sprayed with nonstick cooking spray

| | | |
|---|---|---|
| 1 cup | raspberries | 250 mL |
| 1 tsp | cornstarch | 5 mL |
| 2 tbsp | packed light brown sugar, divided | 30 mL |
| ¹⁄₂ tsp | vanilla extract | 2 mL |
| 3 tbsp | all-purpose flour | 45 mL |
| 3 tbsp | large-flake (old-fashioned) or quick-cooking rolled oats | 45 mL |
| ¹⁄₂ tsp | ground cinnamon | 2 mL |
| 1 tbsp | virgin coconut oil, melted | 15 mL |
| 1 tbsp | milk (dairy or nondairy) | 15 mL |

1. In a medium bowl, coarsely mash half the raspberries with a fork. Add the remaining raspberries, cornstarch, half the brown sugar and vanilla, gently tossing to combine.

2. In a small bowl, whisk together flour, oats, cinnamon and the remaining brown sugar. Add oil and milk, mixing with your fingertips until moist and crumbly.

3. Spoon fruit mixture into ramekins. Sprinkle with oat mixture.

4. Place a piece of foil in bottom of air fryer basket, leaving ¹⁄₂ inch (1 cm) between the foil and the inside edge of the basket (in case of filling bubbling over). Place ramekins in basket. Air-fry for 16 to 21 minutes or until fruit is bubbling and topping is golden brown. Let cool to room temperature before serving.

# Blueberry Clafouti

As the main ingredient in this clafouti — a minimalist French dessert that's a cross between a custard and a tart — blueberries become the belle of the ball.

## Storage Tip

Store the cooled clafouti, loosely covered in foil or plastic wrap, in the refrigerator for up to 1 day.

## Variation

An equal amount of pitted cherries, raspberries, blackberries or diced peaches or pears can be used in place of the blueberries.

- Preheat air fryer to 360°F (180°C)
- Two ³⁄₄-cup (175 mL) ramekins, sprayed with nonstick cooking spray

| | | |
|---|---|---|
| 1 cup | blueberries | 250 mL |
| 1 | large egg, at room temperature | 1 |
| ⅓ cup | milk | 75 mL |
| 1½ tbsp | liquid honey | 22 mL |
| ¼ tsp | almond extract | 1 mL |
| 3 tbsp | all-purpose flour | 45 mL |
| ⅛ tsp | salt | 0.5 mL |
| 1 tbsp | confectioners' (icing) sugar (optional) | 15 mL |

1. Divide blueberries between prepared ramekins.

2. In a small bowl, whisk together egg, milk, honey and almond extract until blended. Whisk in flour and salt until blended. Pour batter evenly over blueberries.

3. Place ramekins in air fryer basket. Air-fry for 15 to 20 minutes or until clafouti are puffed and golden. Transfer ramekins to a wire rack and let cool for 20 minutes. If desired, sprinkle with confectioners' sugar.

# Toffee Apple Hand Pies

Offering a simple but ever-popular pairing, these toffee and apple hand pies are full of seasonal flavors.

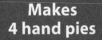

## Makes
### 4 hand pies

**Storage Tip**
Store the cooled pies in an airtight container in the refrigerator for up to 3 days.

• *Preheat air fryer to 360°F (180°C)*

| | | |
|---|---|---|
| 3 cups | finely chopped peeled tart-sweet apples (such as Gala, Braeburn or Cortland) | 750 mL |
| 3 tbsp | granulated sugar, divided | 45 mL |
| ¾ tsp | ground cinnamon | 3 mL |
| 1 | chocolate-covered English toffee candy bar (1.4 oz/40 g), chopped | 1 |
| 1 tbsp | freshly squeezed lemon juice | 15 mL |
| 1 | package (15 oz/425 g) refrigerated rolled pie crusts | 1 |
| 1 | large egg | 1 |
| 1 tbsp | water | 15 mL |

1. In a medium bowl, combine apples, 2 tbsp (30 mL) sugar, cinnamon, toffee and lemon juice.

2. On work surface, unroll 1 pie crust. Cut into 4 equal wedges. Spread ¾ cup (175 mL) filling on each of 2 wedges, leaving a ½-inch (2 cm) border. Brush crust edges with water. Top with the 2 remaining wedges. Press edges firmly with a fork to seal. Cut three small slits in the top of each hand pie.

3. In a small cup or bowl, whisk together egg and water. Brush tops of pies with some of the egg wash and sprinkle with half of the remaining sugar.

4. Place pies in air fryer basket, spacing them evenly. Air-fry for 20 to 25 minutes or until crust is golden brown. Transfer to a wire rack to cool.

5. Repeat steps 2 to 4 with the remaining pie crust, filling, egg wash and sugar. Serve warm or at room temperature.

# Apricot Hand Pies

Apricot season is short, but love for the fruit can endure year-round with the help of dried apricots and apricot jam. Dried apricots are more intense in flavor than fresh apricots, which means every bite of these treats is cause for cheer.

## Makes 8 hand pies

### Tips

The pies are best eaten soon after they are made.

Other varieties of dried fruit, such as peaches, cherries or blueberries, may be used in place of the apricots. Use apricot jam, or use another variety that matches the dried fruit.

Other spices, such as ground cinnamon or allspice, may be used in place of the cardamom.

• *Preheat air fryer to 360°F (180°C)*

| | | |
|---|---|---|
| 1 tbsp | granulated sugar | 15 mL |
| ¼ tsp | ground cardamom or ginger | 1 mL |
| ½ cup | chopped soft dried apricots | 125 mL |
| ½ cup | apricot jam or preserves | 125 mL |
| 1 | can (17.3 oz/490 g) refrigerated large dinner biscuits | 1 |
| | Nonstick cooking spray | |

1. In a small cup, combine sugar and cardamom.

2. In a small bowl, stir together apricots and jam.

3. Remove dough from packaging and separate into biscuits. Using your fingertips or a rolling pin, press or roll each biscuit into a 5-inch (12.5 cm) circle.

4. Place 2 tbsp (30 mL) apricot mixture slightly off-center on each dough circle. Fold biscuits over filling and press edges together with a fork to seal. Prick the top of each hand pie three times with a fork. Spray pies with cooking spray and sprinkle with cardamom sugar.

5. Place half the pies in air fryer basket, spacing them evenly (refrigerate the remaining pies). Air-fry for 10 to 14 minutes or until puffed and golden brown. Transfer to a wire rack and let cool for at least 10 minutes before serving. Repeat with the remaining hand pies. Serve warm or at room temperature.

# Vanilla Cupcakes with Chocolate Icing

Some love vanilla, others love chocolate, but just about everyone loves it when the two are united in delicious harmony. Case in point, these cupcakes. It's a good thing you can only prepare a few at a time — once made, they are hard to resist!

**Makes 4 cupcakes**

**Tip**
For best results, use full-fat sour cream.

- *Preheat air fryer to 330°F (160°C)*
- *8 standard-size foil or paper muffin cup liners*

### Vanilla Cupcakes

| | | |
|---|---|---:|
| 6 tbsp | all-purpose flour | 90 mL |
| 1/2 tsp | baking powder | 2 mL |
| 1/8 tsp | baking soda | 0.5 mL |
| 1/8 tsp | salt | 0.5 mL |
| 1/4 cup | granulated sugar | 60 mL |
| 1/4 cup | unsalted butter | 60 mL |
| 1 | large egg white | 1 |
| 2 tbsp | sour cream | 30 mL |
| 1/2 tsp | vanilla extract | 2 mL |

### Chocolate Icing

| | | |
|---|---|---:|
| 2 tbsp | unsweetened cocoa powder | 30 mL |
| 1 tbsp | boiling water | 15 mL |
| 1 1/2 tbsp | unsalted butter | 22 mL |
| 3/4 cup | confectioners' (icing) sugar | 175 mL |
| 1/2 tsp | vanilla extract | 2 mL |

1. *Cupcakes:* Place one muffin cup liner inside another. Repeat to create 4 doubled liners.

2. In a small bowl, whisk together flour, baking powder, baking soda and salt.

## Storage Tip

Store the iced cupcakes, loosely tented in foil, in the refrigerator for up to 1 day.

## *Variation*

*Almond Cupcakes:* Replace the vanilla in step 3 with ¼ tsp (1 mL) almond extract. Divide 2 tbsp (30 mL) sliced almonds equally over top of batter before air-frying. Omit the icing and sprinkle the cooled cupcakes with confectioners' (icing) sugar.

**3.** In a medium bowl, using an electric mixer on medium speed, beat sugar and butter until blended, light and fluffy, stopping once to scrape the bowl. Add egg white, sour cream and vanilla, mixing on low speed until just blended. Add flour mixture, mixing on low speed until just blended.

**4.** Divide batter equally among the doubled liners.

**5.** Place filled liners in air fryer basket, spacing them evenly. Air-fry for 14 to 18 minutes or until tops are golden and a tester inserted in the center of a cupcake comes out clean. Transfer to a wire rack and let cool completely.

**6.** *Icing:* In a small bowl or cup, whisk together cocoa powder, boiling water and butter until smooth. Stir in confectioners' sugar and vanilla until blended and smooth. Use immediately to ice the cooled cupcakes.

# Lemony Baby Pound Cakes

These petite cakes are a quick and easy version of a spectacular pound cake I remember from my childhood, made and served by a family friend whenever we paid a visit. One taste makes me feel like a kid again.

**Makes 4 servings**

**Tip**

For best results, use full-fat sour cream.

- *Preheat air fryer to 330°F (160°C)*
- *8 standard-size foil or paper muffin cup liners*

### Cakes

| | | |
|---|---|---|
| 1/2 cup | all-purpose flour | 125 mL |
| 1/4 tsp | baking powder | 1 mL |
| 1/8 tsp | salt | 0.5 mL |
| 1/3 cup | granulated sugar | 75 mL |
| 1/4 cup | unsalted butter | 60 mL |
| 1 | large egg | 1 |
| 1 | large egg yolk | 1 |
| 3 tbsp | sour cream | 45 mL |
| 1 tsp | finely grated lemon zest | 5 mL |

### Glaze

| | | |
|---|---|---|
| 3/4 cup | confectioners' (icing) sugar | 175 mL |
| 1/4 tsp | finely grated lemon zest | 1 mL |
| 1 tbsp | freshly squeezed lemon juice | 15 mL |

1. *Cakes:* Place one muffin cup liner inside another. Repeat to create 4 doubled liners.

2. In a small bowl, whisk together flour, baking powder and salt.

3. In a medium bowl, using an electric mixer on medium speed, beat sugar and butter until blended, light and fluffy, stopping once to scrape the bowl. Add egg, egg yolk, sour cream and lemon zest, mixing on low speed until just blended. Add flour mixture, mixing on low speed until just blended.

## Storage Tip

Store the glazed cakes, loosely covered in foil or plastic wrap, in the refrigerator for up to 1 day.

## *Variation*

An equal amount of lime or orange zest and juice may be used in place of the lemon zest and juice in both the cakes and the glaze.

4. Divide batter equally among the doubled liners.

5. Place filled liners in air fryer basket, spacing them evenly. Air-fry for 14 to 18 minutes or until tops are golden and a tester inserted in the center of a cupcake comes out clean. Transfer to a wire rack and let cool completely.

6. *Glaze:* In a small bowl, whisk together confectioners' sugar, lemon zest and lemon juice until smooth. Drizzle each cooled cake with glaze.

# Molten Chocolate Cakes

It's no wonder molten chocolate cakes have remained so popular: they have all of the rich flavor of regular chocolate cake with a warm and luscious chocolate sauce built in. No need to wait for a restaurant visit to have them, as they are a cinch to make in the air fryer.

## Makes 2 servings

### Tip

Do not let the cakes cool in the ramekins for longer than 3 minutes or they will continue to cook from the heat of the ramekins and will no longer have a molten center.

- Preheat air fryer to 390°F (200°C)
- Two ³⁄₄-cup (175 mL) ramekins, liberally sprayed with nonstick cooking spray

| | | |
|---|---|---|
| ¹⁄₃ cup | bittersweet (dark) or semisweet chocolate chips | 75 mL |
| ¹⁄₄ cup | unsalted butter, cut into small pieces | 60 mL |
| 3 tbsp | granulated sugar | 45 mL |
| ¹⁄₂ tsp | instant espresso powder | 2 mL |
| ¹⁄₄ tsp | salt | 1 mL |
| ¹⁄₂ tsp | vanilla extract | 2 mL |
| 1 | large egg | 1 |
| 1 | large egg yolk | 1 |
| 2 tbsp | all-purpose flour | 30 mL |
| 1 tbsp | confectioners' (icing) sugar | 15 mL |

### Suggested Accompaniments

Vanilla ice cream
Whipped cream
Raspberries or sliced strawberries

1. In a medium microwave-safe bowl, combine chocolate chips and butter. Microwave on High for 30 seconds. Stir. Microwave for 30 seconds longer. Vigorously stir for 30 seconds or until chocolate is melted and mixture is smooth. Stir in granulated sugar, espresso powder, salt and vanilla. Let cool for 2 minutes.

2. Stir in egg and egg yolk until blended. Sprinkle flour over batter and stir until completely blended.

**Tip**

You can use 1 tsp (5 mL) instant coffee powder in place of the espresso powder.

3. Divide batter equally between prepared ramekins.

4. Place ramekins in air fryer basket, spacing them evenly. Air-fry for 8 to 13 minutes or until surface of cakes appears dry but a tester inserted in the center comes out with wet batter attached. Transfer to a wire rack and let cool for 3 minutes.

5. Run a knife around edges of ramekins and invert onto individual dessert plates. Sift with confectioners' sugar and serve with any of the suggested accompaniments, as desired.

# Peach Pudding Cakes

Regardless of whether you use frozen or fresh, this pudding cake — serve it with spoons — captures the sunshiny flavor of summertime peaches.

### Tip

Other spices, such as ground cardamom, ginger or allspice, may be used in place of the cinnamon.

### Storage Tip

Store the cooled pudding cakes, loosely covered in foil or plastic wrap, in the refrigerator for up to 1 day.

### Variation

An equal amount of pitted cherries, raspberries, blackberries or blueberries can be used in place of the peaches.

- Preheat air fryer to 350°F (180°C)
- Three 3/4-cup (175 mL) ramekins, sprayed with nonstick cooking spray

| | | |
|---|---|---|
| 2 cups | thawed frozen or fresh sliced peaches | 500 mL |
| 4 tbsp | granulated sugar, divided | 60 mL |
| 1/4 tsp | ground cinnamon | 1 mL |
| 1/2 cup | all-purpose flour | 125 mL |
| 3/4 tsp | baking powder | 3 mL |
| 1/4 tsp | salt | 1 mL |
| 1 | large egg yolk | 1 |
| 2 tbsp | milk (dairy or nondairy) | 30 mL |
| 2 tbsp | unsalted butter, melted | 30 mL |
| 1/2 tsp | vanilla extract | 2 mL |

**Suggested Accompaniments**

Vanilla ice cream

Whipped cream

1. In a medium bowl, combine peaches, 1 tbsp (15 mL) sugar and cinnamon. Divide equally among prepared ramekins.

2. In a small bowl, stir together flour, baking powder, salt, egg yolk, milk, butter and vanilla until blended. Spoon batter over peaches, dividing equally among ramekins. Sprinkle with the remaining sugar.

3. Place ramekins in air fryer basket, spacing them evenly. Air-fry for 20 to 25 minutes or until cake has risen in between the peaches and is golden brown. Transfer ramekins to a wire rack and let cool for at least 10 minutes before serving with suggested accompaniments, as desired.

# Mini Cheesecakes

I love a good cheesecake, but the advance planning required for the regular-size versions (a long bake, followed by a long cooling and then overnight to chill) is vexing. Not so with this version. I've slashed the time and effort dramatically so that homemade cheesecake is ready in no time.

## Makes 4 servings

### Tip
Two large egg whites can be used in place of the whole egg.

### Storage Tip
Store the cooled cheesecakes, loosely covered in foil or plastic wrap, in the refrigerator for up to 2 days.

### Variations
*Chocolate Chip Cheesecakes:* Stir in 3 tbsp (45 mL) miniature semisweet chocolate chips after beating in the egg in step 2.

*Peanut Butter Cheesecakes:* Replace the granulated sugar with an equal amount of packed light brown sugar. Add 2 tbsp (30 mL) creamy peanut butter with the cream cheese.

*Berry Cheesecakes:* Gently press 1 whole raspberry, blueberry or blackberry into the batter after dividing it equally among the liners in step 3.

- *Preheat oven to 350°F (180°C)*
- *8 standard-size foil or paper muffin cup liners*

| 3 tbsp | granulated sugar | 45 mL |
| 8 oz | brick-style cream cheese, softened | 250 g |
| 1/2 tsp | vanilla extract | 2 mL |
| 1 | large egg | 1 |
| 4 | vanilla wafers | 4 |

1. Place one muffin cup liner inside another. Repeat to create 4 doubled liners.

2. In a medium bowl, using an electric mixer on medium speed, beat sugar, cream cheese and vanilla until blended, light and fluffy, stopping once to scrape the bowl. Add egg and mix on low speed until just blended.

3. Place 1 vanilla wafer, rounded side up, in each doubled liner. Divide batter equally among the liners.

4. Place filled liners in air fryer basket, spacing them evenly. Air-fry for 16 to 20 minutes or until cheesecakes are puffed and surface appears dry. Transfer to a wire rack and let cool completely. Refrigerate for at least 1 hour, until cold, before serving.

# Pumpkin Cheesecake Bites

When it comes to favorite flavors, I am a caramel lover first and a chocolate lover second, but after concocting these "bites," I might have to move pumpkin into the top ranks.

## Makes 8 servings

### Tips

While assembling the cheesecake bites, keep the stack of wrappers moist by covering them with a damp towel.

These are best eaten soon after air-frying.

Either regular or reduced-fat ricotta cheese may be used.

An equal amount of ground cinnamon may be used in place of the pumpkin pie spice.

Use oven pads or mitts when shaking the basket.

• Preheat air fryer to 390°F (200°C)

| | | |
|---|---|---|
| 3 tbsp | packed light brown sugar | 45 mL |
| 1 tsp | pumpkin pie spice | 5 mL |
| 1/8 tsp | salt | 0.5 mL |
| 1/2 cup | ricotta cheese | 125 mL |
| 1/3 cup | pumpkin purée (not pie filling) | 75 mL |
| 1/2 tsp | vanilla extract | 2 mL |
| 16 | 3-inch (7.5 cm) square wonton wrappers | 16 |
| | Nonstick cooking spray | |
| | Confectioners' (icing) sugar | |

1. In a medium bowl, whisk together brown sugar, pumpkin pie spice, salt, ricotta, pumpkin and vanilla.

2. Place 1 wonton wrapper on work surface. Spoon 1 tbsp (15 mL) filling into the center of wrapper. Using a pastry brush or a fingertip, moisten the edges of the wrapper with water. Fold in half to form a triangle, pressing the edges to seal. Repeat with 7 more wrappers and filling.

3. Spray both sides of wontons with cooking spray as you place them in the air fryer basket, placing them close together but not touching. Air-fry for 3 minutes, then gently shake the basket. Air-fry for 2 to 4 minutes or until golden brown. Transfer to a plate or wire rack and sprinkle with confectioners' sugar.

4. Repeat steps 2 and 3 with the remaining wonton wrappers and filling.

# Anytime Chocolate Cake

This easy, eggless cake (known for generations as "wacky cake") tastes as rich as rubies, yet is still light, tender and not too sweet. I list the chocolate chips as an option, but I urge you to add them if you have them on hand.

**Storage Tip**

Store the cooled cake, loosely wrapped in foil or waxed paper, at room temperature for up to 1 week. Alternatively, wrap it in plastic wrap, then foil, completely enclosing cake, and freeze for up to 6 months. Let thaw at room temperature for 4 to 6 hours before serving.

*Variation*

Replace the vanilla with 1/4 tsp (1 mL) peppermint extract.

- Preheat oven to 330°F (160°C)
- 6-inch (15 cm) round metal cake pan, sprayed with nonstick cooking spray

| | | |
|---|---|---|
| 1/2 cup | all-purpose flour | 125 mL |
| 1/4 cup | granulated sugar | 60 mL |
| 1 1/2 tbsp | unsweetened cocoa powder | 22 mL |
| 1/4 tsp | baking soda | 1 mL |
| 1/8 tsp | fine sea salt | 0.5 mL |
| 1/3 cup | water | 75 mL |
| 2 tbsp | vegetable oil | 30 mL |
| 3/4 tsp | apple cider vinegar or white vinegar | 3 mL |
| 1/2 tsp | vanilla extract | 2 mL |
| 3 tbsp | miniature semisweet chocolate chips (optional) | |

1. In a medium bowl, whisk together flour, sugar, cocoa powder, baking soda and salt.

2. In a glass measuring cup, combine water, oil, vinegar and vanilla. Pour water mixture and chocolate chips (if using) into flour mixture, stirring until just blended.

3. Immediately pour batter into prepared cake pan.

4. Place pan in air fryer basket. Air-fry for 15 to 19 minutes or until a tester inserted in the center comes out clean. Let cool completely in pan on a wire rack.

# Chocolate Hazelnut Fudge Cake

Chocolate and hazelnut is a favorite combination across Europe (where it is known as *gianduja* or *gianduia*), but it has gained tremendous popularity in North America, too. The reason is largely due to chocolate hazelnut spread, which I've used here as the basis of a lickety-split, lick-your-lips chocolate cake.

## Makes 4 servings

### Tip

For added crunch, sprinkle the cake batter with 2 tbsp (30 mL) chopped hazelnuts before air-frying.

### Storage Tip

Store the cooled unfrosted cake, loosely wrapped in foil or waxed paper, at room temperature for up to 1 week. Alternatively, wrap it in plastic wrap, then foil, completely enclosing cake, and freeze for up to 6 months. Let thaw at room temperature for 4 to 6 hours before frosting and serving.

- *Preheat oven to 350°F (180°C)*
- *6-inch (15 cm) round metal cake pan, sprayed with nonstick cooking spray*

| | | |
|---|---|---|
| 2 | large eggs, at room temperature | 2 |
| 1 cup | chocolate hazelnut spread, divided | 250 mL |
| ¼ cup | all-purpose flour | 60 mL |
| 3 tbsp | miniature semisweet chocolate chips | 45 mL |

1. In a medium bowl, using an electric mixer on medium speed, beat eggs and ¾ cup (175 mL) chocolate hazelnut spread for 2 minutes, stopping once to scrape bottom and sides of bowl, until blended and slightly fluffy. Add flour and chocolate chips, mixing on low speed until just blended.

2. Spread batter in prepared cake pan.

3. Place pan in air fryer basket. Air-fry for 15 to 19 minutes or until a tester inserted in the center comes out clean. Let cool completely in pan on a wire rack.

4. Frost cake with the remaining chocolate hazelnut spread.

# One-Bowl Brownies

A short list of pantry ingredients is all you need to make a quick batch of one-bowl, crave-worthy chocolate brownies.

**Makes 4 servings**

## Storage Tip

Store the cooled brownies in an airtight container at room temperature for up to 1 week. Alternatively, wrap them in plastic wrap, then foil, completely enclosing them, and freeze for up to 6 months. Let thaw at room temperature for 1 to 2 hours.

## Variations

*Gluten-Free Brownies:* Replace the all-purpose flour with an all-purpose gluten-free flour blend.

*Double Chocolate Brownies:* Add 1/3 cup (75 mL) miniature semisweet chocolate chips with the flour in step 2.

*Peanut Butter Swirl Brownies:* After spreading the batter in the pan in step 3, distribute six 1/2-tsp (2 mL) dollops of creamy peanut butter over the surface of the batter. Using the tip of a knife, swirl peanut butter into batter. Air-fry as directed.

- Preheat air fryer to 360°F (180°C)
- 6-inch (15 cm) round metal cake pan, sprayed with nonstick cooking spray

| | | |
|---|---|---|
| 1/2 cup | granulated sugar | 125 mL |
| 1/3 cup | unsweetened cocoa powder | 75 mL |
| 1/4 cup | unsalted butter, cut into small pieces | 60 mL |
| 1/4 tsp | salt | 1 mL |
| 1/2 tsp | vanilla extract | 2 mL |
| 1 | large egg | 1 |
| 1/4 cup | all-purpose flour | 60 mL |

1. In a medium microwave-safe bowl, combine sugar, cocoa powder and butter. Microwave on High for 30 seconds. Stir. Microwave for 30 seconds longer. Vigorously stir for 30 seconds or until well blended. Stir in salt and vanilla. Let cool for 2 minutes.

2. Stir in egg until blended. Sprinkle flour over batter and stir until completely blended.

3. Spread batter evenly in prepared cake pan.

4. Place pan in air fryer basket. Air-fry for 16 to 20 minutes or until surface of brownies appears shiny and dry and a tester inserted in the center comes out with moist crumbs attached. Transfer to a wire rack and let cool for at least 20 minutes. Cut into 4 wedges. Serve warm or let cool completely.

# Butterscotch Blondies

Butterscotch chips stirred into the batter give these brown sugar and butter treats an extra fillip of blondie flavor. Chopping them ensures an even distribution of butterscotch in every bite.

## Storage Tip

Store the cooled blondies in an airtight container at room temperature for up to 1 week. Alternatively, wrap them in plastic wrap, then foil, completely enclosing them, and freeze for up to 6 months. Let thaw at room temperature for 1 to 2 hours.

## Variations

*Gluten-Free Butterscotch Blondies:* Replace the all-purpose flour with an all-purpose gluten-free flour blend. Most major brands of butterscotch baking chips are gluten-free, but double-check the label.

*Toasted Pecan Blondies:* Add ¼ cup (60 mL) chopped toasted pecans with the butterscotch chips.

*Chocolate Chip Blondies:* Replace the butterscotch baking chips with an equal amount of semisweet chocolate chips.

- Preheat air fryer to 360°F (180°C)
- 6-inch (15 cm) round metal cake pan, sprayed with nonstick cooking spray

| | | |
|---|---|---|
| ½ cup | packed light brown sugar | 125 mL |
| ⅛ tsp | salt | 0.5 mL |
| 3 tbsp | unsalted butter, melted | 45 mL |
| ½ tsp | vanilla extract | 2 mL |
| 1 | large egg yolk | 1 |
| ½ cup | all-purpose flour | 125 mL |
| ¼ tsp | baking powder | 1 mL |
| 3 tbsp | butterscotch baking chips, roughly chopped | 45 mL |

1. In a medium bowl, stir together brown sugar, salt, butter and vanilla until well blended. Stir in egg yolk until blended. Sprinkle flour, baking powder and butterscotch chips over batter and stir until completely blended.

2. Spread batter evenly in prepared cake pan.

3. Place pan in air fryer basket. Air-fry for 15 to 19 minutes or until surface of blondies appears dry and a tester inserted in the center comes out with moist crumbs attached. Immediately invert blondies onto a wire rack. Turn blondies over and let cool completely. Cut into 4 wedges.

# Butter Cookies

Six ingredients you undoubtedly have in your cupboard and refrigerator are all that stand between you and a plate of tender, butter-rich cookies.

## Makes 6 cookies

### Storage Tip

Store the cooled cookies in a tin at room temperature for up to 2 days. Alternatively, wrap them in plastic wrap, then foil, completely enclosing them, and freeze for up to 6 months. Let thaw at room temperature for 1 hour.

### Variations

*Gluten-Free Butter Cookies:* Replace the all-purpose flour with an all-purpose gluten-free flour blend.

*Almond Butter Cookies:* Replace the vanilla extract with $1/4$ tsp (1 mL) almond extract.

*Brown Sugar Butter Cookies:* Replace the granulated sugar with an equal amount of packed light brown sugar.

| | | |
|---|---|---|
| $1/4$ cup | granulated sugar | 60 mL |
| $1/4$ cup | unsalted butter, softened | 60 mL |
| $1/8$ tsp | salt | 0.5 mL |
| 1 | large egg yolk | 1 |
| $1/2$ tsp | vanilla extract | 2 mL |
| $1/2$ cup | all-purpose flour | 125 mL |
| | Nonstick cooking spray | |

1. In a medium bowl, using a wooden spoon, vigorously stir together sugar and butter until blended and creamy. Stir in salt, egg yolk and vanilla until well blended. Sprinkle flour over mixture and stir until just blended.

2. Transfer dough to a large square of plastic wrap and form into a 3- by 2-inch (7.5 by 5 cm) log. Securely close ends of plastic wrap and refrigerate for at least 1 hour or freeze for up to 1 month.

3. Preheat air fryer to 360°F (180°C). Tear a piece of foil large enough to cover the bottom of the air fryer basket with $1/2$ inch (1 cm) between the foil and the inside edge of the basket. Spray foil with cooking spray.

4. Slice cookie dough crosswise into 6 equal slices.

5. Place 3 cookies on prepared foil, spacing them 2 inches (5 cm) apart (place the remaining cookies in the refrigerator until ready to air-fry).

6. Place foil with cookies in air fryer basket. Air-fry for 5 to 8 minutes or until surface of cookies appears dry and edges are golden brown. Using a spatula, transfer cookies to a wire rack and let cool completely.

7. Repeat steps 5 and 6 with the remaining cookies.

# Air-Fried Chocolate Crème-Filled Cookies

At times there is nothing finer than the taste of a childhood favorite. You will love the flavor of this classic cookie all over again when it is encased in light, puffy dough and showered with confectioners' sugar.

**Makes 8 pastries**

**Tip**

These treats are best eaten very soon after they are air-fried.

**Variation**

An equal amount of vanilla crème-filled cookies may be used in place of the chocolate.

• *Preheat air fryer to 360°F (180°C)*

| | | |
|---|---|---|
| 1 | can (8 oz/250 g) refrigerated crescent dinner rolls | 1 |
| ½ cup | milk (dairy or nondairy) | 125 mL |
| 8 | chocolate crème-filled cookies | 8 |
| | Nonstick cooking spray | |
| | Confectioners' (icing) sugar | |

1. Remove dough from packaging, keeping it in a cylinder shape (do not unroll). Cut dough crosswise into 16 equal pieces. Using your fingertips, press each piece into a circle slightly larger than a crème-filled cookie.

2. Pour milk into a small bowl or cup. Dunk 1 cookie in milk, shaking off excess (do not soak cookie). Place cookie in the center of a dough circle. Press a second dough circle on top, pinching top and bottom dough circles together to seal. Repeat with the remaining cookies, milk and dough circles. Spray pastries with cooking spray.

3. Place half the pastries in air fryer basket, spacing them 2 inches (5 cm) apart (refrigerate the remaining pastries). Air-fry for 8 to 12 minutes or until puffed and golden brown. Transfer pastries to a wire rack and sprinkle with confectioners' sugar. Repeat with the remaining pastries. Serve warm.

# Crispy Chocolate Hazelnut Ravioli

~~~~~~~~~~~~~~~~~~~~~~~~~~~~~~~~~~~~~~~~~~~~~~~~~~~~~

**Warning: may require finger licking. These crispy on the outside and luscious on the inside bites may have only four ingredients, but they taste out of this world.**

## Makes 4 servings

### Tips

These treats are best eaten very soon after they are air-fried.

While assembling the ravioli, keep the stack of wrappers moist by covering them with a damp towel.

The ravioli can be assembled 1 day in advance. Refrigerate in an airtight container until ready to air-fry.

Use oven pads or mitts when shaking the basket.

• *Preheat air fryer to 390°F (200°C)*

| | | |
|---|---|---|
| 8 | 3-inch (7.5 cm) square wonton wrappers | 8 |
| 1 | large egg, beaten | 1 |
| ½ cup | chocolate hazelnut spread | 125 mL |
| | Nonstick cooking spray | |
| 2 tbsp | confectioners' (icing) sugar | 30 mL |

1. Place 1 wonton wrapper on work surface. Brush edges of wrapper with egg. Spoon 1 tbsp (15 mL) chocolate hazelnut spread into center of wrapper. Fold in half to form a triangle, pressing the edges to seal. Repeat with the remaining wrappers, egg and chocolate hazelnut spread.

2. Spray both sides of ravioli with cooking spray as you place them in the air fryer basket, placing them close together but not touching. Air-fry for 3 minutes, then gently shake the basket. Air-fry for 2 to 4 minutes or until golden brown. Transfer to a plate or wire rack and sprinkle with confectioners' sugar.

# Air-Fried Peanut Butter with Jelly Dipping Sauce

If you were wondering whether peanut butter and jelly could be made any better, the answer is a resounding yes! In this whimsical interpretation (based on deep-fried regional fair and carnival versions), dough is stuffed with sweetened peanut butter centers, air-fried, then dunked in a jelly sauce. It's even better than it sounds!

## Makes 8 servings

**Tip**

These treats are best eaten very soon after they are air-fried.

• *Small baking sheet, lined with parchment paper*

| | | |
|---|---|---|
| ²⁄₃ cup | creamy or crunchy peanut butter | 150 mL |
| ¹⁄₂ cup | confectioners' (icing) sugar, divided | 125 mL |
| ¹⁄₂ cup | grape jelly | 125 mL |
| 1 | can (8 oz/250 g) refrigerated crescent dinner rolls | 1 |
| | Nonstick cooking spray | |

1. In a small bowl, stir together peanut butter and half the confectioners' sugar. Drop mixture by heaping tablespoonfuls (15 mL) onto prepared baking sheet. Freeze for 30 minutes.

2. Preheat air fryer to 360°F (180°C).

3. In a small saucepan, melt jelly over low heat. Remove from heat and cover to keep warm.

4. Remove dough from packaging, keeping it in a cylinder shape (do not unroll). Cut dough crosswise into 16 equal pieces. Using your fingertips, press each piece into a circle slightly larger than a peanut butter mound.

Other nut or seed butters (such as almond butter, cashew butter or sunflower seed butter) can be used in place of the peanut butter.

Other flavors of jelly or jam (such as strawberry, raspberry or plum) can be used in place of the grape jelly.

5. Place 1 frozen peanut butter mound in the center of a dough circle. Press a second dough circle on top, pinching top and bottom dough circles together to seal. Repeat with the remaining peanut butter mounds and dough circles. Spray pastries with cooking spray.

6. Place half the pastries in air fryer basket, spacing them 2 inches (5 cm) apart (refrigerate the remaining pastries). Air-fry for 8 to 12 minutes or until puffed and golden brown. Transfer pastries to a wire rack and sprinkle with some of the remaining confectioners' sugar. Repeat with the remaining pastries and confectioners' sugar. Serve warm with melted jelly.

# Air-Fried Apple Fritters

I love any apple dessert: baked apples, apple pie, apple cake, apple dumplings — you name it. These air-fried fritters are no exception. They have a fraction of the oil and calories of the jumbo apple fritters at donut shops, but are exponentially more delicious.

### Makes 4 fritters

**Tip**

These treats are best eaten very soon after they are air-fried.

- *Preheat air fryer to 390°F (200°C)*
- *8 standard-size foil or paper muffin cup liners*

### Fritters

| | | |
|---|---|---|
| 1/2 cup | all-purpose flour | 125 mL |
| 3/4 tsp | baking powder | 3 mL |
| 1/8 tsp | salt | 0.5 mL |
| 1/8 tsp | ground nutmeg | 0.5 mL |
| 1/4 cup | granulated sugar | 60 mL |
| 1 | large egg white | 1 |
| 1/3 cup | sour cream | 75 mL |
| 1 1/2 tbsp | unsalted butter, melted | 22 mL |
| 1/2 tsp | vanilla extract | 2 mL |
| 2/3 cup | diced peeled tart-sweet apples (such as Gala, Golden Delicious or Braeburn) | 150 mL |
| | Nonstick cooking spray | |

### Glaze

| | | |
|---|---|---|
| 1/3 cup | confectioners' (icing) sugar | 75 mL |
| 1/8 tsp | ground cinnamon | 0.5 mL |
| 2 tsp | unsalted butter, melted | 10 mL |
| 1 tsp | warm water | 5 mL |

1. *Fritters:* Place one muffin cup liner inside another. Repeat to create 4 doubled liners.

2. In a small bowl, whisk together flour, baking powder, salt and nutmeg.

3. In a medium bowl, vigorously whisk sugar and egg white for 1 minute, until frothy. Whisk in sour cream, butter and vanilla. Stir in flour mixture until just blended. Gently stir in apples.

4. Divide batter equally among the doubled liners. Spray tops of fritters with cooking spray.

5. Place filled liners in air fryer basket. Air-fry for 9 to 13 minutes or until tops are golden brown and a tester inserted in the center comes out clean. Transfer to a wire rack.

6. *Glaze:* While the fritters are air-frying, in a small bowl or cup, whisk together confectioners' sugar, cinnamon, butter and water until blended and smooth.

7. Spoon glaze over warm fritters. Let cool for at least 10 minutes. Serve warm or at room temperature.

# Jelly Donut Holes

These miniature jelly-stuffed donut bites require little to no explanation. Frankly, they are far more delicious than anything available at the local donut shop.

**Makes 8 servings**

## Tips

These treats are best eaten very soon after they are air-fried.

Other ground spices, such as cardamom or ginger, may be used in place of the cinnamon. Alternatively, omit the cinnamon.

## Variation

Other flavors of jam, jelly or preserves can be used in place of strawberry. Alternatively, use an equal amount of chocolate hazelnut spread or peanut butter in its place.

- Preheat air fryer to 360°F (180°C)
- 1½-inch (4 cm) biscuit or cookie cutter

| | | |
|---|---|---|
| ¼ cup | granulated sugar | 60 mL |
| ½ tsp | ground cinnamon | 2 mL |
| 1 | can (17.3 oz/490 g) refrigerated large dinner biscuits | 1 |
| 2 tbsp | strawberry jam, jelly or preserves | 30 mL |
| | Nonstick cooking spray | |

1. In a shallow dish, combine sugar and cinnamon.

2. Remove dough from packaging and separate into biscuits. Using your fingertips or a rolling pin, press or roll each biscuit into a 3¼-inch (8 cm) circle. Using the biscuit cutter, cut 3 smaller rounds from each large circle; discard scraps.

3. Using a small sharp knife, slice each round horizontally (parallel to the cutting board) through the center, without cutting all the way through, and open like a book. Spoon ¼ tsp (1 mL) jam onto one side. Fold dough over jam and pinch edges to seal. Spray dough with cooking spray.

4. Place half the donut holes in air fryer basket, spacing them 1 inch (2.5 cm) apart (refrigerate the remaining donut holes). Air-fry for 5 to 8 minutes or until puffed and golden brown. Roll the warm donut holes in cinnamon sugar, transfer to a wire rack and let cool for at least 5 minutes before serving. Repeat with the remaining donut holes and cinnamon sugar. Serve warm or at room temperature.

# Cinnamon Churros

~~~~~~~~~~~~~~~~~~~~~~~~~~~~~~~~~~~~~~

Cinnamon sugar–coated churros — deep fried dough — are found on the streets of Mexico and Spain alike. I have had them in both places, and they are hard to beat. My streamlined version, made simple with frozen puff pastry and the air fryer, may, however, take the prize.

## Makes 18 churros

### Tips

Commercial puff pastry loses it crispness quickly, so it is best to eat the churros shortly after air-frying.

An equal amount of ground cardamom, ginger or pumpkin pie spice can be used in place of the cinnamon.

• *Preheat air fryer to 360°F (180°C)*

| | All-purpose flour | |
|---|---|---|
| 1 | sheet frozen puff pastry (half a 17.3-oz/490 g package), thawed | 1 |
| 3 tbsp | granulated sugar | 45 mL |
| ¾ tsp | ground cinnamon | 3 mL |
| 2 tbsp | unsalted butter, melted and cooled slightly | 30 mL |

1. On a lightly floured work surface, unfold pastry sheet. Cut sheet in half lengthwise. Cut each half crosswise into 1-inch (2.5 cm) wide strips.

2. Place 4 to 5 strips in air fryer basket, spacing them 1 inch (2.5 cm) apart (refrigerate the remaining strips). Air-fry for 10 to 15 minutes or until puffed and golden brown.

3. Meanwhile, in a shallow dish, combine sugar and cinnamon.

4. Remove pastry strips from air fryer. Brush each strip with butter and gently roll in cinnamon sugar. Place churros on a wire rack and let cool for at least 5 minutes.

5. Repeat steps 2 to 4 with the remaining pastry strips, butter and cinnamon sugar. Serve warm or at room temperature.

# Funnel Cakes

Deep-fried funnel cakes are a consistent feature at outdoor festivals and fairs in my adopted state of Texas, and the line to get one is invariably deep. With this easy recipe, you won't have to wait long at all to have one fresh from the (air) fryer. Dusting them with ample amounts of confectioners' sugar is a must!

**Makes
6 funnel cakes**

**Tip**
These treats are best eaten very soon after they are air-fried.

| | | |
|---|---|---|
| 1/2 cup | water | 125 mL |
| 1/4 cup | unsalted butter, cut into pieces | 60 mL |
| 1/8 tsp | salt | 0.5 mL |
| 1/2 cup | all-purpose flour | 125 mL |
| 2 | large eggs | 2 |
| | Nonstick cooking spray | |
| | Confectioners' (icing) sugar | |

1. In a small saucepan, combine water, butter and salt. Bring to a boil over medium-high heat. Reduce heat to medium and vigorously stir in flour. Cook, stirring, until mixture forms a ball. Remove from heat and let cool for 10 minutes.

2. Add eggs, one at a time, vigorously stirring with a wooden spoon after each addition.

3. Preheat air fryer to 390°F (200°C). Tear a piece of foil large enough to cover the bottom of the air fryer basket with 1/2 inch (1 cm) between the foil and the inside edge of the basket. Spray foil with cooking spray.

4. Spoon dough into a large sealable plastic bag. Using scissors, snip a 1/4-inch (0.5 cm) hole in one corner of the bag. Pipe two 3-inch (7.5 cm) circles on prepared foil, spacing them evenly. Fill in circles with swirls and crisscrosses of dough, to resemble funnel cakes.

5. Place foil with dough in air fryer basket. Air-fry for 7 to 11 minutes or until puffed and golden brown. Transfer funnel cakes to a wire rack and generously sprinkle with confectioners' sugar.

6. Repeat steps 5 and 6 with the remaining dough. Serve warm.

# Air-Fried Candy Bars

Deep-fried candy bars began appearing across the pond in England more than a decade ago, and it wasn't long before North Americans followed suit. Now you can try this extravagance with ease using your air fryer, candy bar minis and frozen puff pastry. Prepare to be thrilled.

## Makes 25 pieces

### Tips
The miniature muffin liners help to keep any leaking melted chocolate away from the air fryer basket.

Commercial puff pastry loses it crispness quickly, so it is best to eat the pastries shortly after baking.

### Storage Tip
The filled pastries can be fully assembled and refrigerated, loosely covered in plastic wrap, for up to 1 day before air-frying. Alternatively, freeze the assembled pastries on a baking sheet, then store the frozen pastries in an airtight container in the freezer for up to 2 months. Thaw in the refrigerator overnight before air-frying.

- *Preheat air fryer to 360°F (180°C)*
- *25 miniature foil or paper muffin liners*

| | All-purpose flour | |
|---|---|---|
| 1 | sheet frozen puff pastry (half a 17.3-oz/490 g package), thawed | 1 |
| 25 | miniature (square) chocolate caramel and peanut nougat candy bars, unwrapped | 25 |
| | Confectioners' (icing) sugar (optional) | |

1. On a lightly floured work surface, unfold pastry sheet. With a lightly floured rolling pin, roll into a 10-inch (25 cm) square. Cut into twenty-five 2-inch (5 cm) squares.

2. Lightly brush the edges of each square with water. Place 1 candy bar piece in middle of each square. Fold corners up over candy and firmly press corners together to seal. Place pastries, seam side down, in muffin liners.

3. Place 6 or 7 pastries in air fryer basket, leaving space in between (refrigerate the remaining pastries). Air-fry for 8 to 12 minutes or until pastry is puffed and golden brown. Using a spatula, carefully transfer pastries to a wire rack and let cool for at least 5 minutes before serving. Repeat with the remaining pastries. Sprinkle with confectioners' sugar, if desired.

# Whiskey Bread Pudding

A whiskey-spiked butterscotch sauce is the perfect counterpoint to creamy, chocolate-flecked bread pudding.

**Tip**

An equal amount of semisweet, milk or white chocolate chunks or chips can be used in place of the bittersweet chocolate.

- 6-inch (15 cm) round metal cake pan, sprayed with nonstick cooking spray

**Pudding**

| | | |
|---|---|---|
| 2 | thick slices soft French- or Italian-style bakery bread, torn into small pieces | 2 |
| 2 tbsp | bittersweet (dark) chocolate chunks or chips | 30 mL |
| 1 | large egg | 1 |
| 2½ tbsp | granulated sugar | 37 mL |
| ⅛ tsp | salt | 0.5 mL |
| ½ cup | light (5%) cream | 125 mL |
| 2 tsp | whiskey or bourbon | 10 mL |

**Sauce**

| | | |
|---|---|---|
| 1 tbsp | packed light brown sugar | 15 mL |
| Pinch | salt | Pinch |
| 1 tbsp | unsalted butter | 15 mL |
| 1 tbsp | whiskey or bourbon | 15 mL |
| 1 tsp | light (5%) cream | 5 mL |

1. *Pudding:* Place bread in prepared cake pan. Sprinkle with chocolate chunks.

2. In a small bowl, whisk egg until blended. Whisk in sugar, salt, cream and whiskey until blended. Pour evenly over bread in pan. Place a piece of parchment or waxed paper over pan and press down to help bread absorb liquid. Let stand for 15 minutes.

3. Meanwhile, preheat air fryer to 330°F (160°C).

**Tip**

An equal amount of milk can be used in place of the cream.

4. Remove parchment and place pan in air fryer basket. Air-fry for 13 to 16 minutes or until bubbling and golden brown. Transfer to a wire rack and let cool for 10 minutes.

5. *Sauce:* In a small skillet, combine brown sugar, salt, butter, whiskey and cream. Heat over medium heat, stirring, until butter and sugar are melted. Drizzle over bread pudding.

# Air-Fried Mexican Ice Cream Balls

Here, balls of vanilla ice cream are rolled in a crispy cinnamon and butter coating, mimicking Mexican deep-fried ice cream to delicious effect. More is more with this dessert, so strongly consider some or all of the suggested toppings.

**Makes 3 servings**

**Tip**

An equal amount of crisp rice cereal can be used in place of the corn flakes cereal.

- Two 9-inch (23 cm) pie pans, lined with parchment paper or plastic wrap

| | | |
|---|---|---|
| 1 pint | vanilla ice cream | 500 mL |
| | Nonstick cooking spray | |
| 3 cups | corn flakes cereal, finely crushed | 750 mL |
| 1 tbsp | granulated sugar | 15 mL |
| 1 tsp | ground cinnamon | 5 mL |
| 1 tbsp | unsalted butter, melted | 15 mL |

**Suggested Accompaniments**

Caramel sauce or chocolate sauce
Whipped cream
Maraschino cherries

1. Working quickly, scoop ice cream into 3 equal balls on a prepared pie pan. Place pan in freezer and freeze for at least 2 hours, until ice cream is very firm, or up to 24 hours.

2. Preheat air fryer to 330°F (160°C). Tear a piece of foil large enough to cover the bottom of the air fryer basket with $\frac{1}{2}$ inch (1 cm) between the foil and the inside edge of the basket. Spray foil with cooking spray. Place prepared foil in air fryer basket.

3. In a medium bowl, stir together cereal, sugar, cinnamon and butter until combined.

## Tip

Other flavors of ice cream can be used in place of the vanilla.

4. Spread cereal mixture in prepared air fryer basket and spray with cooking spray. Air-fry for 3 to 6 minutes or until golden and fragrant. Transfer to a shallow dish and let cool completely.

5. Wearing kitchen gloves and working with 1 ball at a time (leave the remaining balls in the freezer), roll each ice cream ball in cereal mixture until well coated. Place in the other prepared pie pan and freeze for at least 30 minutes, until firm, or up to 24 hours. Serve with any of the suggested accompaniments, as desired.

# Air-Fried Banana Splits

Humble bananas are anything but in this decadent dessert. The banana pieces are given a cinnamon-sugar coating, air-fried and finally topped with vanilla ice cream. It's heavenly.

## Makes 4 servings

### Variation

*Gluten-Free Banana Splits:* Replace the panko with an equal amount of crushed gluten-free corn flakes cereal.

• *Preheat air fryer to 390°F (200°C)*

| | | |
|---|---|---|
| ¼ cup | cornstarch, sifted | 60 mL |
| 2 | large firm-ripe bananas, peeled and quartered crosswise | 2 |
| 1 cup | panko (Japanese bread crumbs) | 250 mL |
| 2 tbsp | granulated sugar | 30 mL |
| 1 tsp | ground cinnamon | 5 mL |
| 1 | large egg | 1 |
| | Nonstick cooking spray | |
| 1 pint | vanilla ice cream or frozen yogurt | 500 mL |

### Suggested Accompaniments

Chocolate, caramel or strawberry ice cream sauce

Maraschino cherries

Chopped toasted nuts (such as pecans, peanuts or walnuts)

Whipped cream

1. Place cornstarch in a large sealable plastic bag. Add bananas, seal bag and gently toss until coated.

2. Spread panko in a shallow dish.

3. In a small cup, combine sugar and cinnamon.

4. In another shallow dish, whisk egg.

5. Working with 1 banana piece at a time, remove from cornstarch, shaking off excess. Dip in egg, shaking off excess, then dredge in panko, gently pressing to adhere. Spray with cooking spray and sprinkle with cinnamon sugar. As they are sprinkled, place bananas in air fryer basket, leaving space in between.

6. Air-fry for 5 to 7 minutes or until coating is golden brown. Serve with ice cream and any of the suggested accompaniments, as desired.

# Caramel Corn

Caramel corn does not need reinvention, but there's nothing wrong with a revamp to make it extra-easy to prepare. The even heat flow of the air fryer ensures perfectly crisp (not sticky) caramel corn with minimal effort and cleanup.

## Makes 2 servings

### Tips

An equal amount of pure maple syrup, brown rice syrup or corn syrup can be used in place of the honey.

Use oven pads or mitts when shaking the basket.

### Variation

*Sesame Ginger Caramel Corn:* Replace 1/2 tbsp (7 mL) of the butter with toasted (dark) sesame oil and add 1/2 tsp (2 mL) ground ginger with the vanilla and salt.

• *Preheat air fryer to 300°F (140°C)*

|  | Nonstick cooking spray | |
| --- | --- | --- |
| 2 cups | popped popcorn | 500 mL |
| 1 tbsp | packed dark brown sugar | 15 mL |
| 1 1/2 tbsp | unsalted butter, cut into pieces | 22 mL |
| 1 tbsp | liquid honey | 15 mL |
| 1/4 tsp | vanilla extract | 1 mL |
| 1/8 tsp | salt | 0.5 mL |

1. Tear a piece of foil large enough to cover the bottom of the air fryer basket with 1/2 inch (1 cm) between the foil and the inside edge of the basket. Spray foil with cooking spray. Place prepared foil in air fryer basket.

2. Place popcorn in a medium bowl.

3. In a small skillet, combine brown sugar, butter and honey. Bring to a boil over medium heat, stirring. Remove from heat and stir in vanilla and salt. Immediately pour over popcorn, stirring to coat.

4. Spread popcorn in prepared air fryer basket. Air-fry for 8 to 12 minutes, shaking the basket once or twice, until crisp. Remove from air fryer and let cool completely.

# Air-Fried Whiskey and Cola

Air-fry a beverage? Absolutely, and you needn't be a magician to do it. The trick depends on combining whiskey with vanilla wafer crumbs and toasted pecans, shaping the mixture into balls, and then drizzling with a cola syrup after air-frying. Prepare to be charmed.

## Makes about 10 pieces

### Tips

An equal amount of brown rice syrup or corn syrup can be used in place of the honey.

Two large egg whites can be used in place of the whole egg.

• Preheat air fryer to 390°F (200°C)

| | | |
|---|---|---|
| 1/2 cup | cola | 125 mL |
| 4 tsp | granulated sugar | 20 mL |
| 6 oz | vanilla wafers, finely crushed, divided | 175 g |
| 1/4 cup | finely chopped toasted pecans | 60 mL |
| 3 tbsp | confectioners' (icing) sugar | 45 mL |
| 2 tsp | unsweetened cocoa powder | 10 mL |
| 2 tbsp | whiskey or bourbon | 30 mL |
| 2 tsp | liquid honey | 10 mL |
| 1/4 cup | all-purpose flour | 60 mL |
| 1 | large egg, lightly beaten | 1 |
| | Nonstick cooking spray | |

1. In a small saucepan, bring cola and granulated sugar to a boil over medium-high heat. Boil for 1 minute, then reduce heat to low and simmer, stirring occasionally, for 3 to 5 minutes or until mixture is syrupy. Remove from heat and let cool.

2. In a medium bowl, stir together half the vanilla wafers, pecans, confectioners' sugar and cocoa powder. Stir in whiskey and honey until blended. Form mixture into 1-inch (2.5 cm) balls.

3. Spread flour in a shallow dish.

4. Spread the remaining vanilla wafers in another shallow dish.

5. In a third shallow dish, whisk egg.

**Tip**

Air fryers become very hot, especially when heated to maximum temperature. Use oven pads or mitts when shaking the basket.

6. Working with 1 ball at a time, roll in flour until lightly coated. Dip in egg, shaking off excess, then gently press into wafers. As they are coated, spray balls with cooking spray and place in air fryer basket, leaving space in between. Discard any excess egg and wafer crumbs.

7. Air-fry for 2 minutes, then gently shake the basket. Air-fry for 1 to 4 minutes or until coating is golden brown. Carefully transfer balls to a serving plate and drizzle with cola syrup. Serve warm.

# Sauces, Dips and More

# Sriracha Ketchup

In this easy and versatile condiment recipe, everyday ketchup is transformed into a piquant, boast-worthy dipping sauce that also happens to be fantastic on hamburgers and hot dogs.

### Makes about 1/2 cup (125 mL)

| | | |
|---|---|---|
| 1/2 cup | ketchup | 125 mL |
| 2 tsp | Sriracha | 10 mL |
| 1 1/2 tsp | freshly squeezed lime juice | 7 mL |
| 1/2 tsp | unseasoned rice vinegar | 2 mL |

1. In a small bowl, whisk together ketchup, Sriracha, lime juice and vinegar until blended.

## Tips

White or apple cider vinegar can be used in place of the rice vinegar.

For a more pronounced lime flavor, add 1 tsp (5 mL) finely grated lime zest with the lime juice.

You can use 1 1/2 tsp (7 mL) hot pepper sauce (such as Tabasco) in place of the Sriracha.

## Storage Tip

Refrigerate the ketchup in an airtight container for up to 1 month.

# Creamy Horseradish Ketchup

If you are looking for the perfect all-in-one spread, dip and sauce, this creamy, spicy, sweet ketchup is it.

**Makes about ¹⁄₂ cup (125 mL)**

**Storage Tip**
Refrigerate the ketchup in an airtight container for up to 1 month.

| | | |
|---|---|---|
| ¹⁄₃ cup | ketchup | 75 mL |
| 2¹⁄₂ tbsp | mayonnaise | 37 mL |
| 1 tbsp | prepared horseradish | 15 mL |

**1.** In a small bowl, whisk together ketchup, mayonnaise and horseradish until blended.

### Variation

*Horseradish Chili Sauce:* Replace the ketchup with an equal amount of chili sauce.

# Horseradish Sauce

Spicy horseradish is an unusually good accent for the natural sweetness of shrimp.

**Makes about ²⁄₃ cup (150 mL)**

**Tip**
An equal amount of white wine vinegar can be used in place of the lemon juice.

**Storage Tip**
Refrigerate the sauce in an airtight container for up to 3 days.

| | | |
|---|---|---|
| ¹⁄₂ cup | plain Greek yogurt | 125 mL |
| 1 tbsp | prepared horseradish | 15 mL |
| 1 tbsp | freshly squeezed lemon juice | 15 mL |
| 1 tsp | Dijon mustard | 5 mL |
| | Salt and freshly cracked black pepper | |

**1.** In a small bowl, whisk together yogurt, horseradish, lemon juice and mustard. Season to taste with salt and pepper.

# Redeye Gravy

Redeye gravy is a traditional recipe from the American South, typically made with ham drippings and leftover coffee. Here, butter takes the place of drippings and fresh coffee gives an extra dose of flavor.

**Makes about ²/₃ cup (150 mL)**

### Tip

An equal amount of light (fancy) molasses can be used in place of the brown sugar.

### Variation

*Bacon Redeye Gravy:* Replace the ham with an equal amount of finely chopped cooked bacon.

| | | |
|---|---|---|
| 1 cup | hot strong brewed coffee | 250 mL |
| 1½ tbsp | packed dark brown sugar | 22 mL |
| 1 tbsp | unsalted butter | 15 mL |
| 2 tbsp | finely chopped smoked ham | 30 mL |
| | Salt and freshly cracked pepper | |

1. In a small bowl or cup, stir together coffee and brown sugar. Let cool.

2. In a small saucepan, melt butter over medium heat. Add ham and cook, stirring, for 4 to 5 minutes or until ham is browned and somewhat crispy. Add coffee mixture, stirring to loosen particles from bottom; bring to a boil. Boil, stirring occasionally, for 10 minutes or until reduced by about one-third. Season to taste with salt and pepper. Serve immediately.

# Easy Marinara Sauce

With a rich, home-style flavor punctuated by garlic, basil and balsamic vinegar, this simple marinara sauce is an any-day and everyday winner.

**Makes about 1¹/₂ cups (375 mL)**

| | | |
|---|---|---|
| 2 tbsp | olive oil | 30 mL |
| 2 | cloves garlic, minced | 2 |
| 1¹/₂ tsp | dried basil | 7 mL |
| 1 | can (14 oz/398 mL) tomato purée | 1 |
| 2 tbsp | tomato paste | 30 mL |
| 2 tsp | balsamic vinegar | 10 mL |
| | Salt and freshly cracked black pepper | |

## Tip

If you don't have fresh garlic on hand, you can use 1 tsp (5 mL) garlic powder in its place.

## Storage Tip

Refrigerate the sauce in an airtight container for up to 1 week.

## Variations

*Spicy Marinara Sauce:* Add ¹/₄ tsp (1 mL) hot pepper flakes with the garlic in step 1.

*Chunky Marinara Sauce:* Add ³/₄ cup (175 mL) drained canned petite diced tomatoes with the tomato purée in step 2.

*Fresh Basil Marinara Sauce:* Omit the dried basil. Stir in ¹/₄ cup (60 mL) chopped fresh basil before seasoning with salt and pepper.

1. In a medium saucepan, heat oil over medium heat. Add garlic and cook, stirring, for 1 minute.

2. Stir in basil, tomato purée, tomato paste and vinegar. Reduce heat to low and cook, stirring occasionally, for 10 minutes. Season to taste with salt and pepper.

# Spicy Cocktail Sauce

The perfect partner to so many air-fried foods, this zesty sauce is as impressive and delicious as it is easy to make.

**Makes about ²/₃ cup (150 mL)**

**Tip**

An equal amount of red or white wine vinegar can be used in place of the lemon juice.

**Storage Tip**

Refrigerate the sauce in an airtight container for up to 2 weeks.

**Variation**

*Wasabi Cocktail Sauce:* Replace the horseradish with an equal amount of prepared wasabi, and replace the lemon juice with lime juice.

| | | |
|---|---|---|
| ½ cup | ketchup | 125 mL |
| 1 tbsp | prepared horseradish | 15 mL |
| 1 tsp | freshly squeezed lemon juice | 5 mL |
| ½ tsp | Worcestershire sauce | 2 mL |
| | Salt and freshly cracked black pepper | |

1. In a small bowl, whisk together ketchup, horseradish, lemon juice and Worcestershire sauce. Season to taste with salt and pepper.

# Spicy Mustard Sauce

Packed with bold flavor, this easy mustard sauce is terrific with a wide range of appetizers, but especially with crab cakes.

**Makes about ²/₃ cup (150 mL)**

## Tip
An equal amount of lemon juice can be used in place of the white wine vinegar.

## Storage Tip
Refrigerate the sauce in an airtight container for up to 3 days.

| | | |
|---|---|---|
| 3 tbsp | mayonnaise | 45 mL |
| 2 tbsp | plain Greek yogurt | 30 mL |
| 1 tbsp | whole-grain or Dijon mustard | 15 mL |
| 1½ tsp | white wine vinegar | 7 mL |
| ⅛ tsp | cayenne pepper | 0.5 mL |
| | Salt and freshly cracked black pepper | |

1. In a small bowl, whisk together mayonnaise, yogurt, mustard, vinegar and cayenne. Season to taste with salt and pepper.

# Romesco Sauce

A Spanish sauce made from roasted red peppers and almonds, Romesco is terrific as a sauce for fried shrimp and chicken fingers, as a dunk for french fries or as a spread for burgers and sandwiches.

### Makes about 1½ cups (375 mL)

## Tips

To toast the slivered almonds, preheat the air fryer to 350°F (180°C). Spread the almonds in a single layer in a 6-inch (15 cm) round metal cake pan. Air-fry for 4 to 6 minutes or until fragrant and golden. Let cool completely before using.

An equal amount of red or white wine vinegar can be used in place of the sherry vinegar.

## Storage Tip

Refrigerate the sauce in an airtight container for up to 1 week.

• *Food processor*

| | | |
|---|---|---|
| 1 | clove garlic | 1 |
| ½ cup | slivered almonds, toasted (see tip, at left) | 125 mL |
| 1 tsp | smoked paprika | 5 mL |
| 1 cup | chopped drained roasted red bell peppers | 250 mL |
| ⅓ cup | extra virgin olive oil | 75 mL |
| 1½ tbsp | sherry vinegar | 22 mL |
| 1 tbsp | tomato paste | 15 mL |
| | Salt and freshly ground black pepper | |

1. In food processor, pulse garlic and almonds until finely chopped. Add paprika, roasted peppers, oil, vinegar and tomato paste; process until smooth.

2. Transfer to a small bowl and season to taste with salt and pepper.

# Spicy Apricot Wing Sauce

Lemon juice and Worcestershire sauce amp up the flavor of apricot jam in this easy wing sauce, while horseradish gives it some kick.

**Makes about ¹/₂ cup (125 mL)**

| | | |
|---|---|---|
| ¹/₃ cup | apricot jam or preserves | 75 mL |
| 1 tbsp | prepared horseradish | 15 mL |
| 1 tbsp | freshly squeezed lemon juice | 15 mL |
| 2 tsp | Worcestershire sauce | 10 mL |

**Tip**

An equal amount of white vinegar, apple cider vinegar or unseasoned rice vinegar can be used in place of the lemon juice.

**Storage Tip**

Refrigerate the sauce in an airtight container for up to 1 week.

1. In a small bowl or cup, whisk together jam, horseradish, lemon juice and Worcestershire sauce until blended.

# Lemon Honey Wing Sauce

Honey and a double dose of lemon (both the zest and the juice) add up to a lick-your-fingers wing sauce.

**Makes about ¹/₄ cup (60 mL)**

| | | |
|---|---|---|
| ¹/₂ tsp | finely grated lemon zest | 2 mL |
| 2 tbsp | freshly squeezed lemon juice | 30 mL |
| 1¹/₂ tbsp | liquid honey | 22 mL |
| 1 tbsp | soy sauce | 15 mL |

**Storage Tip**

Refrigerate the sauce in an airtight container for up to 1 week.

1. In a small bowl or cup, whisk together lemon zest, lemon juice, honey and soy sauce until blended.

# Orange Sweet-and-Sour Sauce

It takes no more than a splash each of apple cider vinegar and soy sauce to reconfigure orange marmalade into a boldly flavored sweet-and-sour sauce.

**Makes about
¹/₂ cup (125 mL)**

### Tip
White or unseasoned rice vinegar can be used in place of the cider vinegar.

### Storage Tip
Refrigerate the sauce in an airtight container for up to 1 week.

| | | |
|---|---|---|
| ¹/₃ cup | orange marmalade | 75 mL |
| 1¹/₂ tbsp | apple cider vinegar | 22 mL |
| 1 tbsp | soy sauce | 15 mL |

**1.** In a small bowl or cup, whisk together marmalade, vinegar and soy sauce until blended.

### Variation
*Spicy Sweet-and-Sour Sauce:* Add 2 tsp (10 mL) Sriracha or ¹/₄ tsp (1 mL) hot pepper sauce.

# Hoisin Glaze

Hoisin sauce adds a deep, caramelized flavor to this addictive glaze.

**Makes about
¹/₂ cup (125 mL)**

### Storage Tip
Refrigerate the sauce in an airtight container for up to 3 days.

| | | |
|---|---|---|
| 2 | cloves garlic, minced | 2 |
| ¹/₂ tsp | ground ginger | 2 mL |
| ¹/₄ cup | hoisin sauce | 60 mL |
| 2 tbsp | unseasoned rice vinegar | 30 mL |
| 1 tbsp | soy sauce | 15 mL |
| 1 tsp | toasted (dark) sesame oil | 5 mL |

**1.** In a small bowl or cup, whisk together garlic, ginger, hoisin sauce, vinegar, soy sauce and sesame oil until blended.

# Mango Avocado Salsa

In this festive salsa, creamy avocado and tropical mango take the place of tomatoes. Pair it with everything from shrimp to chicken to chips.

**Makes about 1¹⁄₂ cups (375 mL)**

**Storage Tip**
Refrigerate the salsa in an airtight container for up to 1 day.

**Variation**
Replace the cilantro with an equal amount of fresh mint leaves.

| 1 | small firm-ripe Hass avocado, diced | 1 |
| ¾ cup | chopped fresh or thawed frozen mango | 175 mL |
| ½ cup | packed fresh cilantro leaves, chopped | 125 mL |
| ¼ cup | finely chopped red onion | 60 mL |
| 1 tsp | minced jalapeño pepper | 5 mL |
| ¼ tsp | salt | 1 mL |
| 1 tbsp | freshly squeezed lime juice | 15 mL |

**1.** In a small bowl, combine avocado, mango, cilantro, onion, jalapeño, salt and lime juice.

# Mint Chimichurri

Chimichurri is a bold South American sauce made from herbs, garlic, vinegar and oil. Parsley and cilantro are used most often, but fresh mint makes a vibrant variation that is especially fine alongside lamb.

## Makes about ³/₄ cup (175 mL)

## Tips

White wine vinegar can be used in place of the red wine vinegar.

An equal amount of granulated sugar can be used in place of the honey.

## Storage Tip

Refrigerate the chimichurri in an airtight container for up to 3 days.

## Variations

*Cilantro Chimichurri:* Omit the honey and replace the mint with an equal amount of packed fresh cilantro leaves.

*Parsley Chimichurri:* Omit the honey and replace the mint with an equal amount of packed fresh flat-leaf (Italian) parsley leaves.

• *Food processor*

| | | |
|---|---|---|
| 1 | clove garlic | 1 |
| 1 cup | packed fresh mint leaves | 250 mL |
| ¼ tsp | salt | 1 mL |
| ⅛ tsp | freshly ground black pepper | 0.5 mL |
| ¼ cup | olive oil | 60 mL |
| 2 tbsp | red wine vinegar | 30 mL |
| 2 tsp | liquid honey | 10 mL |

**1.** In food processor, combine garlic, mint, salt, pepper, oil, vinegar and honey; process until blended and smooth.

# Greek Feta Dipping Sauce

You will want to dunk just about everything into this boldly flavored, creamy, tangy and fresh feta sauce.

**Makes about
³/₄ cup (175 mL)**

## Tips

Chopped fresh flat-leaf (Italian) parsley or dill can be used in place of the mint.

An equal amount of chives can be used in place of the green onions.

## Storage Tip

Refrigerate the dipping sauce in an airtight container for up to 3 days.

| | | |
|---|---|---|
| 2 tbsp | finely chopped green onions | 30 mL |
| 1 tbsp | chopped fresh mint | 15 mL |
| ¼ cup | crumbled feta cheese | 60 mL |
| ¼ cup | plain Greek-style yogurt | 60 mL |
| 1 tsp | finely grated lemon zest | 5 mL |
| 2 tbsp | freshly squeezed lemon juice | 30 mL |
| 2 tbsp | extra virgin olive oil | 30 mL |
| | Salt and freshly cracked black pepper | |

1. In a small bowl, stir together green onions, mint, feta, yogurt, lemon zest, lemon juice and oil until blended. Season to taste with salt and pepper.

# Cilantro Lime Dipping Sauce

This showy sauce has much to offer: creaminess from the yogurt and mayonnaise, freshness from the cilantro and lime, and zip from the garlic and pepper.

### Makes about 1 cup (250 mL)

**Tip**

An equal amount of sour cream can be used in place of the Greek yogurt.

**Storage Tip**

Refrigerate the dipping sauce in an airtight container for up to 3 days.

| | | |
|---|---|---|
| 1 | clove garlic, mashed | 1 |
| 2 tbsp | chopped fresh cilantro | 30 mL |
| ⅔ cup | plain Greek-style yogurt | 150 mL |
| ¼ cup | mayonnaise | 60 mL |
| 1 tsp | finely grated lime zest | 5 mL |
| 1 tbsp | freshly squeezed lime juice | 15 mL |
| | Salt and freshly cracked black pepper | |

1. In a small bowl, whisk together garlic, cilantro, yogurt, mayonnaise, lime zest and lime juice. Season to taste with salt and pepper.

# Citrus Soy Dipping Sauce

**Looking for a great sauce to serve with all of your favorite Asian-inspired appetizers? This easy-to-prepare, citrusy recipe is always a winner.**

### Makes about ⅓ cup (75 mL)

## Tips

An equal amount of liquid honey or packed brown sugar can be used in place of the granulated sugar.

Freshly squeezed lemon juice can be used in place of the lime juice.

For a milder sauce, omit the hot pepper sauce.

## Storage Tip

Refrigerate the dipping sauce in an airtight container for up to 1 week.

| | | |
|---|---|---|
| 2 tsp | granulated sugar | 10 mL |
| 2 tbsp | soy sauce | 30 mL |
| 2 tbsp | freshly squeezed orange juice | 30 mL |
| 1 tbsp | freshly squeezed lime juice | 15 mL |
| 2 tsp | toasted (dark) sesame oil | 10 mL |
| ¼ tsp | hot pepper sauce (such as Tabasco) | 1 mL |

1. In a small bowl, whisk together sugar, soy sauce, orange juice, lime juice, sesame oil and hot pepper sauce until sugar is dissolved.

# Honey Mustard Dipping Sauce

Despite the humble assemblage of pantry ingredients, this creamy honey mustard sauce may well become your favorite from this chapter.

**Makes about 2/3 cup (150 mL)**

### Tip
Whole-grain or brown mustard can be used in place of the Dijon mustard.

### Storage Tip
Refrigerate the dipping sauce in an airtight container for up to 2 weeks.

| | | |
|---|---|---|
| ¼ cup | mayonnaise | 60 mL |
| ¼ cup | Dijon mustard | 60 mL |
| 2 tbsp | liquid honey | 30 mL |
| | Salt and freshly ground black pepper | |

1. In a small bowl, whisk together mayonnaise, mustard and honey until blended. Season to taste with salt and pepper.

# Spicy Peanut Dipping Sauce

**Here, peanut butter eschews jelly to become a Thai-inspired sensation.**

**Tip**
You can use ¾ tsp (3 mL) ground ginger in place of the fresh ginger.

**Storage Tip**
Refrigerate the dipping sauce in an airtight container for up to 5 days.

| | | |
|---|---|---|
| 1 | clove garlic, minced | 1 |
| 2 tsp | minced gingerroot | 10 mL |
| 1½ tsp | packed light brown sugar | 7 mL |
| ⅓ cup | ready-to-use chicken broth | 75 mL |
| ¼ cup | creamy peanut butter | 60 mL |
| 1 tbsp | freshly squeezed lime juice | 15 mL |
| 1½ tsp | soy sauce | 7 mL |
| ¼ tsp | hot pepper sauce (such as Tabasco) | 1 mL |

**1.** In a small saucepan, combine garlic, ginger, brown sugar, broth, peanut butter, lime juice, soy sauce and hot pepper sauce. Bring to a boil over medium heat, whisking to combine. Reduce heat and simmer for 2 to 3 minutes or until slightly thickened. Remove from heat, transfer to a small heatproof bowl and let cool to room temperature.

# Asian Dipping Sauce

One of the things I love about soy sauce is its versatility. Here, it shines in a quick and easy dipping sauce accented with nutty sesame, tart vinegar and a hint of sweetness.

**Makes about ⅓ cup (75 mL)**

## Tips

White or apple cider vinegar can be used in place of the rice vinegar.

An equal amount of sherry or unsweetened apple juice can be used in place of the mirin.

## Storage Tip

Refrigerate the dipping sauce in an airtight container for up to 1 week.

| | | |
|---|---|---|
| 1 tbsp | granulated sugar | 15 mL |
| 1 tsp | toasted sesame seeds (optional) | 5 mL |
| 3 tbsp | soy sauce | 45 mL |
| 1 tbsp | mirin (sweet Asian wine) | 15 mL |
| 2 tsp | unseasoned rice vinegar | 10 mL |
| 1 tsp | toasted (dark) sesame oil | 5 mL |

1. In a small bowl, stir together sugar, sesame seeds (if using), soy sauce, mirin, vinegar and sesame oil until sugar is dissolved.

# Creamy Garlic and Herb Dip

Once puréed until smooth, the combination of cottage cheese and buttermilk makes a silky-smooth dip that tastes rich despite being light. Here, the combination is pepped up with fresh herbs, lemon and garlic.

**Makes about 1 cup (250 mL)**

**Tip**

An equal amount of plain yogurt (not Greek-style) can be used in place of the buttermilk.

**Storage Tip**

Refrigerate the dip in an airtight container for up to 3 days.

• *Food processor*

| | | |
|---|---|---|
| 1 | clove garlic, roughly chopped | 1 |
| ¼ cup | packed fresh flat-leaf (Italian) parsley leaves | 60 mL |
| 2 tbsp | chopped fresh chives | 30 mL |
| 1 tsp | freshly grated lemon zest | 5 mL |
| ¼ tsp | salt | 1 mL |
| ⅛ tsp | freshly ground black pepper | 0.5 mL |
| ¾ cup | cottage cheese | 175 mL |
| ¼ cup | buttermilk | 60 mL |

**1.** In food processor, combine garlic, parsley, chives, lemon zest, salt, pepper, cottage cheese and buttermilk; process until smooth.

# Herbaceous Green Goddess Dip

Believed to have been invented in San Francisco during the roaring 1920s, this verdant dip is as fresh and modern as ever.

**Makes about 1¼ cups (300 mL)**

**Tip**
White or apple cider vinegar can be used in place of the white wine vinegar.

**Storage Tip**
Refrigerate the dip in an airtight container for up to 3 days.

- Food processor

| | | |
|---|---|---|
| 1 cup | packed fresh basil leaves | 250 mL |
| ½ cup | packed fresh flat-leaf (Italian) parsley leaves | 125 mL |
| ½ cup | coarsely chopped green onions | 125 mL |
| ¼ tsp | freshly ground black pepper | 1 mL |
| ½ cup | plain Greek-style yogurt | 125 mL |
| ½ cup | mayonnaise | 125 mL |
| 2 tsp | white wine vinegar | 10 mL |
| 1 tsp | Asian fish sauce (optional) | 5 mL |
| | Salt | |

1. In food processor, combine basil, parsley, green onions, pepper, yogurt, mayonnaise, vinegar and fish sauce (if using); process until smooth.

2. Transfer to a bowl and season to taste with salt.

# Bubbling Artichoke Dip

When mixed into a creamy, cheesy base and air-fried until bubbly, artichokes become a fail-proof crowd-pleaser.

**Makes about 1¼ cups (300 mL)**

## Tips

For a milder dip, omit the hot pepper sauce.

You can use 1 cup (250 mL) drained canned artichoke hearts (from a 15-oz/425 mL can) in place of the frozen artichoke hearts.

- Preheat air fryer to 350°F (180°C)
- Food processor
- 6-inch (15 cm) round metal cake pan, sprayed with nonstick cooking spray

| | | |
|---|---|---|
| 1 | clove garlic, roughly chopped | 1 |
| ¼ tsp | salt | 1 mL |
| ⅛ tsp | freshly ground black pepper | 0.5 mL |
| ⅓ cup | cottage cheese | 75 mL |
| ¼ cup | freshly grated Parmesan cheese | 60 mL |
| 3 tbsp | mayonnaise | 45 mL |
| 2 tsp | freshly squeezed lemon juice | 10 mL |
| ¼ tsp | hot pepper sauce (such as Tabasco) | 1 mL |
| 1 | package (9 oz/255 g) frozen artichoke hearts, thawed and chopped | 1 |

1. In food processor, combine garlic, salt, pepper, cottage cheese, Parmesan, mayonnaise, lemon juice and hot pepper sauce; process until smooth. Add artichokes and pulse once or twice, just to combine. Scrape mixture into prepared pan.

2. Place pan in air fryer basket. Air-fry for 20 to 25 minutes or until artichoke mixture is hot and begins to brown. Serve warm.

# Creamy Chipotle Dip

Chipotle peppers are smoked jalapeños, and they have a deep, unmistakable flavor. Here, they star in a quick and creamy dip.

**Makes about 1 cup (250 mL)**

**Tip**

You can use 1 tsp (5 mL) chipotle chile powder in place of the canned chile.

**Storage Tip**

Refrigerate the dip in an airtight container for up to 1 week.

| | | |
|---|---|---|
| 1 tbsp | chopped canned chipotle chile pepper in adobo sauce, seeds removed | 15 mL |
| 1 tbsp | chopped fresh cilantro | 15 mL |
| ½ cup | plain Greek-style yogurt | 125 mL |
| ½ cup | mayonnaise | 125 mL |
| 1 tbsp | freshly squeezed lime juice | 15 mL |
| | Salt and freshly ground black pepper | |

1. In a small bowl, whisk together chipotle, cilantro, yogurt, mayonnaise and lime juice. Season to taste with salt and pepper.

# Goat Cheese Dip

**Delivering a lot of sophistication for very little work, this lickety-split, creamy dip will wow one and all.**

**Makes about 1 cup (250 mL)**

### Storage Tip
Refrigerate the dip in an airtight container for up to 3 days.

• *Food processor*

| | | |
|---|---|---|
| 1 tbsp | chopped fresh chives | 15 mL |
| ½ cup | buttermilk | 125 mL |
| ½ cup | soft goat cheese | 125 mL |
| 2 tsp | prepared horseradish | 10 mL |
| 1 tsp | finely grated lemon zest | 5 mL |
| | Salt and freshly ground black pepper | |

1. In food processor, combine chives, buttermilk, goat cheese, horseradish and lemon zest; process until smooth.

2. Transfer to a bowl and season to taste with salt and pepper.

# Blue Cheese Dressing

The labor required for this dressing is minimal, and it pays tenfold (or more). The delectable (but healthy) result is great paired with Buffalo chicken wings, but the list of options for other combinations is vast.

**Storage Tip**
Refrigerate the dressing in an airtight container for up to 3 days.

**Variation**
*Blue Cheese Dip:* Replace the buttermilk with an equal amount of plain Greek yogurt or sour cream.

• *Food processor*

| | | |
|---|---|---|
| 1 | clove garlic, roughly chopped | 1 |
| Pinch | ground nutmeg (optional) | Pinch |
| ¹⁄₂ cup | crumbled blue cheese (about 2 oz/60 g) | 125 mL |
| ¹⁄₂ cup | cottage cheese | 125 mL |
| ¹⁄₂ cup | buttermilk | 125 mL |
| 2 tbsp | mayonnaise | 30 mL |
| | Salt and freshly ground black pepper | |

1. In food processor, combine garlic, nutmeg (if using), blue cheese, cottage cheese, buttermilk and mayonnaise; process until smooth.

2. Transfer to a bowl and season to taste with salt and pepper.

# Buttermilk Ranch Dressing

Ranch dressing may be great on salad, but it is also a fantastic multitasking dip, dressing and spread for appetizers and main dishes galore.

**Makes about ³/₄ cup (175 mL)**

## Storage Tip
Refrigerate the dressing in an airtight container for up to 3 days.

## Variations
*Buttermilk Dill Dressing:* Reduce the chives to 1 tbsp (15 mL) and replace the parsley with 2 tsp (10 mL) minced fresh dill.

*Cilantro Ranch Dressing:* Reduce the chives to 1 tbsp (15 mL) and replace the parsley with 1 tbsp (15 mL) chopped fresh cilantro.

| | | |
|---|---|---|
| 1 | clove garlic, mashed | 1 |
| 1½ tbsp | minced fresh chives | 22 mL |
| 2 tsp | chopped fresh parsley | 10 mL |
| ½ cup | buttermilk | 125 mL |
| 3 tbsp | mayonnaise | 45 mL |
| 2 tsp | freshly squeezed lemon juice | 10 mL |
| | Salt and freshly ground black pepper | |

1. In a small bowl, whisk together garlic, chives, parsley, buttermilk, mayonnaise and lemon juice. Season to taste with salt and pepper.

# Lemon Herb Aïoli

Aïoli is a Mediterranean sauce made from olive oil, garlic and, in some cases, egg yolks. My version simplifies the preparation by starting with prepared mayonnaise and then adding extra flavor with fresh herbs and lemon.

**Makes about ¹/₂ cup (125 mL)**

### Tip
You can use ¹/₄ tsp (1 mL) dried thyme in place of the fresh thyme.

### Storage Tip
Refrigerate the aïoli in an airtight container for up to 3 days.

| | | |
|---|---|---|
| 1 | clove garlic, mashed | 1 |
| 1 tbsp | chopped fresh parsley | 15 mL |
| 1 tbsp | chopped fresh chives | 15 mL |
| ¹/₂ tsp | minced fresh thyme | 2 mL |
| ¹/₂ cup | mayonnaise | 125 mL |
| 1¹/₂ tbsp | extra virgin olive oil | 22 mL |
| ¹/₂ tsp | finely grated lemon zest | 2 mL |
| 1 tbsp | freshly squeezed lemon juice | 15 mL |

**1.** In a small bowl, whisk together garlic, parsley, chives, thyme, mayonnaise, oil, lemon zest and lemon juice.

# Avocado Aïoli

A cross between guacamole and mayonnaise, this über-creamy, velvety sauce is equally fitting with Mexican food or Mediterranean dishes.

**Makes about ³⁄₄ cup (175 mL)**

### Storage Tip
Refrigerate the aïoli in an airtight container for up to 2 days. Place a piece of plastic wrap directly on the surface of the aïoli to prevent browning.

• *Food processor*

| | | |
|---|---|---|
| 2 | cloves garlic, roughly chopped | 2 |
| 1 | small Hass avocado, diced | 1 |
| ¼ cup | mayonnaise | 60 mL |
| 1 tbsp | extra virgin olive oil | 15 mL |
| 1 tbsp | freshly squeezed lemon juice | 15 mL |
| | Salt and freshly ground black pepper | |

1. In food processor, combine garlic, avocado, mayonnaise, oil and lemon juice; process until smooth.

2. Transfer to a bowl and season to taste with salt and pepper.

# Creole Mayonnaise

You will find versions of spicy mayonnaise like this all across Louisiana, where it is used as an accompaniment for fried fish, shrimp, crawfish and po'boy sandwiches. It's fantastic with french fries and onion rings, too.

**Makes about ½ cup (125 mL)**

**Tip**
Feel free to vary the amount of hot pepper sauce to your liking.

**Storage Tip**
Refrigerate the mayonnaise in an airtight container for up to 2 weeks.

| | | |
|---|---|---|
| ½ tsp | paprika | 2 mL |
| ¼ tsp | dried thyme | 1 mL |
| ½ cup | mayonnaise | 125 mL |
| 1 tbsp | Worcestershire sauce | 15 mL |
| 2 tsp | freshly squeezed lemon juice | 10 mL |
| 1 tsp | hot pepper sauce (such as Tabasco) | 5 mL |

1. In a small bowl, whisk together paprika, thyme, mayonnaise, Worcestershire sauce, lemon juice and hot pepper sauce until blended.

# Sriracha Mayonnaise

The additions of Sriracha and lime juice make for an unusual but ultimately addictive variation on mayonnaise.

**Makes about ½ cup (125 mL)**

**Tip**
Freshly squeezed lemon juice can be used in place of the lime juice.

**Storage Tip**
Refrigerate the mayonnaise in an airtight container for up to 1 month.

| | | |
|---|---|---|
| ½ cup | mayonnaise | 125 mL |
| 1½ tbsp | Sriracha | 22 mL |
| 2 tsp | freshly squeezed lime juice | 10 mL |

1. In a small bowl or cup, whisk together mayonnaise, Sriracha and lime juice until blended.

# Rémoulade

Akin to mayonnaise and aïoli, rémoulade is a creamy French sauce made from hard-cooked (not raw) egg yolks. Flavorings can include curry powder, pickles, fresh herbs and capers, and it is very often served with seafood. Here, store-bought mayonnaise makes preparation simpler.

**Makes about ³/₄ cup (175 mL)**

### Tip
Regular Dijon mustard can be used in place of the whole-grain Dijon mustard.

### Storage Tip
Refrigerate the rémoulade in an airtight container for up to 3 days.

| | | |
|---|---|---|
| 1 | small clove garlic, mashed | 1 |
| 2 tbsp | chopped fresh flat-leaf (Italian) parsley | 30 mL |
| 1 tbsp | minced fresh chives | 15 mL |
| 1 tbsp | finely chopped dill pickle | 15 mL |
| ½ cup | mayonnaise | 125 mL |
| 1 tbsp | whole-grain Dijon mustard | 15 mL |
| 1 tsp | freshly squeezed lemon juice | 5 mL |
| | Salt and freshly cracked black pepper | |

1. In a small bowl, whisk together garlic, parsley, chives, pickle, mayonnaise, mustard and lemon juice. Season to taste with salt and pepper.

# Tartar Sauce

Parsley, capers, mustard and lemon add just the right amount of flavor and texture to mayonnaise to make this sauce a classic accompaniment to seafood.

### Makes about 1/2 cup (125 mL)

**Tip**
An equal amount of finely chopped dill pickle can be used in place of the capers.

**Storage Tip**
Refrigerate the sauce in an airtight container for up to 1 week.

| | | |
|---|---|---|
| 2 tsp | chopped fresh parsley | 10 mL |
| 1/3 cup | mayonnaise | 75 mL |
| 1 tbsp | finely chopped drained capers | 15 mL |
| 1 tsp | freshly squeezed lemon juice | 5 mL |
| 1/2 tsp | Dijon mustard | 2 mL |

1. In a small bowl, stir together parsley, mayonnaise, capers, lemon juice and mustard.

# Index

**Library and Archives Canada Cataloguing in Publication**

Saulsbury, Camilla V., author
    175 best air fryer recipes / Camilla V. Saulsbury.

Includes index.
ISBN 978-0-7788-0551-9 (paperback)

    1. Hot air frying. 2. Cookbooks. I. Title. II. Title: One hundred seventy-five best air fryer recipes.

TX689.S29 2016          641.7          C2016-903968-4